P9-ARD-463

WRITING FOR DIGITAL MEDIA

Writing for Digital Media teaches students how to write effectively for online audiences—whether they are crafting a story for the Web site of a daily newspaper or a personal blog. The lessons and exercises in each chapter help students build a solid understanding of the ways that the Internet has introduced new opportunities for dynamic storytelling as digital media have blurred roles of media producer, consumer, publisher and reader. Using the tools and strategies discussed in this book, students are able to use their insights into new media audiences to produce better content for digital formats and environments.

Fundamentally, this book is about good writing—clear, precise, accurate, filled with energy and voice, and aimed directly at an audience. *Writing for Digital Media* also addresses all of the graphical, multimedia, hypertextual and interactive elements that come into play when writing for digital platforms. Learning how to achieve balance and a careful, deliberate blend of these elements is the other primary goal of this text.

Writing for Digital Media teaches students not only how to create content as writers, but also how to think critically as a site manager or content developer might about issues such as graphic design, site architecture, and editorial consistency. By teaching these new skill sets alongside writing fundamentals, this book transforms students from writers who are simply able to post their stories online into engaging multimedia, digital storytellers.

For additional resources and exercises, visit the companion Web site for *Writing for Digital Media* at **www.routledge.com/textbooks/9780415992015**.

Brian Carroll is Associate Professor of Journalism at Berry College and Adjunct Professor in the School of Journalism and Mass Communication at the University of North Carolina. He is author of *When to Stop the Cheering? The Black Press, the Black Community, and the Integration of Professional Baseball* (Routledge, 2006).

WRITING FOR DIGITAL MEDIA

Brian Carroll

Routledge
Taylor & Francis Group

NEW YORK AND LONDON

First published 2010
by Routledge
270 Madison Ave, New York, NY 10016

Simultaneously published in the UK
by Routledge
2 Park Square, Milton Park, Abingdon, Oxon OX14 4RN

Routledge is an imprint of the Taylor & Francis Group, an informa business

© 2010 Brian Carroll

Typeset in Classical Garamond and Myriad by
Florence Production Ltd, Stoodleigh, Devon
Printed and bound in the United States of America
on acid-free paper by Edwards Brothers, Inc.

All rights reserved. No part of this book may be reprinted or
reproduced or utilised in any form or by any electronic, mechanical,
or other means, now known or hereafter invented, including
photocopying and recording, or in any information storage or
retrieval system, without permission in writing from the publishers.

Trademark Notice: Product or corporate names may be trademarks
or registered trademarks, and are used only for identification and
explanation without intent to infringe.

Library of Congress Cataloging in Publication Data
Carroll, Brian, 1965–.
  Writing for digital media/Brian Carroll.
      p. cm.
   Includes bibliographical references and index.
  1. Online authorship.   I. Title.
  PN171.O55C37 2009
  808′.002854678—dc22

ISBN10: 0-415-99200-1 (hbk)
ISBN10: 0-415-99201-X (pbk)
ISBN10: 0-203-89431-6 (ebk)

ISBN13: 978-0-415-99200-8 (hbk)
ISBN13: 978-0-415-99201-5 (pbk)
ISBN13: 978-0-203-89431-6 (ebk)

CONTENTS

INTRODUCTION

In the digital age, we are all consumers and producers, readers and publishers alike. The Internet has made it possible for anyone to publish his or her writing online almost instantaneously for all the world to read.

The evolution of digital media has introduced both unprecedented challenges and opportunities for media corporations and organizations. The unique way that digital media tools and technologies combine (or *converge*) skill sets—such as written, visual, and interactive storytelling—has also posed a new challenge for journalism and mass communication schools and departments training future media professionals.

This book guides students through the landscape of new media convergence, pointing them toward the best practices and techniques of writing and editing for an online audience, and helping them to take full advantage of the new opportunities offered by digital media.

Understanding our increasingly fragmented online audiences and exploring how different media behave—their unique limits and possibilities—will help students develop content that is ideally suited for digital formats and environments. Students will analyze the technical and rhetorical possibilities of online environments, including interactivity, hyperlinking, spatial orientation and non-linear storytelling. Students will also learn practical skills to help them succeed in writing and editing for specifically online environments.

First and foremost, this book is about writing—clearly, precisely, accurately, with energy and voice, and for specific audiences. Fortunately, good writing is valued online, and unfortunately it is still just as hard to find good writing online as it is in print. Specifically, this book is about writing in and for digital environments and about communicating effectively in those online environments, which often are populated with graphical content, multimedia and hypertextual, interactive elements. Learning how to achieve a careful, deliberate balance of these elements is a primary goal of this book, and accomplishing it will require new skills, intuitions and sensitivities. The premium on good writing has not changed, but the process or activity of reading has; people accessing information online are not reading as much as they are scanning, surfing, moving and navigating. Web writers, therefore, are engineers of spaces and places in addition to being communicators with and through words.

The point of view taken in this book is that we all are content creators and writers, whether or not we are part of a larger content development and management team. We are principally writers, therefore. Sometimes, though, the point of view is that of a site editor, someone charged with maintaining consistent editorial, graphic design and management policies for a Web site or group of sites. As editors, we are surrogates for the site's potential reader. As such, this book's approach is journalistic, seeing convergence and multi-media in terms of journalism first and foremost.

This book does not assume the point of view of development team members in graphic design, site architecture, code writing or marketing, therefore, though as site editors we strive for knowledge in and sensitivity to those skill sets. Whether content creators or site editors, we recognize that more than anything we are storytellers. Throughout history humans have taught, learned, entertained and communicated with stories, and this has held constant across media. Stories transmit information and transfer experience. This book, therefore, emphasizes digital storytelling and upholds the value of narrative, which also underlines the value of a journalistic approach to information-gathering, writing, editing and publishing online. Journalism, in other words, well serves the journalist and non-journalist alike, especially online, where the democracy of production and publishing is even threatening the relevance of such distinctions.

Specifically, this book aims to:

- further develop students' **abilities to write** clearly, precisely, accurately, with energy and voice, and for specific online audiences;
- teach journalism and communication students **practical skills** for writing and developing content for digital publishing and delivery;
- teach how to **purposefully blend** text, graphical content, multimedia and hypertextual, interactive elements;
- explore how trends in personal publishing, especially blogging, and social networking are **forcing change** in journalism and other information industries;
- give students a comprehensive resource for online journalism, one that deals with digital media as their own distinct forms of communication rather than merely adjuncts to print or broadcast.

Writing for Digital Media is primarily for journalism students, particularly those enrolled in courses in online journalism, but the content is also aimed at students learning to develop content, both textual and visual, for Web delivery in a variety of contexts. It is somewhat broad-based, therefore, reflecting the ongoing convergence of roles and jobs of and for content producers, online journalists, Web writers and online editors. There is no such thing as a "typical" Web writer or content developer, an ambiguity that demands fresh approaches to pedagogy and to industry practice.

A quick word on what this book is not: it is not a technical guidebook for students looking to master Flash, javascript, php or, more generally, multimedia development. (There are many other textbooks devoted to the software side of things.) Instead, this is a writing text first and last.

While placing an emphasis on understanding the fundamentals of good Web site and page design, this textbook primarily focuses on writing skills as the foundation for writing specifically for digital media, and is designed particularly for use in online journalism courses. This book comes at a time of unprecedented upheaval and change in journalism teaching and in the journalism industry itself. Journalism schools and departments are grappling with the question of how to address the shift from print and broadcast to digital delivery of converged content, and this book hopes to help educators overcome that challenge by connecting the basics of good writing and journalism with the unique challenges and opportunities of writing specifically for digital media.

Structurally, this book is divided into three sections. The first section, **Foundations (Chapters 1 through 2)**, is devoted to the fundamentals of writing well and the elements of journalism. After laying the ground rules for good writing, the second section, **Practice (Chapters 3 through 6)**, introduces students to the special skills and techniques needed to create content for digital environments and online publications. **Chapter 3: Screen Writing: Online Style and Techniques** establishes the general rules and conventions of writing for an online audience. **Chapter 4: Headlines and Hypertext** emphasizes the importance of providing good organization and clear navigation tools for online readers. **Chapter 5: Designing Places and Spaces** discusses how to plan, organize and update a Web site or online publication appropriately to attract an audience and keep readers coming back. **Chapter 6: Getting It Right: Online Editing, Designing and Publishing** focuses on the fundamentals of online editing and publishing, from copyediting to page design. The final section, **Contexts (Chapters 7 through 11)**, looks at personal publishing, citizen journalism, legal issues and questions specific to online communication, and business communication and its environments. The **Afterword: Core Values of Online Journalism** reflects upon the lessons of the book and encourages students to practice online journalism that is **accurate, reasonable, transparent, fair** and **independent**.

A number of pedagogical features appear in each chapter to encourage students to further explore and build upon the lessons of the book. These features include:

- **Chapter Objectives**: These brief points clearly establish the learning goals for each chapter.
- **Chapter Introductions**: A concise paragraph at the start of each chapter outlines the major topics discussed in the chapter and how they connect to chapter objectives, along with historical and cultural context.
- **Chapter Assignments**: These writing exercises ask students to apply the skills, critical perspectives and best practices introduced in each chapter.

- **Online Resources**: These links connect students to relevant Web sites where they can learn more about the topics discussed in each chapter.

This book owes a great debt to Patrick Lynch's and Sarah Horton's *Web Style Guide 3* from Yale University Press (2009). This book refers to their text and to its companion Web site. Also important to the development of this book were *Web Writing, Web Designing* by Margaret W. Batschelet, from Longman (2001), and Mark Briggs's *Journalism 2.0* from the Knight Citizen News Network (2007; http://www.kcnn.org/resources/journalism_20/).

By way of acknowledgments, the author would like to thank Richard Cole, Paul Jones, Louise Spieler, Rachel Lillis and Deb Aikat at the School of Journalism & Mass Communication at the University of North Carolina at Chapel Hill; John Conway at WRAL.com in Raleigh, NC; Ryan Tuck at *The New York Times*; and Matt Byrnie at Routledge. For help finding typos and other copy demons, the author would like to thank Danny Lineberry and Marcie Barnes. For their expert indexing, profound gratitude to Diane Land and Nicole Nesmith. Finally, a big "thank you" to the many students of UNC's JoMC 711, Writing for Digital Media, whose collective intelligence and wisdom of the crowds heavily influenced this work.

PART I
FOUNDATIONS

1   ON WRITING WELL

I sometimes think that writing is like driving sheep down a road. If there is any gate to the left or right, the readers will most certainly go into it.
C.S. Lewis, novelist

But words are things, and a small drop of ink falling like dew, upon a thought, produces that which makes thousands, perhaps millions, think . . .
Lord Byron, *Don Juan*

If, for a while, the ruse of desire is calculable for the uses of discipline soon the repetition of guilt, justification, pseudo-scientific theories, superstition, spurious authorities, and classifications can be seen as the desperate effort to "normalize" formally the disturbance of a discourse of splitting that violates the rational, enlightened claims of its enunciatory modality.
Homi K. Bhabha, Professor of English, Harvard University, "Mimicry and Man"

Chapter Objectives

After studying this chapter, you will understand how to:

- use the basic rules of good writing;
- determine the intended audience and write specifically for that audience;
- correctly apply the fundamentals of grammar, style, and usage;
- avoid common writing problems.

Introduction

Whether a person is writing a news story, novel, letter-to-the-editor or advertising copy, the principles of good writing are the same. Different media place different burdens and responsibilities on writers, but the reason behind writing is always to communicate ideas in your head to an audience through words. Does Professor Homi K. Bhabha's sentence above communicate his ideas clearly? Can you understand what he means by efforts to normalize the disturbance of a discourse of splitting? Perhaps that's why this sentence was awarded second prize in the annual "Bad Writing Contest." Bad writing, like Bhabha's prize-winning example, obfuscates and confuses; it promotes misunderstanding and perhaps even apathy. This chapter provides a foundation for good writing, including sections on grammar, spelling and punctuation, as it aims to help students identify weaknesses in their writing, then to offer help and resources to improve in those weak areas.

The Medium is the Message: A Brief History of Writing

The writing tools of today—computers and word processing software, primarily —are a far cry from the earliest writing instrument, a caveman's stone. Think for a moment about how the innovation of clay tablets, the first portable writing artifact, changed the written record of human history. Now consider texting, twitter or the phone-enabled mobile Web and the ways these and other Internet-enabled technologies and tools are changing the way people communicate today. The tools that we use *to* communicate affect *how* and *what* we communicate. This book pays special attention to writing in the digital environment, but we will look as far back as the beginning of writing itself for timeless lessons on writing well, whether you're using a stone or a tablet PC.

In approximately 8500 BC, clay tokens were introduced to make and record transactions between people trading goods and services. An alphabet of sorts began to emerge to record what was being traded. A clay cone, for example, represented a small measure of grain. A sphere represented a larger measure. A cylinder signified the transaction of an animal. Writing evolved, therefore, by transferring literal depictions into abstract forms.

The alphabet that we would recognize today was invented around 2000 BC. Jews in Egypt used 27 hieroglyphs to produce this recognizable alphabet, assigning to each of the simple hieroglyphs a sound of speech. This phonetic alphabet led to the Phoenician alphabet, the "great-grandmother" of many Roman letters used today in roughly 100 languages worldwide (Sacks 2003).

At about the same time, papyrus and parchment were introduced as early forms of paper. The Romans wrote on papyrus with reed pens fashioned from the hollow stems of marsh grasses. The reed pen would evolve into the quill pen around AD 700. Though China had wood fiber paper in the 2nd century AD, it would be the late 14th century and the arrival of Gutenberg before paper became widely used in Europe. So what we think of as writing's main use—language communication—was a low priority for a long, long time, in part because literacy remained so rare. Until Gutenberg, there was not much for the average person to read—mainly inscriptions on buildings and coins. When Gutenberg began printing books, scholars estimate that there were only about 30,000 books in all of Europe. Fast forward only 50 years and Europe could count between 10 million and 12 million volumes and witness a rapid increase in literacy. The democratization of knowledge generates along with it advances in literacy.

In 286 BC, Ptolemy I launched an ambitious project to archive all human knowledge. His library in Alexandria, Egypt, housed hundreds of thousands of texts. None survive today. Invaders burned the papyrus scrolls and parchment volumes as furnace fuel in AD 681, so some of history's lessons here should be obvious:

- Make a copy.
- Back up your data.
- Beware of invaders.

Although Korea was first to make multiple copies of a work, Johannes Gutenberg gets most of the credit in histories of printing. In 1436, he invented a printing press with movable, replaceable wood letters. How much Gutenberg knew of the movable type that first had been invented in 11th-century China is not known; it is possible he re-invented it. Regardless, these innovations, which combined to create the printing process and the subsequent proliferation of printing and printed material, also led to a codification of spelling and grammar rules, though centuries would be required to agree on most of the final rules (and we are still arguing, of course).

New communication techniques and technologies rarely eliminate the ones that preceded them, as Henry-Jean Martin pointed out in his *History and Power of Writing* (1994). The new techniques and technologies redistribute labor, however, and they influence how we think. These early tools—pen and paper—facilitated written communication, which, like new communication technologies today, arrived amidst great controversy. Plato and Socrates, for instance, argued in the 4th century BC against the use of writing altogether. Socrates favored learning through face-to-face conversation over anonymous, impersonal writing. Plato feared that writing would destroy memory. After all, why make the effort to remember or, more correctly, to memorize something when it is already written down? In Plato's day, people could memorize tens of thousands of "lines" of poetry, a practice still common in Shakespeare's day many centuries later. Think for a moment: What have *you* memorized lately? Plato also believed that the writer's ideas in written form would be misunderstood. When communication is spoken, the speaker is present to correct misunderstanding, and the speaker has control over who gets to hear what. If you have ever had an email terribly misunderstood—or read by entirely the wrong person—these ancient concerns might still find sympathy today.

Another ancient Greek, Aristotle, became communication's great hero by defending writing from its early detractors. In perhaps one of the earliest versions of the "if-you-can't-beat-'em, join-'em" argument, Artistotle argued that the best way to protect yourself and your ideas from the harmful effects of writing was to become a better writer yourself. Aristotle also saw the potential of writing as communication, as a means to truth, and therefore a skill everyone should learn. Aristotle believed that with truth at stake, honesty and clarity were paramount in writing. These values perhaps are as important, and just as rare, in the 21st century as they were in the 4th century. Aristotle also was the first to articulate the concept of "audience," which has been variously defined ever since. He instructed rhetoricians to consider the audience before deciding on the message (Vandenberg 1995). This consideration more than any other distinguishes communication from expression for expression's sake, a distinction perhaps best understood by comparing visual communication to art, or journalism to literature.

Printing quickly became crucial to education by making it possible to produce multiple copies of the same text. With the availability of multiple copies, you could distribute the same text to many individuals, allowing readers separated by time and space to refer to the same information. With the advent of the printing press, no longer were people primarily occupied by the task of preserving information in the form of fragile manuscripts that diminished with use.

The book changed the priorities of communication, and the book, like any communication technology, has attributes that define it. These include:

- **Fixity**. The information contained in a given text is fixed by existing in many copies of the same static text.
- **Discreteness**. The text is experienced by itself, in isolation, separated from others. If there is a footnote in a book directing a reader to a reference or source material, the reader has to go get that material, physically, by going to the library or filling out an interlibrary loan request, expending time and perhaps money.
- **Division of labor**. The author or creator and the reader or audience perform distinctly different tasks, and the gulf cannot be crossed. The book is written, published, distributed and then perhaps bought or borrowed and read.
- **Primacy for creativity and originality**. The value set embodied by books does not include collaboration, community or dialogue, values impossible in a medium that requires physical marks and symbols on physical surfaces such as paper.
- **Linearity**. Unless it is a reference book, the work likely is meant to be read from front to back, in sequence, one page at a time. After hundreds of years of familiarity with this linearity, non-linear forms have found it difficult to gain acceptance.

Compare and contrast the book's fixed attributes to Web content, for which all writing and all content development depends on a process of generating lines and lines of computer code. Web pages can be static, or writing on or for the Web can be dynamic, increasing or decreasing in size, changing in font and color and presentation. Web "pages" aren't even pages; what you are actually viewing on screen is a picture of a page.

Web space is non-linear, with changing borders and boundaries. Unlike a book, the Web is scaleable and navigable, a space people move through rather than a series of pages read in a particular order. Online readers can easily subvert planned sequences of "reading" by accessing information in any order they wish (or click). The Web also is networked. Think about how the search function alone has changed use or consumption of Web documents compared to books, with search engines allowing a viewer to navigate directly to page 323 of a document and to begin reading there. Technology changes the way an artifact is used, read, stored, searched, altered and controlled. These changes are not necessarily progress, though often they can be.

The idea that a technology is not inherently good or inherently evil, that its virtues and liabilities evolve as its contexts change, is an important assumption that this book makes, one that underpins many of the book's other assumptions. Though a commonly held view, it is not necessarily true that the book is somehow natural while the Internet is somehow unnatural. Gutenberg's printing press was revolutionary as a technology; the Internet, too, as the product of hundreds of technologies, is revolutionary.

Principles of Good Writing

When asked what he would do first were he given rule over China, Confucius is believed to have said:

> To correct language . . . If language is not correct, then what is said is not what is meant. If what is said is not what is meant, then what ought to be done remains undone. If this remains undone, morals and art will deteriorate. If morals and art deteriorate, justice will go astray. If justice goes astray, the people will stand about in helpless confusion. Therefore, there must be no arbitrariness in what is said. This matters about everything.

This section aims to help you better understand the principles of good writing. These principles transcend any particular media, principles important no matter the medium and no matter the audience. Below is a list of some of these fundamentals, realizing that writing is a process of pre-writing, writing, editing, revising, editing again, revising again and evaluating. Each fundamental is paired with an exercise or two demonstrating the instructional point being made. The exercises are designed to help you think like a writer. The "want" to write starts now.

 Be Brief

> *I have made this letter longer than usual only because I have not had the time to make it shorter.*
> Blaise Pascal, 17th-century philosopher

Writing should be clear and concise. Readers need little reason *not* to read further, and this is especially and painfully true online. Prune your prose.

Exercise 1.1

Here are some samples of cluttered writing. Re-write the sentences to convey the same meaning, but with fewer words, perhaps using a sentence or phrase you have seen somewhere else.

Example: The essential question that must be answered, that cannot be avoided, is existential, which is, whether or not to even exist.

Solution: To be or not to be, that is the question.

Try these:

- People should not succumb to a fear of anything except being fearful in the first place; and we should stick together on this so we can't be defeated.
- The male gender is so different from the female gender that it is almost as if the two are from completely different planets.
- There were two different footpaths in the forest, one that had been cleared by foot traffic and another that obviously fewer people had used. I decided to take the one that fewer people had used, and it really made a big difference.

 Be Precise

> *When I use a word it means exactly what I say, no more and no less.*
> Humpty Dumpty in *Through the Looking-Glass*

Use the precise word that your meaning requires, not one that is close or, worse, one that sounds close. A dictionary and thesaurus should never be far away (and online, they never are). Examples:

- "A sense of trust was **induced**"—no, trust is enabled or rewarded or encouraged, it is not induced.
- "Put into **affect**"—no, put it into effect, though A might affect B.
- "She was **surrounded** by messages"—perhaps she was inundated with messages, or drowning in information, but surrounded by a ring of messages? No.
- "He was **anxious** to go to the game"—he was probably eager, not anxious, unless he was playing in the game, in which case it is possible he indeed was anxious, or worried.
- "He watched a **random** TV show"—perhaps he arbitrarily chose a show to watch, but it likely wasn't "random" at all; a broadcaster determined with great precision what to air and when. Random has a specific meaning, which is that each and every unit in a population had an equal statistical chance of being selected.
- "In lieu of this new information, we should . . ."—no, *in light of* the new information . . . "In lieu of" means "in the absence of."

Exercise 1.2

Write a sentence for each of the words in the pairings of words below. The sentences should illustrate the differences in meaning or nuance in each pairing:

Example:

deduce: From the blood on the glove, he deduced that the murderer was left-handed.

infer: By leaving her bloodless glove on the table, she inferred her innocence.

- ambiguous
- ambivalent

- healthy
- healthful

- conscience
- conscious

- apprise
- appraise

- disinterested
- uninterested

- affect
- effect

 Be Active

> *Just do it.*
> Ad slogan for Nike

Though there are times when passive voice is appropriate, too much yields writing that is lifeless. Habitually writing in the passive is what we want to avoid. In the passive, which uses a form of the verb *to be* and a past participle, the subject is acted upon. An example:

- The baseball player fielded the ball (active).
- The ball was fielded by the baseball player (passive).

The second sentence is longer and therefore more difficult to read.

Exercise 1.3

Re-write the following two sentences to make them active and more descriptive.

> *Example*: Exhausted and bleary-eyed, I somehow negotiated the winding staircase, spilling me into my bed. Work would have to wait for a fresh day.
>
> *Solution*: I was tired, so I finished my work and went up to bed.

- The labor leaders were frustrated by the latest offer which forced them to go through with the strike.
- She walked into the room without saying a word, sat down and looked at me.

Be Imaginative

You have to try very hard not to imagine that the iron horse is a real creature. You hear it breathing when it rests, groaning when it has to leave, and yapping when it's under way . . . Along the track it jettisons its dung of burning coals and its urine of boiling water; . . . its breath passes over your head in beautiful clouds of white smoke which are torn to shreds on the track-side trees.

Novelist Victor Hugo, describing a train

Analogies, similes and metaphors are like sutures and scalpels. In expert hands, they can be transformative. In the hands of quacks, however, somebody is going to get hurt, to use a bad though not mixed metaphor.

For the poet Maya Angelou, social changes have appeared "as violent as electrical storms, while others creep slowly like sorghum syrup." For French novelist Colette, the skyscrapers of Paris resembled "a grove of churches, a gothic bouquet, and remind us of that Catholic art that hurled its tapered arrow towards heaven, the steeple, stretching up in aspirations." Dorothy Parker, a riotously funny writer, once declared, "His voice was as intimate as the rustle of sheets." (She also wrote that "brevity is the soul of lingerie.")

Visualize analogies and metaphors when writing them, as well as the images they conjure. Are they apt and effective in conveying their intent? Be warned, however, that mixed metaphors are not only inaccurate, they distract the reader and discredit the writer. "He smelled the jugular." ESPN broadcaster Chris Berman actually said this in 2002 describing a playoff football game. (To hold a broadcaster to the standards of the written word is unfair, but it makes the point about how easily metaphors can go wrong.) In addition, global audiences will have great difficulty with metaphors and analogies. Great care should be exercised when employing them, using them only where they *help* communicate an idea and do not *hinder* understanding, or worse, offend and alienate.

Berman's example points to another danger—clichés. It is easy to settle for a cliché, but doing so is like arriving a day late and a dollar short, like taking candy from a baby, like picking low-hanging fruit. Because at the end of the day, when all is said and done, laziness is perhaps the writer's greatest enemy.

Avoid these clichés *like the plague*:

- last but not least;
- give 110 percent;
- untimely death (think about this one just for a moment);
- brutal rape (what would its opposite be, a friendly rape?);
- few and far between;
- stick to the game plan;
- off the wagon, on the wagon or circling the wagons.

Exercise 1.4

Think of some more clichés—the more the merrier. If you need inspiration, more clichés than you can shake a stick at can be found at the American Copy Editors Society Web site, http://www.copydesk.org/words/cliches.htm.

Exercise 1.5

Describe the Internet using analogy in two different sentences, each with a different emphasis in meaning. For attempts at this from the past, think information superhighway, cyberspace or getting a Second Life.

Example: As an information superhighway, the Internet too often resembles a Los Angeles cloverleaf during rush hour.

 ## Be Direct

I am hurt. A plague o' both your houses! I am sped.
Mercutio in *Romeo and Juliet*

Shakespeare knew how to deliver a verbal punch with a stab of brevity. The short sentence can affect emphasis and power in writing. Ernest Hemingway perfected this skill: *"He knew at least twenty good stories ... and he had never written one. Why?"* And an example from another rhetorical master, Rev. Dr. Martin Luther King, Jr.: *"This is our hope. This is the faith with which I return to the South to hew out of the mountain of despair a stone of hope."*

In King's quote, the brief introductory sentence sets up the sentence of normal length following. In Hemingway's, the abrupt question "Why?" adds emphasis to the character's flaw under examination. The short sentence (Hemingway's was one word) also can be used for transition. For Shakespeare, Mercutio's words are his last, like final, choking gasps for air.

 ## Be Consistent

Failing to use parallel structure is one of the most common problems in writing. Here are some examples of this:

Good: One cannot think well, love well, sleep well, if one has not dined well.
Bad: One cannot think well, have love, fall asleep, if dinner was bad.

Good: Jane likes hunting and fishing.
Bad: Jane likes to hunt and fishing.

Sentences should be balanced and faithful to a reader's subconscious expectations in terms of the physical act of reading. Parts of a sentence with coordinating conjunctions (*and*, *but* or *for*, *nor*, *yet*, *so*), therefore, should be joined in consistent fashion.

Exercise 1.6

Re-write the following sentences to make them parallel in structure.

- Delta promises a bounty of flights that are on time, have convenient connections and offer a well-balanced in-flight meal.
- Heroes in movies are always wealthy, always get the girl, wear high fashion and usually arrive at the scene about two seconds after the bad guy has left.
- Speaking of movies, telephones in movies are always knocked over if they wake up a character, never ring more than three times before getting answered, and get restored by frantically tapping on the cradle and shouting, "Hello? Hello?"

Just as laziness or lack of care prevents good parallel structure, verb tenses should not mysteriously change mid-sentence, nor should the singularity or plurality of subjects or objects being described or discussed.

 Be Aware

Here are some common pitfalls you'll want to be sure to avoid when writing:

- **plagiarism**—both intentional and inadvertent; it is almost impossible to over-cite, so when in doubt, cite the source;
- **stereotyping**—"journalists are cynical";
- **oversimplifying**—rarely is a choice either/or; rarely does a question or issue have *only* two sides;
- **generalizing**—"All computer users struggle with addiction." Every last one of them? Be wary of *all*, *none*, *nobody*, *always*, *everything*;
- **jumping to conclusions**—see *generalizing*;
- **faulty logic** or **circular arguments**—using the Bible, for example, to justify one's Christian faith; however the Bible is fine for *explaining* Christian faith;
- **overuse of pronouns and articles**—"this," "these," "those," "he" or "she." Which one(s)? Who? What are you talking about? Don't risk confusing the reader.

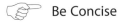 **Be Concise**

What difference does it make if you live in a picturesque little outhouse surrounded by 300 feeble minded goats and your faithful dog . . .? The question is: Can you write?

Ernest Hemingway

Exercise 1.7

Hemingway could write, obviously. He once wrote a short story in six words. "For sale: baby shoes, never worn." He called it his best work. The task in this exercise is to do as Hemingway did, to write a short story in just six words. This will force you to be most judicious and deliberate in choosing your words. Here are some examples, from *Wired* magazine's November 2006 issue:

"Failed SAT. Lost scholarship. Invented rocket."—William Shatner.

"Computer, did we bring batteries? Computer?"—Eileen Gunn.

"Vacuum collision. Orbits diverge. Farewell, Love."—David Brin.

"Gown removed carelessly. Head, less so."—Joss Whedon.

An example of good writing

To consider how to improve your own writing (and thinking), consider some of the problems in writing George Orwell observed in his essay, "Politics and the English Language," an essay as timely today as the day it was published more than 50 years ago:

- staleness of imagery;
- lack of precision or concreteness;
- use of dying (or dead) metaphors;
- use of "verbal false limbs," such as "render inoperative" or "militate against";
- pretentious diction (words like *phenomenon, element, individual*);
- use of meaningless words.

Orwell wrote that a scrupulous writer will ask himself at least four questions in every sentence that he writes:

1 What am I trying to say?
2 What words will express it?
3 What image or idiom will make it clearer?
4 Is this image fresh enough to have an effect?

And he will probably ask himself two more:

1 Could I put it more shortly?
2 Have I said anything that is avoidably ugly?

Finally, in cautioning against "prefabricated phrases" and "humbug and vagueness generally," Orwell's essay provides writers with several points of advice:

1 Never use a metaphor, simile, or other figure of speech which you are used to seeing in print.
2 Never use a long word where a short one will do.
3 If it is possible to cut a word out, always cut it out.
4 Never use the passive where you can use the active.
5 Never use a foreign phrase, a scientific word or a jargon word if you can think of an everyday English equivalent.

To Orwell's last point, take a look at a concurring judicial opinion written by Supreme Court Justice Robert H. Jackson in a First Amendment case from 1945, *Thomas v. Collins*. Revel in Jackson's directness, in how accessible the language is compared to the legal jargon that characterizes many if not most court opinions. The case had to do with the constitutionality of a Texas law requiring labor organizers to register with the state before soliciting memberships in a union. From p. 323 of the decision:

> As frequently is the case, this controversy is determined as soon as it is decided which of two well established, but at times overlapping, constitutional principles will be applied to it. The State of Texas stands on its well settled right reasonably to regulate the pursuit of a vocation, including—we may assume—the occupation of labor organizer. Thomas, on the other hand, stands on the equally clear proposition that Texas may not interfere with the right of any person peaceably and freely to address a lawful assemblage of workmen intent on considering labor grievances.
>
> Though the one may shade into the other, a rough distinction always exists, I think, which is more shortly illustrated than explained. A state may forbid one without its license to practice law as a vocation, but I think it could not stop an unlicensed person from making a speech about the rights of man or the rights of labor, or any other kind of right, including recommending that his hearers organize to support his views. Likewise, the state may prohibit the pursuit of medicine as an occupation without its license, but I do not think it could make it a crime publicly or privately to speak urging persons to follow or reject any school of medical thought. So the state, to an extent not necessary now to determine, may regulate one who makes a business or a livelihood of soliciting funds or memberships for unions. But I do not think it can prohibit one, even if he is a

salaried labor leader, from making an address to a public meeting of
workmen, telling them their rights as he sees them and urging them to
unite in general or to join a specific union.

This wider range of power over pursuit of a calling than over speech-
making is due to the different effects which the two have on interests
which the state is empowered to protect. The modern state owes and
attempts to perform a duty to protect the public from those who seek for
one purpose or another to obtain its money. When one does so through
the practice of a calling, the state may have an interest in shielding the
public against the untrustworthy, the incompetent, or the irresponsible,
or against unauthorized representation of agency. A usual method of
performing this function is through a licensing system.

But it cannot be the duty, because it is not the right, of the state to
protect the public against false doctrine. The very purpose of the First
Amendment is to foreclose public authority from assuming a guardianship
of the public mind through regulating the press, speech, and religion. In
this field, every person must be his own watchman for truth, because the
forefathers did not trust any government to separate the true from the false
for us (*West Virginia State Board of Education v. Barnette*, 319 U.S. 624).
Nor would I. Very many are the interests which the state may protect
against the practice of an occupation, very few are those it may assume
to protect against the practice of propagandizing by speech or press. These
are thereby left great range of freedom.

This liberty was not protected because the forefathers expected its use
would always be agreeable to those in authority, or that its exercise always
would be wise, temperate, or useful to society. As I read their intentions,
this liberty was protected because they knew of no other way by which
free men could conduct representative democracy.

(Opinion available: http://supreme.justia.com/us/323/516/case.html)

The first thing you may notice is how Jackson is present with you through his
writing. He is speaking to you, you right there. He isn't "performing," trying
to impress you with rhetorical flourishes.

Jackson's intellect as a jurist is on display here, as are his voice and method
of thinking. He first identifies what he sees as the core issue. He presents the
facts. He identifies the principles by which he will decide. He decides, then
he explains in such a way that we non-lawyers can understand him. In short,
Jackson says what he means and means what he says. Sherwood Anderson
wrote that "the danger lies in the emptiness of so many of the words we use."

Getting Started: Putting Your Ideas in Words

Mindful of how writing has evolved (and why), inspired by Pascal, Hemingway, Shakespeare and Orwell, finally it is time to write. The following steps
will help us get started.

A. Get the Idea: Determine Your Purpose

- **Brainstorm**: write down whatever might be related to the task, even if it seems irrelevant at the moment. There is no judgment in brain-storming, which, to use a sailing metaphor, is akin to producing your own wind. As the Latin proverb goes, "If there is no wind, row!" The best way to get some ideas, at least one good idea, is to generate a lot of ideas.
- **Cluster**: similar to brainstorming, this is more for visual people. Put the main idea in the middle of the page, then link related ideas, then related ideas to those related ideas, and so on. The ideas should radiate out from a conceptual center.
- **Free write**: write down the thesis or purpose statement at the top of the page, then write under it all the ideas that flow from that thesis, including sources, questions to pursue and things *not* to do.

B. Map It Out

- What is the topic?
- What is/are the main point(s)?
- Who is the primary audience? Are there secondary audiences?
- What is the specific purpose of the writing? (What is the goal?)
- What sources will be used?
- What method will be used to gather the information?

A *word about audience*: There is much more on audience in Chapter 5, but even now it is critical to know who the readers will be or to whom the content is being targeted. This knowledge should influence topic, tone, complexity and a host of other content issues. To help, here are some things to think about adapted from a worksheet put together by long-time literary agent Laurie Rozakis (1997):

1 How old are your readers?
2 What is their gender?
3 How much education do they have?
4 Are they mainly urban, rural or suburban?
5 In which country were they born? How much is known about their culture and heritage?
6 What is their socio-economic status?
7 How much does the audience already know about the topic?
8 How do they feel about the topic? Will they be neutral, oppositional, or will this be more like preaching to the choir?

The answers to all of these questions might not yet be available, which is fine. The point is to consider the readers or users* as completely as possible before writing. (*A better term for readers/users/consumers is desperately needed. Online, we do not merely read. Presumably most of us are not addicted to the Net. And content online is not like a bag of potato chips. What do we call the people who visit our blogs and Web sites and interact with our content? Inter-actors, perhaps? Hmm . . .)

C. Outline and Storyboard It

Outlining helped prepare this very section on writing. After answering the basic questions, it makes sense to then organize how the content will be presented to readers. Similar to home-building, the outline or blueprint can be used to organize the work, especially when different pieces of the project are being done at different times by different people. This blueprint can always be changed, and it does not have to be an elaborate outline replete with Roman numerals and series of alphabetized lists. Even a visual map, using circles, for example, might do the trick. Reverse-outlining, or outlining after the piece is written, can also be very useful, revealing structural flaws or a better order for the information.

Before getting to work, writing students are advised to buy or borrow a writing handbook like the one most of us used in English composition as first-year undergraduates. Examples include *The Everyday Writer*, by Andrea A. Lunsford (this book's author's favorite); *The Longman Handbook for Writers and Readers*; *Rules for Writers*; or *When Words Collide* (Lunsford 2009; Anson and Schwegler 2009; Hacker 2009; Kessler and McDonald 1984). Most every major publisher has one.

D. Revise It. Then Revise It Again

Plan time for revisions. As Hemingway famously said, "All first drafts are [crap]," so give yourself time and room to fail. The only reason for a first draft is to have something to revise. And be tenacious! Editing and revising takes patience and perseverance.

During the revision process, question the decisions you made in writing the first draft. Re-consider, critique and question:

- Your first paragraph. Re-write your first paragraph from an entirely different perspective, sit back and see which beginning you like better. For that alternate beginning, try thinking sideways! In other words, come at the subject from an entirely different angle.
- Your last paragraph. Re-write your last paragraph, your landing, as well.
- The one or two sentences you absolutely love. Highlight these and delete them. Is your writing stronger without your precious darlings there preening for attention? (The lesson here is to remove anything that is merely for effect, to impress, to be admired as witty or clever. Hemingway described prose not as interior decoration but as architecture.)

- Your adjectives. Look for redundancy, for empty descriptives, like "the long hallway" or "the deep, blue ocean."
- Your adverbs. Often one good verb is far better than a verb–adverb combination. Example: "He ran briskly across the field." Try: "He galloped in pursuit." While revising for adverbs, you might also reconsider your verb choices. Highlight all your verbs in one color and all of your adverbs in another. Re-think your choices.
- Clichés. Get rid of them.
- Ambiguity, vagueness, generalities. If you are not quite sure what a passage means, your reader most definitely won't either. Cut it out.

You might also read your piece with the following catalog of common writing problems at hand. The product of years of grading and editing undergraduate student writing, this list, which is in no particular order, will keep your writing out of potholes.

1 "Media" is a plural term. "Medium" is singular. So media *are*; a medium *is*. Even senior journalism and mass communication students haplessly struggle with this basic usage.

2 Avoid ethnocentric references such as "we" or "our" or "us" or "our country." It assumes too much, and it communicates exclusivity. Assume as little as possible. Many readers might not consider themselves members of any one person's "us" or "we" or "our." What of immigrants, green card aliens, international students? What does "us" even mean? Be precise instead.

3 Singular–plural agreement is a very common writing problem.

   —Example 1: "The government is wrong when they tell us what to do." The government is an "it." People who work for governments are a "they."
   —Example 2: "A, B and C are a predictor of future behavior." No, they are predictors. There are three of them.
   —Example 3: "The surfer is able to read the article themselves." Word processing makes moving words around so easy—too easy, in fact. Writers oftentimes lose track of agreement with so much cutting and pasting.

4 Beware of imprecise, even reckless use of personal pronouns such as "they," "their," "them" and "it." Often these are used at the sacrifice of clarity. Which "they" is being referenced? Most articles include discussion of more than one group. Which "them"? What "it"? "Their" refers to ownership, but by whom? The writer knows the words' references because they flowed from the writer's head. The reader, however, likely will be confused. A second reading or edit can reveal the vagueness of many of these usages. Night-before or on-deadline writing is notorious for producing this kind of carelessness and imprecision.

5 Use the right word, not just a good word. This was discussed earlier in the chapter.

6 A related issue, imprecision with adjectives. "A lot" . . . "more and more" . . . "massive amounts" . . . "very detrimental" . . . "a great deal." None of these suffice. Instead be specific, precise and show supporting evidence for such statements and judgments.

7 Do your part to prevent semi-colon abuse! Semi-colons, colons, commas, hyphens and dashes each have their own specific purposes. A writer's handbook is valuable in figuring them out. The comma, for example, is "a small crooked point, which in writing followeth some branch of the sentence & in reading warneth us to rest there, & to help our breth a little" (Richard Mulcaster, writing in his 1582 volume, *The First Part of the Elementarie*). A common apostrophe problem pits "its" v. "it's." "It's" is a contraction. "Its" is possessive.

8 After beginning a quote, make sure you end it, somewhere, sometime. It is a common mistake to begin a quote but then to forget the close quotes, effectively putting the rest of the treatise into the quotation. This is the writing equivalent of flicking on your turn signal, turning, then leaving it blinking the rest of the way down the highway. Other motorists are laughing at you!

9 A related issue, orphaning quotes. Quotes should all have parents, so be sure to identify this parentage. Orphan quotes are quotations dropped into an article without identification of the speaker or writer or source. There should be a source in the narrative ("said the inspections officer" or "the Civil War historian wrote").

10 Another related issue, stringing quotations together. The writing can quickly become a very thin piece of string merely holding other people's work together. The writer should be providing some pearls, as well, which means taking the time to integrate and weave the parts into a coherent, meaningful whole. Rarely is there benefit in merely grafting in quoted material just because it is on topic and seems worded more ably than the writer thinks he or she could pull off him- or herself. Writers should avoid subletting their space to others.

11 Hyphens pull together, like staples; dashes separate. "Twin-engine plane": hyphen, for a compound adjective. "She was—if you can believe this—trying to jump out of the car!": dashes, to separate the parenthetical phrase. In general, dashes should be avoided. They have no agreed upon rules and therefore are or can be a sign of laziness.

12 More editing required. After something has been written, long or short, even a single blog post, walk away. Go to the coffee shop and sip a latte. Go for a jog. Once refreshed, return to the writing and edit. Revise. Re-work. Improve. All good writers do this. Of course, it takes planning.

The Online Effect

Email, texting, social networking, IM and chat arguably are having a corrosive effect on writing. The informality of writing for these online environments is "seeping into . . . schoolwork," according to a study by the Pew Internet & America Life Project, in partnership with the College Board's National Commission on Writing. Nearly two-thirds of 700 students surveyed acknowledged that their electronic communication style, which primarily is an informal, interpersonal style, found its way into school assignments. About half said they sometimes omitted proper punctuation and capitalization in their schoolwork, while a quarter said they used emoticons. These are alarming trends, calling for more education on the different styles that should be employed for different forms or kinds of communication.

Chapter Assignments

1 Produce a writing sample. The choice of subject is entirely yours. You could, for example, write a short travelogue piece about somewhere you have recently visited. An opinion piece on some question or issue of the day, such as U.S. immigration policy or whether online communication has eroded language skills, also is an option. You could even review a movie, play or book.

   Length: about 700 words.

   Be sure to include:

   (a) a headline summarizing the work;
   (b) identification of the audience(s) for whom it is intended;
   (c) an abstract (a one- or two-sentence summary of your piece);
   (d) a list of key words a search engine might use to find this writing piece online.

2 Students should pair up and work together to improve the writing of one another. This exercise can be extremely valuable, and from both perspectives, that of being critiqued and that of (gently) critiquing. Some might be nervous or uncomfortable critiquing a classmate, especially early in a course, but students should not fret. Be civil and constructive, and demonstrate that you have or are developing a tough skin. Writing improvement demands a great deal of constructive criticism and therefore an increasingly thick skin and short memory.

   Workshop partners should have at their disposal a writing handbook and this text. It does not matter which handbook; they cover the same general topics. Each student will use the handbook to analyze his or her own writing and that of the assigned workshop partner(s).

   Length: about 500 words, but this word count is admittedly arbitrary.

Online Resources

Elements of Style (original 1918 ed.) by William Strunk, Jr.
  http://www.bartleby.com/141
  A free, online edition of *the* classic guide to writing well.

"More Clichés Than You Can Shake a Stick At"
  http://www.copydesk.org/words/cliches.htm
  A list of journalistic clichés compiled by Mimi Burkhardt on the Web site
  for the American Copy Editors Society.

Poynter Institute's Writer's Toolbox
  http://poynter.org/subject.asp?id=2
  Tips and best practices from, and blogs by, some of Poynter's writing
  faculty, including Roy Peter Clark and Chip Scanlan.

Purdue University's Online Writing Lab
  http://owl.english.purdue.edu/
  Style guides, writing and teaching helps, and resources for grammar and
  writing mechanics.

Sources

Chris M. Anson and Robert Schwegler, *The Longman Handbook for Writers and Readers*, 5th ed. (New York: Longman, 2009).

Jacques Barzun, *Simple & Direct* (New York: Harper & Row, 1984).

Homi K. Bhabha, "Mimicry and Man," in Homi K. Bhabha, *The Location of Culture* (New York: Routledge, 2004).

E.L. Callihan, *Grammar for Journalists* (Radnor, PA: Chilton Publishing, 1979).

John Dufresne, *The Lie that Tells a Truth* (New York: Norton, 2003).

Elizabeth Eisenstein, *The Printing Press as an Agent of Change: Communications and Cultural Transformations in Early-Modern Europe* (Cambridge: Cambridge University Press, 1980).

P. Elbow, "Revising with Feedback," in P. Elbow, *Writing with Power* (New York: Oxford University Press, 1981).

Michelle Esktritt, Kang Lee, and Merlin Donald, "The Influence of Symbolic Literacy on Memory: Testing Plato's Hypothesis," *Canadian Journal of Experimental Psychology*, 55 (March 2001): 39–50.

Fred Fedler, John R. Bender, Lucinda Davenport, and Michael W. Drager, *Writing for the Media* (Oxford: Oxford University Press, 2001).

Diana Hacker, *Rules for Writers*, 5th ed. (New York: St. Martin's, 2009).

Lauren Kessler and Duncan McDonald, *When Words Collide: A Journalist's Guide to Grammar and Style* (Belmont, CA: Wadsworth Publishing, 1984).

George P. Landow, *Hypertext 2.0* (Baltimore: Johns Hopkins University Press, 1997).

Tamar Lewin, "Informal Style of Electronic Messages is Showing Up in Schoolwork, Study Finds," *New York Times*, April 25, 2008: A12.

Gunnar Liestol, Andrew Morrison, and Terje Rasmussen, eds., *Digital Media Revisited* (Cambridge, MA: MIT Press, 2003).

Andrea A. Lunsford, *The Everyday Writer*, 4th ed. (New York: St. Martin's, 2009).

Elizabeth McMahan and Robert Funk, *Here's How to Write Well* (Boston: Allyn and Bacon, 1999).

Henry-Jean Martin, *The History and Power of Writing* (Chicago: University of Chicago Press, 1994).

John Pavlik and Shawn McIntosh, "Convergence and Concentration in the Media Industries," in *Living in the Information Age*, Erik P. Bucy, ed. (Belmont, CA: Wadsworth Publishing, 2005): 67–72.

Laurie Rozakis, *Complete Idiot's Guide to Creative Writing* (New York: Alpha Books, 1997).

David Sacks, *Language Visible: Unraveling the Mystery of the Alphabet from A to Z* (New York: Broadway Books, 2003).

Lynne Truss, *Eats, Shoots & Leaves* (New York: Gotham Books, 2004).

Peter Vandenberg, "Coming to Terms," *English Journal*, 84 (April 1995): 79–80.

Rick Williams and Julianne Newton, *Visual Communication: Integrating Media, Art, and Science* (New York: Lawrence Erlbaum, 2007).

Gary Wolf, "The Great Library of Amazonia," *Wired* magazine, December 2003: 215–21.

2 DIGITAL MEDIA VERSUS ANALOG MEDIA

The Web is jam-packed with empty, incoherent, ill-organized, meaningless, repetitive pages. Gunk. Spam. Junk. Crap. It gives the Web a bad name.
Rachel McAlpine, Web designer and author

If you don't know how to communicate with words, you're in the wrong business.
Don Hewitt, executive producer of CBS-TV's *60 Minutes*

Chapter Objectives

After studying this chapter, you will be able to:

- understand the similarities and differences in reading styles for Web audiences and print media audiences;
- evaluate credibility in digital media;
- write in such a way that facilitates online reading through scanning;
- encourage and enhance readership through interactive, multimedia pages;
- explain what XHTML is and how it works.

Introduction

In this chapter, writing for the Web and the credibility of information on the Web are compared with writing for and credibility in traditional print media. Web users do not merely *read* online content, they *interact* with it, because unlike print media, online media are not static or one-way, or at least they shouldn't be. Hypertext allows this interaction, or "reading," to be non-hierarchical and non-linear, more like entering a matrix and moving around within it than reading left to right, line by line. "Writers of hypertext . . . might be described as the designers and builders of an information 'space' to be explored by their readers," Carolyn Dowling wrote in 1999, when new media were in fact new. Interactivity, multimedia, space-building and the credibility of these information *spaces* are the emphases here. HTML and XHTML, the languages of Web page construction, are also introduced.

The more things change, the more things . . .

Think for moment about how much our understanding of how to structure information can be traced to the way information is presented in books. In some fundamental ways, writing for the Web is similar to writing for traditional print media. The fact that writing appears on a computer screen rather than in a bound book does not diminish the writing's need to be clear, concise, complete and correct. Good writing is valued in Web content as much as it is for any other type of content. It may seem as if there is more poor writing on the Web because there simply is so much content posted online. Anyone with a computer and an Internet connection can publish to the Web, so many do. What has been produced in any medium across time largely has been mediocre or worse, perhaps 90 percent of it or more. Online, that 90 percent of lower quality material seems like a great deal more because there is so much available and accessible at any time, from anywhere. We can quickly surf through or to several Web sites in minutes, much more quickly than "surfing" through a dozen or so books down at the public library or corner bookstore. So quality still counts online, and it is still rare online.

Also unchanged by newer, digital media are many of the important roles of the writer. These roles include:

- **Communicator of a message**: How many Web sites fail to make a point, any point? The skilled Web writer conveys a message in provocative, clever, amusing, interesting or profound ways.
- **Organizer of information**: Never has this been more important, with the barrage of information facing interactors each and every day. Decisions must be made about what is most important and, in leaving information out, what is not important enough. Good Web writers help readers make order out of all the information.
- **Interpreter**: The message has to be right for the medium, tailored to leverage the medium's strengths and to mitigate its weaknesses.

The Web has changed the reader's expectations, however. The notion of timeliness, for example, has been completely redefined. Information can be disseminated instantly, so it is, and to audiences that have become conditioned to receive immediate coverage of breaking news events. Major news organizations adopting live blogging and even the twitter microblogging software to provide coverage almost in real time are examples.

This has led to a higher tolerance for error, recognizing that breaking stories and immediacy in reporting are breeding grounds for rumor and hearsay. But because there is no end to the news cycle, readers have come to expect continuous updates of big, breaking stories. As Kovach and Rosenstiel reminded, people "crave news out of basic instinct . . . They need to know what is going on over the next hill, to be aware of events beyond their direct experience" (Kovach and Rosenstiel 2007: 15).

The New York Times

Thursday, February 18, 2010   Last Update: 4:53 AM ET

Proximity, too, has changed, with geographically based definitions of locality being replaced or at least augmented with those that have more to do with affiliation, profession and areas of interest. Because online delivery facilitates immediacy, audiences have grown accustomed to offerings and options in multimedia—photos, audio, video, games, graphics and Flash movies. Audiences demand more because the medium can deliver more.

Roger Parker wrote that the Web "permits you to immediately communicate great amounts of selective and updated information in color at remarkably low cost" (Parker 1997: 4). The immediacy of the Web means content can be updated, added to, deleted and refreshed weekly, daily or hourly, which compares to the months or even years required to publish a book.

"Great amounts" refers to the nominal cost of publishing to the Web, costs that have little to do with how much is being published. For print publications, on the other hand, printing costs increase proportionally with the amount being published. "Selective" implies interactivity and non-linearity. Interactors determine what to read and in what order, which puts a premium on navigation. And these are interactors addicted to movement as they click manically through sites and pages. Finally, "color" marks another point of departure for Web content because color costs no more than black-and-white, a luxury print publishers do not have.

Credibility

All three of the important roles of the online writer described above as Communicator, Organizer, and Interpreter rely upon the writer's credibility. The ways in which credibility is established, maintained and measured are changing online as compared to traditional media. Given the preponderance of Web page publishers and the relative ease of publishing, in many ways source credibility has become an even bigger issue on the Web than it is in other media.

In communication, credibility is one of the areas or topics of study originating with the ancient Greeks. Systematic empirical research, however, began only in the 1930s and 1940s because of interest during wartime in learning how to persuade, developing propaganda and harnessing the power of radio. One reason for such sustained interest by news media in credibility research is the long-term decline in newspaper readership, which has been connected to a diminishing of credibility over time.

There was no widely agreed definition of credibility for some time, as communication researcher Philip Meyer pointed out. Meyer surveyed credibility research in mass communication and developed an index for the two key dimensions of credibility that he identified in the literature: "believability" and "community affiliation" (Meyer 1988: 588). Believability is based on the notion that news media present accurate, unbiased and complete accounts of news and events. Community affiliation encompasses a news organization's efforts in unifying and leading the community it serves, efforts that require some degree of harmony in outlook or perspective. Meyer's two dimensions are important in suggesting that the public can disapprove of the way a media outlet or source covers a story but still believe what it says.

The Internet boom fueled interest in research on credibility in online media. Many if not most of these newer studies suggest that those who do look online for their information deem what they find on the Web as more credible than that found in traditional media. Increasing numbers of Americans are accessing the Web for information, and studies examining Web credibility show that the more people go online, the more credible they evaluate the information they find there. In fact, the amount of time a person spends online might be the single best predictor of that person's perceptions of credibility for an online medium. "The more users rely on Weblogs, the higher their assessments of credibility," in spite of the fact that bias is recognized and even seen as a virtue by blog readers. Blog readers are "seeking out information to support their views and are likely to consider information they receive from blogs as highly credible," found researchers Thomas J. Johnson and Barbara K. Kaye (2004: 631, 633, 634; the researchers found that only 3.5 percent of respondents considered blogs "not at all" credible or "not very credible", p. 630).

Bias

Some research has shown that the credibility of blogs has to do with bias—that is, the inclusion of the writer's perspective in blogs rather than its absence in traditional news media following the model of journalistic objectivity. As one blogging journalist put it, "Veteran journalists know that the objectivity ethos is the 'big lie' of their profession . . . journalists are beholden to various points to view" (Zachary). Geneva Overholser, professor at the University of Missouri School of Journalism, told the authors of *blog!* that 2005 would be remembered as the year "when it finally became unmistakably clear that 'objectivity' has outlived its usefulness as an ethical touchstone of journalism" (Kline and Burstein 2005: 9).

Identification

Identification is a key communication concept that helps us understand how blogs can generate trust from readers. While communication theorists since the writings of Aristotle have focused singularly on the role of persuasion in public discourse, Kenneth Burke called into question traditional notions by introducing a theory grounded in identification. As Burke explained, "You persuade a man insofar as you talk his language by speech, gesture, tonality, order, image, attitude, idea, *identifying* your way with his" (Foss *et al.* 1985: 158). Burke said that humans are uniquely individualized beings, but when their interests are joined, or one perceives or is persuaded to believe that they are joined, then identification occurs, a description that resonates at the individual level with what Meyer's concept of community affiliation described above. Burke added that one is "both joined and separate, at once a distinct substance and consubstantial with another," with consubstantiality rooted in the notion of a perceived "sameness" (p. 158). Burke provides insight into the apparent resurgence of authenticity and genuineness as significant factors in establishing credibility.

Blogs represent an important step for journalism outlets in generating more audience by offering more expression by individual voices. The "everyday person" voice of many blogs encourages identification versus the dispassionate, clinical voice of traditional media. These voices provide a sense of presence with the reader in a way traditional media's detachment, in part the result of allegiance to professional norms such as objectivity, prevents. Americans have also said that they want more interactivity, transparency and accountability in their journalism ("The State of the News Media" 2006). With interactive media, the roles of sender and receiver are interchangeable, the distinctions between the two less meaningful, and this blur or blend is being welcomed by blog readers.

Transparency

Web writers should aim to adopt more of the principles and techniques of blogging, including the practice of transparency. Blog readers respond to authors' willingness to disclose their personal politics and biases, their readiness to acknowledge error and to incorporate or consider new information, and the sharing of and pointing to original source materials that go into their posts.

There is evidence that traditional media institutions are awakening to the need for greater transparency. *New York Times* executive editor Bill Keller acknowledged in 2005 that his newspaper can no longer argue "reflexively that our work speaks for itself . . . We need to be more assertive about explaining ourselves—our decisions, our methods, our values, how we operate" (*New York Times*, July 4, 2005: C1, C4). Echoing Keller's sentiments, Richard Sambrook, director of the BBC World Service and Global News Division, said, "We don't own the news anymore. This is a fundamental realignment of the relationship between large media companies and the public" (*Durham Herald*, October 5, 2005).

Of course, allowing journalists to acknowledge and even base comments on their biases, as well as to point to and otherwise reveal source materials, is to relinquish control, and institutions are reticent to yield control. New York

University journalism professor Jay Rosen, however, argues that this new regime of control allows individual journalists themselves to be involved in creating trust, to be at the point of the transaction of trust with the reader, rather than merely rely upon the institutional trust of the publication and/or brand. In doing so, this new regime actually empowers journalists because they can now add to the organization's reputational capital rather than merely spend it or ruin it, addressing then at the individual journalist level the key problem of eroding credibility.

Accountability

Number three on the public's "to do" list for journalism—accountability—requires that news organizations explain themselves, or are clearer with readers and interactors about how they operate and what service to the public interest looks like in terms of journalistic standards. A backlash against objectivity, and general misunderstanding of even what it is, pushed editors and publishers on the defensive. At the Harvard conference on blogging, Rosen said that mainstream journalism is "dying" in part because it has insisted on objectivity and, in the process, has "killed the human voice." Blogs, he argued, mark the return of "real human voices" and "real human conversations over the Web" (Jay Rosen, "Bloggers vs. Journalists is Over", PressThink [January 21, 2005], available: http://journalism.nyu.edu/pubzone/weblogs/pressthink, accessed June 10, 2006). A big question for news organizations, then, is how to adhere to professional standards, such as ethical news-gathering and balance in the overall presentation of perspectives, to name just two, but at the same time communicate in "real human voices." For a public to hold a news organization accountable, that public must first know to what standards that organization is holding.

Improving credibility

Credibility studies suggest several elements that can give users confidence in a site and its content. Briefly, these include:

- Easy-to-use, intuitive site navigation
- User-friendly site design
- High-quality graphics
- Good writing
- Full contact information and a way to get to it on every page
- Expertise in the subject area
- Links outside to other, relevant Web sites.

One of the goals of Stanford University's Persuasive Technology Lab (http://credibility.stanford.edu/) is to understand those design elements that have an impact on credibility. The lab's Web credibility project found that a broad range of design decisions ranging from visual elements to information architecture to the use of advertisements can powerfully influence whether visitors are likely to find a site credible. Like human communicators, Web sites benefit (or suffer) based upon their appearance. Among the project's findings:

- First impressions online are important. People tend to determine the credibility of a site based upon how professional they think the site looks. This means, among other things, making sure there are no typographical errors.
- Having an organization's name in the URL increases credibility.
- Designers should make sure there is a clear distinction between information and advertising. For the information, the source should be identified and the authors' credentials presented.
- Navigation should be intuitive.
- Everything should work, so check for broken links, prevent down time and ensure that all graphics quickly, successfully download.
- Choose the company you keep. Links to or affiliations with other organizations, whether online or off, can impact credibility.

Stanford itemized a multitude of factors that affect credibility. Each of these factors, which are presented in rank order of importance or potential impact, can be placed into one of the above general guidelines.

A credible site . . .

1   has proven useful to you before;
2   is by or for an organization that is well respected;
3   provides a quick response to your questions;
4   lists the organization's physical address;
5   has been updated since your last visit;
6   gives a contact phone number;
7   appears professionally designed;
8   gives a contact email address;
9   is arranged in a way that makes sense to you;
10 provides comprehensive information that is attributed to a specific source;
11 lists authors' credentials for each article;
12 has articles that list citations and references;
13 is linked to a site you think is credible;
14 states its privacy policy;
15 features design appropriate to its subject matter;
16 sends emails confirming transactions you make;
17 has search capabilities;
18 links to outside materials and sources;
19 was recommended by a news media outlet, such as newspaper, magazine or email newsletter;

what if you are a newspaper?

20 advertises on the radio, billboards or other media;
21 contains user options and reviews;
22 provides live chat with a representative of the company or organization;
23 appears on the first page of search engine results;
24 selects content according to your preferences;
25 appears first when listed by a search engine;
26 recognizes that you have been there before;
27 displays an award it has won;
28 has a URL that ends with ".org";
29 has ads that match the topic you are reading about;
30 is designed for e-commerce transactions.

Generally, there are two Web site categories that typically have consistently low credibility, according to the Stanford lab's research: Web sites with commercial purposes and those that give the impression, real or imagined, that they have been produced by amateurs. People assign much less credibility to a site they know is trying to sell them something. More than one ad on a page, no matter whether or not the site is primarily commercial, can greatly decrease credibility. If a site is going to have ads, they should be for reputable products or organizations. The more reputable the ad, the more credibility it carries. Technical errors and less-than-frequent updates are typical problems for amateur sites, as are non-professional appearances and less adequate contact information.

Diminishing credibility for a site, in rank order from greatest to least, according to Stanford's research:

The site . . .

1   makes it hard to distinguish ads from content;
2   is rarely updated with new content;
3   automates pop-up ads;
4   is difficult to navigate;
5   links to a site you think is not credible;
6   has a link that doesn't work;
7   has a typographical error;
8   is sometimes unexpectedly unavailable;
9   uses a domain name that does not match the company's name;
10 represents a company that is having financial or legal difficulties;
11 has one or more ads on each page;
12 requires a paid subscription to gain access;
13 provides comprehensive information that is not attributed;
14 is hosted by a third party;
15 has a commercial purpose;
16 requires you to register or log in.

Readability and Scan-ability

If credibility is communicated and evaluated differently on the Web than in print, it should not surprise us. The technologies that enable the Web, the Internet and the computer interface have affected human communication in many ways, changing attention spans and even the process of reading. The online reader sits with hand on mouse while scanning text on a monitor that is an uncomfortable distance away, as writer Dale Dougherty wrote. His "Three-second Rule" holds that a site has approximately three seconds to download properly, present itself and engage the viewer . . . or else. Count off three seconds while staring at a Web page that is loading and you will probably agree. One-one thousand, two-one thousand, three . . .

If the experience of reading online is fundamentally different, then online writing should be fundamentally different as well. Web writers must get to the point. Brevity is valued in all media but can be the utmost priority on the Web, in particular the mobile Web that is accessed on personal digital assistants, cell phones and other hand-helds with punishingly small screens. Think for a moment about those who will be asked to write news for delivery to and on these tiny display screens for people on the move.

Rachel McAlpine, author of *Web Word Wizardry: A Guide to Writing for the Web and Intranet* (2001), advised that to successfully write for the Web, "You need to switch from 'think paper' mode to 'think Web' mode." Web users are "monsters of impatience," she observed, making the challenge of Web writers to hold a reader's attention. Like the television remote, the mouse button means content developers are always a click away from oblivion. With McAlpine's notion of the "Web mode" in mind, consider a few points of departure for Web content as compared to that for print media.

Unlike ink on paper, the Web is ephemeral. The context and the purpose, then, should be made readily clear. This is especially true because many Web users often are hunting for a specific kind of information. They are not, by contrast, interested in curling up by the fire for a cozy night with an iBook and the digital version of *The Adventures of Sherlock Holmes*. Online users often have an immediate need for information. This premium on specificity is unique to the Web, which, because of the low costs of publishing, allows for "narrowcasting" or micro-publishing, as well as broadcasting. Content for small, targeted audiences is common on the Web, as the spectacular growth in blogging and explosion of widgets and applications for Facebook and the iPhone underline.

A related point concerns the harsh reality that for most people Web content is appearing on a computer screen. CRT screens make reading unnatural, as compared to the comparatively pleasant experience of ink on paper, so Web writers should be sensitive to contributing to eyestrain. The discomfort of reading via computer explains why Web users scan content rather than reading word for word. Scanners need clues, signposts and highlights, so content should be shaped for scanning. This means, among other things, using headings, deckheads, subheads, hyperlinks, lists and some changes in font or type. Though publishing space is theoretically unlimited online, long blocks of text will simply not be read.

If there is a lot of content to present, it should be layered, or arrayed to permit drilling, skipping and scanning. Readers online typically want to read only as much as they have to; layering allows them to read as much or as little as they want.

These information layers can include:

- Headlines (or titles), subheads and sub-subheads
- One-sentence teasers and lead-ins
- Brief summary paragraphs
- Visuals, photos, graphics
- Audio or video clips
- Related stories
- Related links.

Layering is a response to the reality, the documented fact that Web users do not read. They scan, hurtling through Web space searching for something they need. One usability study, by Jakob Nielsen ("How Users Read on the Web"), showed that perhaps 79 percent of Web users merely scan any new page they download. Nielsen found that only 16 percent reported reading word for word. With these figures in mind, Nielsen recommends several page characteristics to enhance "scan-ability":

- Highlighted key words
- Hypertext links
- Typeface variations
- Use of color
- Subheadings
- Bulleted lists like this one
- Paragraphs with one idea each
- Information in inverted pyramid style
- Brevity. Nielsen recommends half the word count (or less) than conventional writing, one of his more controversial recommendations.

Rather than creating a story or article, online editors, then, are striving to present story packages that link related content. Readers can delve into the package as deeply as they like, and they can access the content in the order they like. The goal is to create a visually and intellectually appealing site that tells a story in such a way that the advantages of the medium are maximized and its disadvantages minimized. For an example of storytelling that intentionally uses particular media to tell pieces of a larger story, the pieces that make the most sense for those media, take a look at the Chauncey Bailey Project, located at http://www.chaunceybaileyproject.org/ and the result of a

collaboration among San Francisco Bay Area journalists, media organizations and university journalism departments.

The Project deploys different media that work together to tell a rich, complicated story and to provide the necessary historical, social, cultural and personal contexts of and for that story. No one medium is an afterthought: Video achieves intimacy and brings interactors into the "present" of historical events. An interactive timeline engages interactors and supplies historical context and a sense of the sequence of events. Text provides the narrative, as well as the very complex interrelationships between actors in this drama, which centers on the case of a journalist gunned down in Oakland in August 2007.

Nielsen mentioned using color, which is among the Web's advantages. Full color is both available and affordable on the Web; in fact, it is free. Other advantages online:

- Available space (both on a single page, navigable by scrolling, and on multiple pages, which cost no more to create or publish and can be interlinked any number of ways)
- Navigation (readers move through your space, making the distance between two pages or sites inconsequential)
- Hypertextuality
- Multimedia, or multiple channels of information
- 24/7 availability and accessibility
- Opportunity to update, revise and expand any number of times
- Distribution (no trees are killed, no trucks have to roll, no tapes must be archived)
- Feedback (email, hit counts, trackbacks, chat).

Among the Web's disadvantages:

- Lack of portability (although this is rapidly changing, with no small debt for this owed to Apple's iPhone; other mobile producers are scrambling to enable the mobile Web, as well)
- Space. It is much more difficult to build a space than to lay out a newspaper or tape a broadcast news segment. Think about how difficult it can be to merely navigate a brochure or a road atlas, for example.

Think of how many man and/or woman hours the Chauncey Bailey Project required.

- Technical issues and the lack of standards for browsers, computers, colors, text sizes and type, etc.
- Time (how long does it take for a photo in the newspaper to download? It's already there.)
- Competition (for attention and time). Remember, you have three seconds to load and engage.

In a study by the Poynter Institute (www.poynter.org/eyetrack2004/index. htm), researchers tracked users' eye movements, in particular those of people who read newspapers online. Their findings can help to guide how to produce content and lay out that content on Web pages. Here is but a sampling of what the Eyetrack researchers found.

Headlines

Dominant headlines most often draw the eye upon entering the page, not photographs, especially when placed in the upper left quadrant of the Web page. Photographs, unlike in print, are not ideal entry points. Text rules on computer screens, generally, both in terms of when it is viewed and in how much time is spent interacting with it. A user's eyes most often fixate in the upper left first, before hovering, then moving left to right. This schematic from the study shows these general attention patterns:

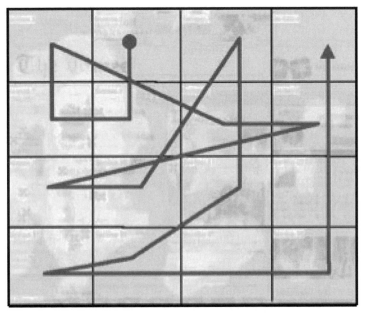

Source: Outing and Ruel (2004).

The schematic demonstrates how Web users focus on a small area and therefore filter out other information. It also demonstrates another counter-intuitive trend: Smaller headlines are more highly read while larger headlines are merely scanned. Large headlines are sometimes perceived as graphical elements, which explains the lack of attention they claim online. Small type, therefore, is preferred in most instances. Think of your favorite blogs. The text in those blogs likely is fairly small. The Poynter study showed that smaller type encourages focused viewing, while larger type promotes scanning.

Headlines and decks (or blurbs)

When a headline is bold and presented in the same size as the deck or the blurb of explanatory text below it, both are read. When the head is larger, however, and the blurb text is on a separate line, readers skip the blurb. Underlined heads further discourage testers from viewing the blurb/deck. Here is an example of a headline that would likely be read, but that would discourage readership of the deckhead below it:

Space shuttle launches on key mission

Discovery safely in space for exploratory mission to Mars

CAPE CANAVERAL, Fla.—The space shuttle Discovery roared off its Florida launch pad and soared into orbit on Tuesday on a key mission whose failure could end the U.S. shuttle program prematurely. After two weather postponements during the week-end, skies cleared at the Kennedy Space Center and allowed NASA to successfully launch Discovery on just the second shuttle flight since the destruction of the shuttle Columbia and the deaths of seven crew members in February 2003.

Headline writing, therefore, is terribly important. Poynter found that "FCUK," for example, was very highly read, and it is little wonder. The interposition of letters from the familiar, from the vulgar, catches the user's eye. "Craig's List" in another headline was highly read in the San Francisco-based study, which, too, makes sense; craigslist.com is based in San Francisco. Good head-lines engage and stir interest.

A summary of other Eyetrack study findings

- Navigation placed at the top of the home page performed best, and by a wide margin, outperforming navigation on either side or at the bottom.

- Shorter paragraphs are more highly read than long ones, by a factor of two.
- The one-column format is more highly read than those with more than one column of text.
- Summary descriptions are popular, so put them in bold. The boldface introductory graph is read 95 percent of the time.
- When graphical ads are not ignored, 0.5 seconds to 1.5 seconds is all the time they get. Text ads, however, get nearly 7 seconds, underlining text's primacy online.
- Mug shots are ignored.
- The average size of photos on news sites is 230 pixels wide and 230 deep, which, surprisingly, is not the golden triangle photography in print traditionally strives for. These photos online are attended to by 70 percent of visitors.
- Clean, clear photos with human faces perform best. People like people.
- Text is most useful when conveying facts, names, places, information.
- Multimedia is most useful when conveying new, unfamiliar, conceptual information. Process is best communicated with multimedia, ideally animation with text.
- The best, most readable fonts online include Arial, Courier, Georgia and Verdana. Also no surprise. Verdana, for example, was developed for Microsoft by type-master Matthew Carter, and sans serif fonts generally render better in the pixilated environments of online.

Linking

Paper has a fixed structure. Hypertextual environments, in contrast, do not. Think about how online content can be arranged and how easily that structure can be completely subverted. Web writers are not merely presenting a narrative, with a beginning, a middle and an end: they are building spaces. As content producers, we need to think of the possibilities that readers might want to pursue, and anticipate the many directions Web users may want to pursue. A useful metaphor here is home-building. You enter into a foyer and see several rooms and doors. You need to have a reasonable expectation of what to expect to find behind each door and how to navigate throughout the house.

One of the mistakes inexperienced Web writers make is to assume that everyone enters a site through the home page. Writers may assume that the visitors know the context of all the other pages on the site. Often, this is not the case, so each and every page should be designed and written with this consideration in mind. Each page should be able to stand on its own as independent, self-contained content that does not require readers to only access a Web site through a prescribed sequence.

Search engines, RSS feeds, socially networked news recommendation systems like Digg's and Facebook's, and email referrals increasingly are taking users directly to individual articles. Google, for example, can direct Web searches to specific pages, sometimes deep within a site or larger document. Both the *Los Angeles Times* and *The Washington Post* report that most of their news stories online are accessed directly. Therefore, the carefully crafted home pages of those news sites are never seen by most online readers accessing their news stories. For the same reasons, each and every page of a site should prominently display a link or route back to the home page, indicating in the process how the page relates or belongs to the whole of the larger site.

Links, then, provide jumping-off points within these spaces, and they can provide access to information throughout the Web. No other medium allows a reader to jump so easily to another story, another source, even another subject altogether. We should link to related content to allow the reader to pursue the subject rather than simply moving to the next story. One of the best sites at doing this is Wikipedia, which layers information and links it to logical and intuitive next-level sites and artifacts. The "Florence Cathedral" entry in Wikipedia demonstrates effective layering, with a "contents" list, hyperlinked terms and, at the bottom, a list of other resources.

Florence Cathedral

From Wikipedia, the free encyclopedia
(Redirected from Florence cathedral)

Coordinates: 43.773232°N 11.255992°E

The **Basilica di Santa Maria del Fiore** is the cathedral church (*Duomo*) of Florence, Italy, begun in 1296 in the Gothic style to the design of Arnolfo di Cambio and completed structurally in 1436 with the dome engineered by Filippo Brunelleschi. The exterior of the basilica is faced with polychrome marble panels in various shades of green and pink bordered by white and has an elaborate 19th century Gothic Revival facade by Emilio De Fabris.

The cathedral complex includes the Baptistry and Giotto's Campanile. The three buildings are part of the UNESCO World Heritage Site covering the Historic Centre of Florence and are a major attraction to tourists visiting the region of Tuscany. The basilica is one of Italy's largest churches, and until the modern era, the dome was one of the largest in the world, being surpassed in width only by that of the Pantheon in Rome. It remains the largest brick dome ever constructed.

Facade

Contents [hide]

1 History
2 Dome
3 Façade
4 Main portal
5 Interior
6 Crypt
7 Other burials
8 See also
9 Notes
10 References
11 External links

References   [edit]

- Bartlett, Kenneth R. (1992). *The Civilization of the Italian Renaissance*. Toronto: D.C. Heath and Company. ISBN 0-669-20900-7 (Paperback).
- King, Ross (2000). *Brunelleschi's Dome*. Penguin Books. ISBN 0-14-200015-9.
- Jepson, Tim (2001). *The National Geographic Traveler, Florence & Tuscany*. National Geographic Society. ISBN 90-215-9720-9.
- Henry A. Millon (ed.) (1994). *Italian Renaissance Architecture: from Brunelleschi to Michelangelo*. London: Thames and Hudson. ISBN 0-500-27921-7.
- Montrésor, Carlo (2000). *The Opera del Duomo, Museum in Florence*. Mandragora.
- Wirtz, Rolf C.. *Kunst & Architektur, Florenz*. Köneman, 2005. ISBN 3-8331-1576-9.
- Marica S. Tacconi, *Cathedral and Civic Ritual in Late Medieval and Renaissance Florence: The Service Books of Santa Maria del Fiore*. Cambridge: Cambridge University Press, 2005. ISBN 13 978-0-521-81704-2

External links   [edit]

- L'Opera del Duomo, Firenze
- Brunelleschi's Dome - en
- "The Cathedral". *The Florence Art Guide*. 2004. Retrieved on July 14 2006.
- "Duomo". *Minosh Photography*. Retrieved on July 14 2006.
- Rick Edmondson's Unfinished Buildings
- Pictures, history, facts, opening hours and prices
- Duomo Museum
- Horner, Susan; Horner, Joanna (December 27, 2005). "Chapter III: The Cathedral - Exterior". *Walks in Florence*. Retrieved on July 14 2006.

Wikimedia Commons has media related to: *Santa Maria del Fiore (Florence)*

Headlines themselves can be linked, but Eyetrack research shows that linked headlines are more often scanned than read versus unlinked headlines. A site can also embed the links within the story's text, like this:

> <u>Apple</u> unveiled its new hand-held device at the <u>Consumer Electronics Show</u> in Las Vegas.

If the links are embedded in the text, readers can click what interests them without having to wait for the end of the story to get to where the links are clustered. However, this also allows readers to abandon the story in pursuit of the linked material. Whether to encourage this flight or not through linking is one of many debates concerning online content. When you link, do you trigger a new browser window? This keeps your site in the background, but it annoys readers by cluttering their desktops. Another issue or debate: How many subjects should you link? You could conceivably link everything.

Many news sites include as a sidebar to a story or at the end of the story a menu of links for related information, stories and sites:

> <u>Apple Computers</u>
> <u>Consumer Electronics Show</u>
> <u>Technology Roundup</u>
> Profile: <u>Steve Jobs</u>

The *Wall Street Journal* presentation of baseball's steroid scandal is another example of layering and of nesting a menu of related content with the lead element, in this case the news story of the Mitchell Report.

Online writers should consider carefully how, when and where to link within their stories and presentations. Before linking to another site, ask what the reward for following that link will be for the reader. This consideration will prevent gratuitous linking. Think also about the text you are using to display the link. Does it give the reader a readily apparent clue as to what the hyperlinked page will contain? Finally, double-check both the link text and the linked-to material to make sure neither will mislead or confuse the reader. No one likes false advertising.

The three main reasons you might link to another article or site are to provide attribution, to provide context for your article, and to reward readers with something extra or another layer or dimension to the story. If you are writing about a celebrity's divorce, for example, link to the court papers and prenuptial agreement. For a story on the new Supreme Court nominee, link to several of that nominee's more important judicial opinions.

Cite sources, supporting documents, empirical research and reports, and corroborating accounts. Linking to archival coverage is one way to contextualize a story, providing the background and longer narrative into which your story falls. Definitions, explanations, maps and artifacts, too, can add context to your story.

WWGD: What Would Google Do?

Web writers should think in terms of key words when composing headlines, subheads and hyperlinks, and we should anticipate and use the choice of vocabulary of our interactors. Text for the Web, therefore, must be rich in key words, the keys to Google's search engine. Perhaps a useful metaphor here is rock climbing. Web users set out to scale an information mountain. The more key words Web writers can provide, the more words that jut out even slightly from the smooth face of the mountain, the more places the reader can grab on, step up and keep moving. These key words also provide Google's and the other search engines' algorithms the keys to finding information and ranking it in findings. Journalists can check how popular specific key words are and get suggested alternatives by using Google's AdWords Keyword Tool, or paid services like WordTracker.com or Keyword Discovery.com.

Google, in particular, looks for key words, particularly in the title bar that sits atop a browser window and in meta tags in the HTML code that created the page, but also within the content itself. The primacy online of key words is in part attributable to AOL (key word: AOL), Google and Web searching in general.

A ranking from Google, in near-real time, of what computer users nationally are searching is shown on the next page.

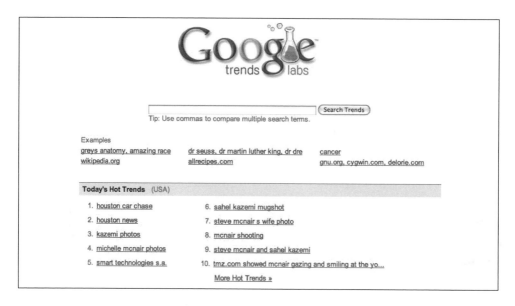

Think Interactive, Write International

Web writing should take advantage of the Web's capacities for interactivity, and it should be created with a potentially international audience in mind. Visitors could come from anywhere, which provides yet another reason for short sentences, an active voice and simple, concrete words. "Small flowers crack concrete," as the anonymous word picture describes.

The interactive and multimedia dimensions of Web pages mean that Web writers often are responsible for elements that were previously left to specialized editors, copyeditors, graphic artists and even computer programmers. Web writers should attend to titles, alt tags (the text that shows up when a graphic fails or is downloading), even a Web page's meta tags, which are used by most search engines as one means to rank pages. Online writers and editors, like the journalists described in the previous chapter, have to be jacks-of-all- (or jacks-of-many-) trades. Online media editors have been called *multimedia journalists*, which is a useful term, describing people who utilize multimedia to tell a story. When developing content, the question must be asked: What will best convey this information? A story? A graphic? A video or audio clip? All of the above? Web writers, then, are called upon to think in visual as well as written terms and concepts.

Using Lists

Using lists is another way for Web writers to emphasize certain information or to help readers follow a particular sequence. Like hyperlinks, lists also facilitate scanning. Lists help to break up the text and to highlight key points or items.

A few general guidelines when creating lists:

- Present all list items consistently, and in almost every way, including approximate length, structure, phrasing, spacing, indentation, punctuation, cap style and font. If you start one with a two-word teaser, for example, begin all of the listed items with a two-word teaser (an example: Safety First: Be sure to switch off all electrical . . .).
- Make each and every item in the list grammatically similar, as well. If you do not use a verb in the first item, do not use verbs in any of the items. Perhaps the most common problem or pitfall in creating lists is inconsistency in grammar, verb tense and phrasing.
- Be careful with punctuation, resisting the temptation to over-punctuate. A good general rule is to punctuate only with commas when the items in the list are not written in complete sentences; with semi-colons if they are complete sentences.
- When and where possible, omit articles ("a," "an," "the") from the beginning of your list items.
- When and where possible, keep the list to approximately six to eight items. Higher list item counts risk losing the reader's interest. (Did you read all of the Stanford Persuasive Technology Lab's lists of factors earlier in this chapter? Be honest!) Think about sub-dividing longer lists and consolidating shorter ones.
- Consider the order in which you present the elements of the list. Is the sequence important? In those cases you may want to number the parts of the list to make that sequence clear, while in other cases that won't be necessary.
- Avoid overusing lists. Too many erode any one's effectiveness or impact.

Tools and Technology: The Medium is the Message

Text online can be presented in non-linear, multimedia environments, and the various media invariably become part of the overall message. Neil Postman, author of *Amusing Ourselves to Death* (1985), observed that a technology, any technology, is

> to a medium as the brain is to the mind. Like a brain, a technology is a physical apparatus. Like the mind, a medium is a use to which a physical apparatus is put . . . Only those who know nothing of the history of technology believe that technology is entirely neutral.
>
> (Postman 1985: 84)

Let us consider the various media and what they offer, beginning with television, to think about what Postman was describing. The medium of television operates with or through its own rhetoric, a rhetoric predicated on a few essential qualities. Because screens are typically small—and even smaller on the Web—TV emphasizes characters and set pieces rather than sweeping epic dramas. For the big stories, we turn to motion pictures, which are shown in multi-speaker rooms with wall-size screens. Because TV delivers moving images, its rhetoric is about experiencing something, and experiencing it now. TV knows only one verb tense—the present. TV's rhetoric is incapable of helping us process a great deal of information or think rationally about complex topics. For this reason, TV must entertain. Because TV is turned to for entertainment, it must ask nothing of its audience. Even multi-part series allow viewers to drop in in the middle and quickly figure out what is going on. Because many can view a program simultaneously in different geographic locations and, when crisis strikes, as it often does, TV specializes in enabling a sort of societal communion, a ritualized viewing. Think of the coverage on September 11, 2001, or Princess Diana's funeral, or the last episode of *Seinfeld*. In important ways, the rhetoric of the medium becomes part of the message itself.

So, when deploying video online, content producers should think through why they are deploying moving images, and they should carefully consider what part of the story the rhetoric of video is best suited to deliver. The Chauncey Bailey Project, for example, offers archival video of the TV coverage of Bailey's killing and the ensuing investigation. This takes interactors back to the originating events and allows them to experience them. The still photography offers poignant, resonant images to gaze at, to reflect on and consider. The text explains. And the possibilities continue to multiply.

Video

Bigger, better bandwidth and improvements in streaming video and audio are cutting download and waiting times. Short clips usually are preferred, however, to minimize download times, to mitigate streaming interruptions, and because of interactors' punishingly short attention spans. YouTube, for example, does not allow videos of lengths longer than ten minutes, though the impulse for that likely is more to avoid copyright infringement suits and conserve server space than to accommodate short attention spans.

Think of the rhetorical possibilities of video, then opportunistically offer video when and where it makes sense. YouTube provides short tutorials on producing and editing video (http://youtube.com/video_toolbox), as does CNN for its "i-Report" citizen media micro-site (http://www.cnn.com/exchange/ireports/toolkit/index.html and http://www.cnn.com/exchange/ireports/toolkit/tips.html#video). CNN also gives tutorials on taking photography and on recording audio.

Other tutorials for shooting and editing video include those from:

- the *Online Journalism Review*: http://www.ojr.org/ojr/wiki/video/;
- the University of California Berkeley's School of Journalism: http://journalism.berkeley.edu/multimedia/tutorials/vidcams/;
- C|Net: http://reviews.cnet.com/4520-6500_7-5510172-1.html?tag=txt.

Flash movies

Flash presentations can combine text and pictures, video and audio, interactive buttons, and animated charts and graphs. Flash employs vector graphics, which require less data than do raster graphics, so Flash does not require a lot of bandwidth. And it's cool. But so what? Does it inform? Is animation the best way to make a point or engage users? Too often it is used merely as eye candy, rendering it a mere distraction. Flash animation is best suited to explaining new concepts, breaking down complex processes and chains of events, and demonstrating how to. Adobe provides a series of Flash movies to show Flash users how to make a Flash movie, for example, taking something fairly complex and sequential, breaking it down, and making it visible. Flash is ideal for presenting ideas or narrative in a linear sequence, allowing users to view Flash movies like motion pictures, and it can be used to accommodate non-linear, reader-directed storytelling, as well. Two cautions: Flash movies should not loop endlessly; viewers should be able to skip or avoid them. And sound should not play automatically. These defaults tend to annoy people.

Also, be aware that Flash does require a browser plug-in. While browser software often automatically updates users' browsers for the latest plug-ins, not all browsers are always up to date. When a user's browser is out of date, they will be asked to update their browser's plug-in before they can view the Flash animation. Any time users are required to take action, like updating or downloading software, before they can view content, the audience for that content will dwindle.

Photo slideshows

Still images best tell some stories or parts of stories because they enable a lingering gaze, a connection with the subject. Stills can rely on iconic messages implicit even in their composition, like the Madonna-and-child implicit in Dorothy Lange's *Migrant Woman* photograph taken in 1936.

Available are a multiplicity of easy-to-use slideshow software programs, such as Soundslides, iPhoto, Flickr, Picasa, Slide and Pickle.

Discussion and chat

To be human is to be social. For this reason, discussion, chat, instant messaging, texting and bulletin boards have been very popular wherever community is offered or claimed. Online newspapers have embraced these technologies to foster dialogue and make connections, and they are but two dimensions to the larger trend toward Web 2.0 social networking applications and platforms, a trend epitomized by Facebook, MySpace, Bebo, twitter and LinkedIn, among others.

Not every story should be accompanied by forums or discussion boards, however, and when and where they are unmonitored, the discourse can become nasty. Stories very emotional in nature, that elicit strong responses from interactors are perhaps those best amplified with discussion, where interactors can share their experiences, voice their reactions and continue the narrative. Stories on hot button issues or almost anything on sports or politics often prove the most problematic in inviting invective and just plain meanness. As with all media and technologies, social tools should be carefully and purposefully offered.

Computer Code: The Building Blocks of Web Pages

HTML Web pages

Computer programming codes like HTML and, increasingly, XHTML and CSS are the principal languages of the Web. Even if many Web writers may not need to use code to build sites from scratch, they should be aware of how code works and how it makes Web content manifest in a browser window. For example, did you realize that even text on a computer screen isn't really text? Computer code assembles the tiny building blocks of pixels to form the letters that you see on screen.

The code languages used most often to make interactive or hypertextual content are HTML (and its revision or evolution, XHTML, or neXt-generation HTML), XML (eXtensible Hypertext Markup Language) and CSS (Cascading Style Sheets). Web writers do not necessarily need to become proficient in these Web programming languages, though it certainly helps. Some companies do require their Web writers to know how to hand-code pages, but most sites use authoring software programs and Web page templates to speed the process.

Most online journalists, or journalists writing for and publishing to online news sites, use content management systems, or complex systems designed to largely automate publishing to the Web by multiple contributors. These systems handle all sorts of Web content, from text files to audio, photo and video, and they allow anyone within an organization to see all of the files, all of the content. Conceptually though, knowing these languages is a tremendous asset in understanding the limitations and capabilities of the Web environments for which the content is being developed and in troubleshooting problems.

Also important to news organizations migrating online are application programming interfaces (APIs), which are programming tools that allow one site or program to interact with or otherwise accommodate other sites or programs. Facebook famously opened up its environment to third-party applications, while Apple allows anyone to develop and offer an application for and via its iPhone. Similarly, APIs allow third-party development and collaboration on or for news organizations, which are seeking to leverage the popularity of such sites as YouTube, Facebook and Ning.com, to name just three examples. APIs give developers controlled access to the Web sites. Of course, opening up a network means surrendering some control, but in return this open sourcing provides vastly more readers access to the news company's content, as well as the ability to re-combine that content with other information and services.

In addition to HTML, XHTML and CSS, Web pages might employ XML, especially for data-rich content; Flash and its engine, actionscripting; JavaScript; Ajax; Spry; and Fireworks. XML, or eXtensible Markup Language, is used to enhance XHTML by using attribute tags to categorize information. For example, an XML tag can tell other computers and search engines whether a certain piece of text is a phone number, a job application, an order form, an invoice or whatever the coder writes into the language. Special search engines can then index documents in XML with great accuracy, regardless of the operating system or computer being used. XML is quickly becoming standard, particularly in electronic commerce, so certainly Web writers should become familiar with it.

To put those new to Web design at ease, XHTML is only marginally different from HTML, using stricter coding formats and borrowing from XML's syntax or language rules. To see these languages in use, you can go to almost any Web page, right click (PC) or control click (Mac), choose "view page source" (or its equivalent, depending on which browser you are using) and browse the code. HTML and XTML use tags, such as <body>. CSS uses brackets and semantic style directions:

```
{
    background-color: #000000
}
```

This simple CSS command sets a page's background color at black, using the hexadecimal (or six-character alphanumeric code) for the color black. CSS also supports semantic instructions:

```
{
    background-color: black
}
```

For Web-based media environments, including blogs, extranets and intranets, learning at least the basics of HTML can aid design and streamline content development. HTML and XHTML source codes are what make Web pages behave or, when the code is faulty, they are what cause the pages to misbehave. In the code are instructions to browsers, including what to show and how to show it. In short, HTML, or HyperText Markup Language, does just what its name implies: marking up language to allow browsers and, more importantly, those using browsers to interact with that language. This markup allows hyperlinks, or references in the code to other sites, Web pages or other places within the same Web site or page (called anchors). This markup allows images to appear on or in the page, though an image is never truly a part of the Web page. The Web page can merely be coded or built to make it seem as if the image is knitted into its fabric. In reality, that image is and forever will be a separate file, explaining why we often see evidence of missing graphics or partials of graphics.

To introduce HTML and XHTML, here is a look at a few very basic tags (commands appearing inside angle brackets < >) that are used to build most Web pages. After showing the tags, we will break down what they are and how they work:

```
<html>
<head>
<title>A primer on HTML source code</title>
<meta name="description" content="learning about HTML">
</head>
<body bgcolor="FFFFFF">
<h1><font: Georgia, Arial, sans serif>The basics of HTML</h1><p>

We are learning about the basic tags used in generating Web pages. These tags
and content should always be in a simple text document, not in Word or
WordPerfect. Once we are done, we can save the file, then open the document
in a browser from our local hard drive.

</p>
</font>
</body>
</html>
```

Eight tags were used in the small sample above; two of them are essential. The <html> tag tells browsers they can read the code by signifying that the page is in HTML format. The </html> turns the HTML off, or closes the document. The <body> tag directs the browser what to display in the browser window. Most tags come in pairs, one to turn a feature or behavior on and one to turn it off again, much like light switches. <strong>, for example, turns on boldface type. Adding a forward slash turns the behavior off again:

</strong>. Failure to add the "off" tag would render whatever followed also in boldface, the equivalent to Grandpa forgetting to switch off his turn signal after making the turn. The tag </body>, then, ends the section viewable through the Web browser.

The <head> indicates header information, such as the title of the Web page, the information that appears in the browser at the very top; it does not signify a headline. The <h1> tag turns on a heading, which is or can be like a headline, and specifies the size. The </h1>, then, would turn it off. The <body bgcolor> tag specifies a background color for the page, which in this case is white (#FFFFFF). Each of the Web's 256 colors are assigned hexadecimal codes, or six letter-number combinations. For example, black is #000000 and brown is #CC6600.

Any tag with a "/" in it is called an "off" tag. An example: <p> starts a paragraph, while </p> turns the same feature off, ending the paragraph. The font is specified with a <font> tag, then turned off with </font>. Arial font would begin <font face="Arial">. When the font changes, Arial would be turned off, </font face="Arial">.

As their name suggests, meta tags apply to the entire site. The term also comes from the fact that meta tags provide data about data. Their content does not direct the browser and is not, therefore, displayed in a browser. These tags direct search engines in how to sort the site, its pages and content by providing key words, descriptions and the like. They also cue other programmers by providing authorship information, copyright information and general design notes. A common meta tag sequence might look like this one, from the *Online Journalism Review* (http://www.ojr.org):

<meta name="description" content="News, commentary and help for online publishers and bloggers, from the USC Annenberg School for Communication.">

Here are a few more common tags used in XHTML:

- Paragraph break: <p> </p>
- Line break:
 (this XHTML tag actually is both the opening and closing tags; by adding the forward slash, the tag also "closes" or turns off the line break command)
- Horizontal rule: <hr> </hr>
- <strong>something written in boldface</strong>
- <em>something appearing in italics</em>
- <a href= "http://www.cubanxgiants.com">something hyperlinked to the CubanXGiants Web page</a>
- Unordered list:
  — <ul>
  — <li> laptops
  — <li> desktop PCs
  — </ul>

- Ordered list:
  — <ol>
  — <li> dolphins
  — <li> panthers
  — <li> jaguars
  — </ol>

Inserting anchors, which are used for internal page navigation, is easy. Anchors are internal hyperlinks, or links that take a reader to another part of the same Web page or to a specific section in another page of the same Web site. Here is what an anchored page would look like in code, a page of FAQs:

```
<a href="#question1">Where do I find out more about Crohn's?</a>

<a href="#question2">Where does the support group meet?</a>
```

Below, where the answers to the questions are presented, an anchor would be inserted just before each answer, a piece of code that is not visible in the browser. The anchor, which is signified by using the number sign—#—is merely a marker that enables the hyperlink—question1—to work, or to have a place to link. The two anchors for the two questions above would look something like this:

```
<a NAME="question1"></a>Crohn's disease is a condition that afflicts . . .

<a NAME="question2"></a>The group meets in Rex Hospital . . .
```

The <a NAME> refers to the name you gave the anchor in the hyperlink at the top of the page.

Perhaps the biggest difference between HTML and XHTML is that in the latter all tags require a closing or off tag. In HTML, a command such as <p> to create a new paragraph does not require a closing tag, </p>. And this is intuitive. Creating a paragraph creates an extra line break, an execution that would not seem to require an "off" command or closing tag. It is a single operation. But XHTML is stricter, and one manifestation of this lower tolerance is the requirement that all tags, all executions, have opening *and* closing tags.

Another manifestation is the prohibition in XHTML on capital letters. That same paragraph tag in HTML could be either <p> or <P>. Not so in XHTML. Finally, XHTML varies by requiring quotation marks (single or double) for all attribute values. For example, in HTML, a tag reading <td rowspan=3>, indicating a table with three rows, would be acceptable. In XHTML, the specification requires quotation marks: <td rowspan="3">. Why do these differences matter? Eventually, XHTML will likely replace HTML and browsers will begin supporting HTML less and therefore requiring XHTML to properly render Web pages.

CSS is an incredibly powerful coding language that is used for two primary purposes: coding individual Web pages with a more semantic or intuitive syntax than is used in HTML/XHTML, and to create "parent" style sheets that can be applied to an infinite number of "children," or pages that refer to the style sheets for their attributes. In other words, CSS can be used merely to indicate (or declare) something simple, like the typeface on a Web page:

```
{
font-family: Verdana, Arial, Helvetica
}
```

Or, CSS can be used to generate entire style sheets that determine attributes for any page referring to that style sheet. A change made to the one style sheet, which is uploaded to the Web along with all its children, will ripple out into all of those pages referring to the style sheet. For large sites, CSS saves an enormous amount of time, contributes to consistency and prevents error. These are just some of the reasons CSS has quickly been adopted by designers and supported by browsers and authoring programs.

The goal in this section was merely to provide a taste of HTML/XHTML and CSS, or just enough so that Web writers would not be intimidated by these authoring languages. The Web design or HTML section of any local bookstore will have a dizzying depth and breadth of literature available on the topic. It is enough for now to learn what XHTML tags are and how they operate in an HTTP (HyperText Transfer Protocol) environment such as the Web. Many will prefer to hand-code because of the precision this control offers; others would rather save time in page-building by using Web authoring software packages such as Dreamweaver, Microsoft FrontPage or Firefox's developer, therefore leaving more time for other tasks.

There are hundreds of Web sites designed to help you learn and use HTML, XHTML and CSS. Particularly since it was combined by Adobe with PhotoShop and InDesign with Adobe's purchase of Macromedia, Dreamweaver is the recommended Web authoring software. Borrowing source code from sites that allow it also is a good method for generating HTML/XHTML code, provided Web authors seek and receive permission to "borrow" or "honor." Certainly the Internet ethos has been one of sharing, which is one reason a right-click on a Web page allows anyone to see or read or use the code.

A Brave New World

What is journalism? As it has been discussed here, journalism can be seen as storytelling with a purpose. Ah, but what's the purpose? "To provide people with information they need to understand the world," wrote Bill Kovach and Tom Rosenstiel (2007: 189). First we have to find the information, then we seek to make it meaningful, relevant and engaging. Then and only then are we ready to think about which media to use to tell the story, or the different parts of the story. Likewise, really good storytelling doesn't begin when we sit down at the computer to start coding Web pages, upload video or write a lead paragraph. Good storytelling begins when we find fresh sources, when we think of fresh questions, when we find authentic voices, when we pursue truth.

Chapter Assignment

This chapter's assignment has two parts.

1   First, revise your Chapter 1 writing sample based on the feedback and help you receive from your workshop partner(s) and from the instructor. Feel free to continue dialoging with your workshop partner(s) and/or the instructor during this revision process.

2   Second, begin formatting the piece for online readership. The purpose here is merely to get started, so do not worry at all about how sophisticated your formatting is or about the limits of your knowledge of XHTML or CSS. The important thing at this stage is to conceptualize how the information should be presented online.

A blogging software can be very helpful in this exercise, particularly since most offer an HTML or Code view, which will show you all of the code generated to create the Web presentation

Use this chapter to inform your formatting. You will need to know or experiment with some XHTML, or have some familiarity with a Web authoring software package like Dreamweaver or Mozilla, both of which offer CSS support. Both Blogger.com and WordPress also accept HTML coding, provided you first select "Edit HTML" or "Code" (rather than "Compose" or "Visual"). If you use the shortcut buttons in your blog software, be sure to inspect or view the code to learn something of how the formatting is added.

Online Resources

Arts & Letters Daily
http://www.aldaily.com/
A great example of a site for all writers and readers.

Living Internet
http://www.livinginternet.com
A comprehensive site about all things Internet.

Purdue University Online Writing Lab
http://owl.english.purdue.edu
Style guides, writing and teaching helps, and resources for grammar and writing mechanics.

Useit.com

http://www.useit.com

Jakob Nielsen's site, for usability studies and a wealth of intelligence on design.

Webgrammar

http://www.webgrammar.com/writing.html

An excellent online writing source.

Additional Web Resources

For learning basic HTML/XHTML, including publishing to the Web:

- **Dave's Site**
  http://www.davesite.com/webstation/html/
- **HTML Goodies**
  http://www.htmlgoodies.com/
- **Webmonkey**
  http://www.webmonkey.com
- **HTML Guides/References from NASA**
  http://heasarc.gsfc.nasa.gov/docs/heasarc/Style_Guide/html.html
- **Peachpit Press**
  http://www.peachpit.com/topics/topic.aspx?st=61442.

For more on CSS, visit webstandards.org or O'Reilly Publishers.

Keep an eye out, too, for OPML (Outline Processor Markup Language) and Ajax (Asynchronous JAvascript with XHTML). In short, CSS is the W3C-approved method for adding to and enriching the visual presentation of Web documents, allowing Web authors to mimic the sophisticated layout and pagination of desktop publishing with clean, easy-to-maintain scripts.

In addition, the Knight Digital Media Center at UC-Berkeley has a brief tutorial on using Soundslides to create slideshows with audio, including how to convert audio files to MP3 format, a common problem in putting these presentations together: http://multimedia.journalism.berkeley.edu/tutorials/webdesign/using-soundslides/.

Sources

Brian Brooks and Jack Sissors, *The Art of Editing* (Boston: Allyn & Bacon, 2001).

Richard Craig, *Online Journalism* (Toronto: Thomson, 2005).

Dale Dougherty, "Don't Forget to Write," Webreview.com; available: http://www.webreview.com/1997/10_10/strategists/10_10_97_6.shtml.

Carolyn Dowling, *Writing and Learning with Computers* (Camberwell, Vic., Australia: Acer Press, 1999).

Jeff Glick, "When, How to Tell Stories with Text, Multimedia," Poynter Institute (2004); available: http://poynterextra.org/eyetrack2004/jeffglick.htm.

Bill Kovach and Tom Rosenstiel, *The Elements of Journalism: What Newspeople Should Know and the Public Should Expect* (New York: Three Rivers Press, 2007).

Patrick Lynch and Sarah Horton, *Web Style Guide 2* (New Haven, CT: Yale University Press, 2001). Also available: http://www.webstyleguide.com/.

Rachel McAlpine, *Web Word Wizardry: A Guide to Writing for the Web and Intranet* (Berkeley, CA: Ten Speed Press, 2001). McAlpine also has a companion Web site that is very good, Quality Web Content, available: http://www.webpagecontent.com.

John Morkes and Jakob Nielsen, "Concise, SCANNABLE, and Objective: How to Write for the Web" (1997); available: http://www.useit.com/papers/webwriting/writing.html.

Jakob Nielsen, "How Users Read on the Web," available: http://www.useit.com/alertbox/9710a.html. "Observations on Multimedia Features," Poynter Institute (2004); available: http://poynterextra.org/eyetrack2004/multimediafreeforall.htm.

Steve Outing and Laura Ruel, "What We Saw Through Their Eyes," Poynter Institute (2004), available: http://poynterextra.org/eyetrack2004/main.htm.

Neil Postman, *Amusing Ourselves to Death: Public Discourse in the Age of Show Business* (New York: Penguin, 1985).

Jeff Small, "When It Comes to Homepages, It is Polite to Stare," Poynter Institute (2004); available: http://poynterextra.org/eyetrack2004/jaysmall.htm.

Anthony Tedesco, "Adapt Your Writing to the Web," *The Writer*, 114, no. 5 (May 2001): 16.

Sources for section on credibility

R. Ambrester, "Identification Within: Kenneth Burke's View of the Unconscious," *Philosophy and Rhetoric*, 7 (1974): 205–16.

American Society of Newspaper Editors, "Examining Our Credibility" (Washington, DC: ASNE and Urban & Associates, 1999).

—— "Journalism Values Handbook" (Washington, DC: ASNE Ethics and Values Committee and The Harwood Group, 1995).

—— "Journalism Values Institute: Insights on the Values" (Washington, DC: ASNE Ethics and Values Committee and The Harwood Group, 1996).

—— "Newspaper Credibility: 206 Practical Approaches to Heighten Reader Trust" (Washington, DC: ASNE Credibility Committee, April 1986).

—— "Newspaper Credibility: Building Reader Trust" (Washington, DC: ASNE Credibility Committee and Minnesota Opinion Research Inc., April 1985).

—— "The Newspaper Credibility Handbook" (Washington, DC: ASNE Journalism Credibility Project, 2001).

—— "Timeless Values: Staying True to Journalistic Principles in the Age of New Media" (Washington, DC: ASNE New Media and Values Committee and The Harwood Group, April 1995).

G.D. Baxter and P.M. Taylor, "Burke's Theory of Consubstantiality and Whitehead's Concept of Concrescence," *Communication Monographs*, 45 (1978): 173–80.

William A. Benoit, "Comparing the Clinton and Dole Advertising Campaigns: Identification and Division in 1996 Presidential Television Spots," *Communication Research Reports*, 17, no. 1: 39–48.

C. Bullis and B.W. Bach, "Are Mentor Relationships Helping Organizations? An Exploration of Developing Mentee–Mentor Organizational Identifications Using Turning Point Analysis," *Communication Quarterly*, 37 (1989): 199–213.

Kenneth Burke, *A Rhetoric of Motives* (Berkeley, CA: University of California Press, 1962).

—— *Language as Symbolic Action: Essays on Life, Literature, and Method* (Berkeley, CA: University of California Press, 1966).

R.H. Carpenter, "A Stylistic Basis of Burkeian Identification," *Today's Speech*, 20 (1972): 19–24.

G. Cheney, "The Rhetoric of Identification and the Study of Organizational Communication," *Quarterly Journal of Speech*, 69 (1983): 143–58.

G. Cheney and P. Tompkins, "Coming to Terms with Organizational Identification and Commitment," *Central States Speech Journal*, 38 (1987): 1–15.

Jonathan Cohen, "Defining Identification: A Theoretical Look at the Identification of Audiences with Media Characters," *Mass Communication & Society*, 4, no. 3 (2001): 245–64.

Bryan Crable, "Rhetoric, Anxiety, and Character Armor: Burke's Interactional Rhetoric of Identity 1," *Western Journal of Communication*, 70, no. 1 (January 2006): 1–22.

D. Day, "Persuasion and the Concept of Identification," *Quarterly Journal of Speech*, 46 (1960): 270–3.

Andrew J. Flanigin and Miriam J. Metzger, "Perceptions of Internet Information Credibility," *Journalism & Mass Communication Quarterly*, 77, no. 3 (2000): 515–39.

Sonja K. Foss, Karen A. Foss, and Robert Trapp, *Contemporary Perspectives on Rhetoric* (Prospect Heights, IL: Waveland Press, 1985).

Jennifer Greer, "Evaluating the Credibility of Online Information: A Test of Source and Advertising Influence," *Mass Communication & Society*, 6 (2003): 11–28.

Jennifer Greer and Donica Mensing, "US News Web Sites Better, but Small Papers Still Lag," *Newspaper Research Journal*, 25, no. 2 (Spring 2004): 98–112.

Carl I. Hovland, Irving L. Janis, and Harold H. Kelley, *Communication and Persuasion: Psychological Studies of Opinion Change* (New Haven: Yale University Press, 1953).

Thomas J. Johnson and Barbara K. Kaye, "Cruising is Believing? Comparing Internet and Traditional Sources on Media Credibility Measures," *Journalism & Mass Communication Quarterly*, 75 (1998): 325–40.

—— "Using is Believing: The Influence of Reliance on the Credibility of Online Political Information among Politically Interested Internet Users," *Journalism & Mass Communication Quarterly*, 77 (2000): 865–79.

—— "Webelievability: A Path Model Examining How Convenience and Reliance Predict Online Credibility," *Journalism & Mass Communication Quarterly*, 79 (2002): 619–42.

—— "Wag the Blog: How Reliance on Traditional Media and the Internet Influence Credibility Perceptions of Weblogs among Blog Users," *Journalism & Mass Communication Quarterly*, 81, no. 3 (2004): 622–42.

John Kirk, "Kenneth Burke and Identification," *Quarterly Journal of Speech*, 47, no. 4 (December 1961): 414–15.

David Kline and Dan Burstein, *blog! how the newest media revolution is changing politics, business and culture* (New York City: cds books, 2005).

J.C. McCroskey, "Scales for the Measurement of Ethos," *Speech Monographs*, 33 (1966): 65–72.

——— "A Survey of Experimental Research on the Effects of Evidence in Persuasive Communication," *Speech Monographs*, 55 (1969): 169–76.

John C. Meyer, "Humor as a Double-Edged Sword: Four Functions of Humor in Communication," *Communication Theory*, 10, no. 3 (August 2000): 310–31.

Philip Meyer, "Defining and Measuring Credibility of Newspapers: Developing an Index," *Journalism Quarterly*, 65 (1988): 567–74, 588.

Roger C. Parker, *Guide to Web Content and Design* (New York: MIS Press, 1997).

"The State of the News Media," Journalism.org (2006), available: http://www.journalism.org (accessed February 21, 2007).

P.K. Tompkins, J. Fisher, D. Infante, and E. Tompkins, "Kenneth Burke and the Inherent Characteristics of Formal Organizations: A Field Study," *Speech Monographs*, 42 (1975): 135–42.

Mark Wright, "Burkeian and Freudian Theories of Identification," *Communication Quarterly*, 42, no. 3 (Summer 1994): 301–10.

G. Pascal Zachary, "A Journalism Manifesto," AlterNet (February 9, 2006), available: http://www.alternet.org/story/31775 (accessed February 13, 2006).

PART II
PRACTICE

3   SCREEN WRITING
Online Style and Techniques

Man is the great pattern-maker and pattern perceiver. No matter how primitive his situation, no matter how tormented, he cannot live in a world of chaos.
Edmund Carpenter, media theorist

Only 16 percent read word by word.

Jakob Nielsen, Web design expert

Chapter Objectives

After studying this chapter, you will be able to:

- understand how writing techniques and style should be informed by the online environments in which the content will be presented;
- plan, organize and test content for an interactive audience, and help that audience navigate to and through the information;
- cultivate a sensitivity to the global reach of the Web and the implications of that reach in producing content that can be quickly, readily apprehended.

Introduction

In this chapter we discuss how to plan and map sites, pages and content before zeroing in on the content itself, when the chapter then shifts to a discussion of style in three dimensions—general online style, writing style (and tone), and visual style. To help clarify the style guidelines and how they become manifest in pages, we look at a few case studies.

General Online Style

Online presentation and the styles that guide it are different from those that are employed for print publications. In print, the document forms a whole; the reader is focused on the entire set of information. On the Web, however, each page should be able to stand alone, acknowledging that many will land directly on that page and bypass the home page. On the Web, any one Web page is potentially an island. In fact, visitors might arrive on any page within a site, before seeing any other part of the site. Search engines permit and in many cases encourage this direct or interior access. Each Web page should, therefore, explain its topic and suggest its content without requiring a user to read previous or subsequent pages. Ubiquitous, consistent navigational schemes throughout a site help pages stand alone.

Writers and readers interact with the material on Web pages through the process of visual communication. Visual design, then, refers to the structured, deliberate (and deliberative) process of planning for this interaction. Though the term "document design" can mean much the same as visual communication, document design may also refer to matters of language. Certain types of paragraph and sentence structure, for example, are considered in the process of document design as developers look for those structures that have been shown to be easily understood by readers. Content producers should be involved at all of these levels of design and development, of course, making visual communication part of the writer's task. After all, visual elements affect how readers interact with the words and even whether they will interact at all.

Writing Style

The Web puts unique burdens on the writer, in particular because the exercise of "reading" is so fundamentally different online compared to print. Research conducted by Jakob Nielsen indicates that Web users read about **25 percent more slowly** on screen than on paper. This means they also read less . . . much less, so writing for the Web must be concise and direct, attributes that will facilitate surfing and scanning.

Nielsen has recommended a word count for online writing that is **about half** the standard word count for a similar piece of writing developed for a print publication (www.useit.com). There is little agreement on word counts among Web writers and editors, but Nielsen does make the important observation that Web users simply find it more taxing to read on a monitor, which emits light into our irises, than it is to read ink on paper.

If site visitors read less, if they are in a hurry, if they most often are on task, then putting the most information up top would also seem wise. The first screen of information, or about 30 text lines for most computers, should organize and telegraph what is in the rest of the document, recognizing that users do not like to scroll. Visitors will use the material presented first—the material in a headline or a list, for example—to help determine whether they want to read any further. For this reason, as Chapter 2 emphasized, the inverted pyramid style used by most newspapers for hard news is a useful style for online, one that addresses the need for writers to present the most important facts or ideas first.

For these reasons, seek to write in a news-you-can-use format. Surfers often are hunting, searching for information on how to lose weight or save money, for example. Rarely are they aimlessly browsing in search of beautiful prose. Zen with the fact that your readers are not choosing you because you are great, but because you have something they need.

Tone

Research shows that Web users are turned off by "the pitch," or marketing and advertising language. They tend to rank sites that use what could be termed "marketingese" as less credible than sites that do not, which recommends an objective or "just-the-facts" tone. Web writers must earn a reader's trust, which can be rapidly lost through exaggerated claims, boastful language or over-the-top sales pitches. Marketing slogans and unsupported claims, particularly in content otherwise designed or presented as neutral information, come across as tacky and unprofessional, much like the spam clogging our email "IN" boxes.

Short sentences, active verbs, direct statements and inverted pyramid presentations help maintain the right tone, one that may come naturally to practiced journalists who know that every word counts. Bloggers, on the other hand, have demonstrated some of the best and worst of online writing. Some are wonderfully concise with expert, judicious use of hyperlinking, while others simply ramble.

Plain English Wanted

Web pages are read globally in all time zones, so the language should be simple and straightforward. Of course, the other option is to translate the copy into several foreign languages, but about one billion people name English as their second, third or fourth language. Simple and straightforward demands plain English. No confusing acronyms or gobbledygook terms. No legal-sounding verbiage. Use short sentences and simple, common, concrete words wherever possible.

Web writers striving to be sensitive to global audiences will also avoid slang, idioms, culturally bound metaphors, clichés, colloquial expressions and phrasal verbs. Phrasal verbs are those that consist of two or more words, such as "pick up," "pick away at," "let on" and "go on about." They are more difficult to understand for those for whom English is a second language. Also to be avoided are ambiguous pronouns, particularly gender-based pronouns, because not all languages handle these in the same ways.

Those who have traveled abroad know that dates are presented differently in different countries and different cultures. In the United States, for example, dates commonly follow a month, day, year sequence (01/11/65 for January 11, 1965, for example). Many countries, however, including most in Asia, present the day first, then month, followed by year. The U.S. date in January 1965 reads in Asia as if it were November 1, 1965. Confusion can be prevented simply by presenting dates in full: 11 January 1965. Phone numbers (country codes, area codes, regional codes, etc.) and currencies present similar challenges. Think for a moment of the term "dollar." Whose dollar? Taiwan's? Australia's? The United States'? Zimbabwe's?

Visual Style

The hallmarks of good visual style, like good writing style, include simplicity, service to message (or content) and service to audience. Minimalist artist Frank Stella famously said, "What you see is what you see." Stella could have been instructing Web designers, because navigation isn't a feature of a Web site, navigation is in important ways the essence of a Web site. Even the term— "site"—signals Web documents' attributes and roles as spaces. Yes, they are discursive surfaces—we "write" on them. But they are also places, or sites, at which site visitors move about, looking, searching, sometimes reading. These visitors should always have a clear sense of where they are, and of how where they are relates to the rest of the site. This is accomplished with clear, ubiquitous, consistent navigation (Lynch and Horton 2001).

How do we accomplish this?

- **Present clear navigation aids throughout the site.** Visitors should be able to easily return to the home page from anywhere else in the site.
- **Present consistent navigation aids.** Every Web page should contain at least one link, and all should link back to the entry page. Each page should communicate through its navigational links how it relates to the site as a whole.
- **Give visitors direct access.** Provide them with the information they want in the fewest possible steps.
- **Direct but do not distract.** Graphics, multimedia and hyperlinks should be used deliberately and not gratuitously.
- **Keep it simple and scannable (KISS).** Interface metaphors, like the envelope icon for email, should be simple, familiar and logical to the audience.

The MiniUSA site (www.miniusa.com) is a fine example of the last directive to keep site content simple and scannable. Mixing Flash movies with straight text, the site quickly orients the visitor and presents information where the visitor would expect to find it (not unlike the dashboard in the Mini cars).

Navigation is at the heart of the site, which re-configures *all* of its information depending on what is clicked. The visual elements—mostly cars—also help to simplify navigation and communicate change. (See p. 61.)

Simplicity and Clarity

The MiniUSA site should be noted also for its judicious use of graphics. There aren't many, keeping the site simple and uncluttered, and those that do appear

are sized and positioned for impact. They direct the visitor's attention by interacting with the text and by prioritizing information. The site's Flash enables navigation and content to be layered, very clearly arraying a great deal of information in front of the viewer on a single page.

The use of Flash here also minimizes download times, which is a key concern whenever designers contemplate graphics. Flash is efficient with bandwidth, using compressed files and typically small graphical file sizes. The downside is that users must have an updated Flash plug-in on their computers and browsers.

Web designers Lynch and Horton warn against what they call "clown pants," or too much graphic embellishment. It is an exquisite metaphor. Horizontal rules, graphic bullets, icons and other visual markers have their purpose, but they should be used sparingly and with a clear sense of purpose. Where everything is garish, nothing in particular is emphasized. Less often truly is more. What sort of first impression would you make by walking into a job interview wearing clown pants, over-sized red shoes and a big red nose? You'd certainly make an impression, but probably not the right one. Web sites that overuse or misuse graphics, features and special effects can also make a bad first impression by trying too hard to stand out.

Three general principles can guide your visual style:

- Make content easy to find (navigation).
- Make it easy to read.
- Make it aesthetically (or visually) appealing.

Repetition

Repetition and consistency help visitors by orienting them and reassuring them. Imagine you have been zapped into the middle of a high-rise office building in Manhattan. You have no idea what floor you are on. You have no idea why you are there. You have no idea how to get out. What you would most like is to be in the lobby, at a reception desk or at least looking at a directory with floor and office numbers, preferably near the elevators. A consistent approach to layout and navigation on the Web enables visitors to quickly learn that layout and to predict the location of information. So, when choosing graphics, layouts, typographies and illustrations, and when building navigation, be consistent in both substance and style.

Repetition and consistency also help produce unity and a consistent rhythm in terms of how the site is viewed and used, much as they do in print publications. Repetition of elements, in organization and in navigation, can yield an impressive overall impression. Think for a moment of your favorite magazine. Notice the ways that the selection and placement of text and images, the typography and text size, the use of color, and other design elements help to set a mood and establish a rhythm for the magazine that affects how you react to and move through the content. Why might these design factors encourage you to flip through a copy of *US Weekly* but linger over an article in *The New Yorker*, for example? These design considerations work similarly online. Visit Nike.com, for example, and race through the many high-energy product presentations and celebrity athlete biographies. Next, visit Adobe.com to sit back, watch and listen to Adobe tell its own story with vivid color Flash presentations with audio. Repetition is not boring, therefore, or at least it doesn't have to be. Repetition can give a site a consistent graphic identity that reinforces a distinct sense of "place," which then makes that site more memorable. A few case studies hopefully will help amplify some of these points

Case Study 1: C|Net (www.cnet.com)

The news package from C|Net on Real ID identification demonstrates effective visual style by expertly using links, headlines, navigation content and layering. The story's byline is linked to the reporters' email addresses, which has become standard practice for news sites. Supporting and related information is linked to down the right side, in sections that include "What Is," "Stories in this Series," "Previous Coverage," "Related Coverage," and a credit section. We should expect to see a lot more credits as news organizations more properly attribute all of the components of work that have to come together in a multimedia presentation. The era of the single byline is coming to a close. These sidebar lists give readers multiple layers at which to engage with the topic.

Macro site navigation is positioned at the top of the screen and at the bottom (not shown), and the tabular format shows clearly where a reader is located within the site:

- Top layer: C|Net
- Second layer: sections of the site
- Third layer: sub-sections of the News section
- Fourth layer: the individual story.

Note the relatively high number of linked words, which appear in a lighter tint in the illustration below. This high number makes sense given the complexity of the story. A reader likely would want to reference some of the terms used in the narrative.

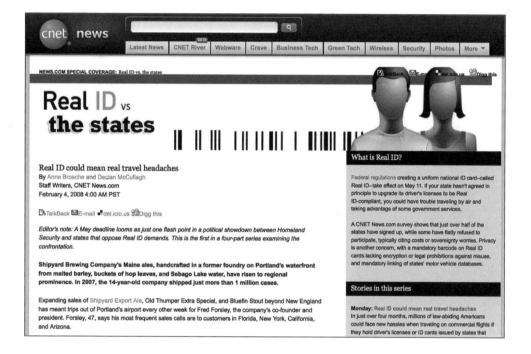

The use of graphics and the way the page is organized help readers easily move through the individual page and throughout C|Net. The interactive map feature is another layer of information, engaging readers at a level potentially much closer to home.

Remember that the computer screen typically is smaller and has different dimensions than most news publications' printed pages. Many graphic designers create page grids that look great on their jumbo computer monitors, forgetting that most users cannot display more than about half of the designers' Web layout at any one time. Remember also that only a fraction of Web surfers scroll the page vertically—*ever*! And few are willing to scroll vertically *and* horizontally.

Ever larger computer screens have given designers more flexibility. Web pages 850 pixels wide and 500 pixels deep now are acceptable; only a few years ago 650 pixels by 350 pixels was a standard size for non-scrolling pages. A letter-sized 8.5-inch by 11-inch document, by contrast, would be 670 by 535, if measured in pixels. These parameters likely will continue to change, presenting a design challenge to Web developers, who have to keep the many monitor sizes, resolution grades, browser sizes and connection speeds in mind.

Case Study 2: Razorfish (www.razorfish.com)

Two examples of Web site layouts that establish appropriate spatial relationships within their elements, and within the 850 by 500 limits, are Apple.com and Razorfish. Each site shows sensitivity to common screen sizes and locates content, navigation and graphics accordingly.

Note the macro site navigation across the top with special content listed and linked at left. Simple graphics, lots of white space for air, and a consistent scheme and layout help users quickly get to the information they need. The site also uses a nifty unfolding Flash-generated graphic to cue site navigation and create suspense.

Case Study 3: Google (www.google.com)

The majesty of Google's home page has always been its simplicity and un-adorned utility, and this simplicity has actually increased over time rather than following the more obvious, nearly ubiquitous trend of increasingly clutter. First, the Google top layer search page from 2006, see page 65 (top).

Next, the home page from 2009, see page 65 (foot).

In either case, Google provides its navigation, a dominant image with the corporate color scheme used throughout the site for consistency, additional functionality on the right, and only the necessary verbiage, all in a very tight

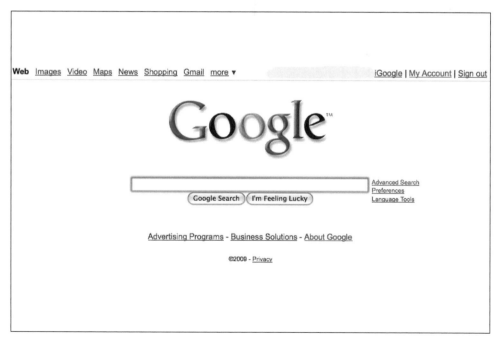

space with lots of white space for a sense of visual rest. The purpose of Google drove its home page design. Its form is its function. There are no clown's pants here.

Planning the Pages

The minimalist elegance of the Google home page is no accident; good Web sites and good Web pages are the products of planning. **Site planning**, or mapping, is the equivalent to creating an architectural blueprint before any mortar is made. The activity of developing a site map forces the Web developer to think through how individual pages, sections, and elements of content are going to relate to each other, which is a necessary first step before creating navigation. A site map either lists or, better yet, graphically presents the pages and sections of a site, with lines connecting those pages and sections that will link to one another.

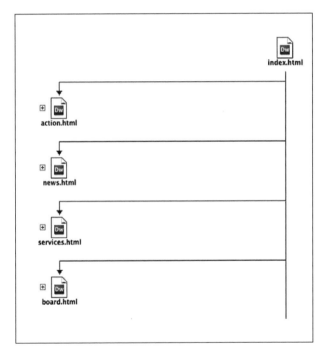

A simple site map showing the pages that link from or off a site's home page.

After mapping out a site, a good next step is to begin **storyboarding** individual pages. The term "storyboard" comes from a practice in filmmaking in which story conceivers graphically map out the content of the movie—the story—on a series of placards or posters. These storyboards can be and often are very crude visual representations of what will populate individual Web pages. They are cheap, easy to make, and they take relatively little time to generate, so there is really no reason not to storyboard. Wading into Web authoring with a general idea but no storyboards often results in a great deal of wasted time building pages or even entire sites that later prove unworkable and/or that are not scalable. Rookie page designers end up designing themselves into a corner, while storyboarding allows them to spot imbalances and to see problems and issues relating to unity before these problems are knitted into the page design.

More specifically, storyboarding involves placing and positioning design elements and content on paper, even if it is merely positioning the major pieces. To the degree possible, both the elements and the content should be described, even fonts, sizes and colors. Each storyboard or page design should effectively lead a reader's eye through the page. Readers will first see only basic shapes, dominant colors and big masses of text. They will pick up the foreground first, then background content. Only after this orientation do they see specific elements and text, deciding at that point on what to focus attention. A storyboard helps the designer see what readers will see. A storyboard helps plot out the precious real estate on the screen, as well.

Storyboards should show a discernible hierarchy of headlines and subheadlines (or second-order headlines); a consistency in color usage; and a logical map or path for the reader's eye. Text should be broken up, and there should be some breathing room for the page's elements. Graphics should not be used gratuitously but only in service to the intent of the page. In developing storyboards, a good rule-of-thumb for internal pages is for content to account for between 50 percent and 80 percent of a page's design space, leaving no less than 20 percent of the space for navigation. This guideline does not apply to home pages, however, where introducing the navigational scheme might require more space.

To prioritize the content, Jakob Nielsen's usability studies results suggest a useful method: Evaluate all of the design elements on the page, even eliminating them one at a time, if only hypothetically. If the design works better or even the same without the element, leave it out. Less is often more.

Unfortunately there is no way of knowing the size of the screen on which users are viewing the pages, and no way of determining the monitor's color sophistication. For this reason, a "lowest-common-denominator" approach is recommended, unless you are targeting a specific group about which more is known vis-à-vis the computers and browsers its members are using. Assume a low baseline and use resolution-independent pages, which allow designs to adapt to the screen size. Using percentage-based sizing in frames and tables rather than fixed, pixel-based sizes, for example, can be an effective way to accomplish a flexible design format. Of course, table cells that are not fixed also are not predictable, possibly re-arranging or re-configuring a design in unpredictable ways. Good designers test and re-test their pages on PCs and Macs, viewing pages in Internet Explorer, Safari, Firefox and others (and in older versions of each), and on monitors or computer screens of various sizes.

After storyboarding, for each and every Web page, think about the following:

- **What:** a title (the text that appears on the browser's top bar, which also is the text that appears when users add the site to their "favorites"; this heading should make absolutely clear what the page is about).
- **Who:** author's identity and institutional affiliation (individual author and/or institution; think of the information any bibliographic citation would require).
- **When:** a creation and/or revision date ("last updated 01/01/09," for example).
- **Where:** at least one link to the local home page.
- **How:** additional navigation, ubiquitous navigation, layered navigation.

Usability

Your Web pages will reach the world, and they will be searched and archived for perpetuity. You were careful planning, mapping and storyboarding your content. Likewise after development, demonstrate care by making sure your pages work. Do the graphics appear in the right places and render in correct ways? Do links work? Are there formatting or layout issues? Usability expert Steve Krug advises that even a little usability research is better than none. Allowing even one other person to test your pages and to read your content can provide valuable feedback to inform updates and changes.

When undergraduate students of a Web design class at Berry College in Mount Berry, Georgia, were asked to develop a Web site for the local Habitat for Humanity chapter, the class first met with the chapter's executive director to discuss his goals for the site.

To guide that discussion, the class prepared a list of questions:

1. What do you definitely want the site to do?
2. What do you definitely want the site NOT to do?
3. When are you hoping to have a working site up on the Web? What deadline do you suggest?
4. Who will host the site? (How will we publish the site to the Web?)
5. What graphics or art do you have? What art do you want to use (logos, photos, charts)? What art do you know you do not want to use, or cannot use?
6. What content do you have or are you planning to get?
7. Of these elements, what will be frequently and/or routinely updated?
8. Which parts of the site will be temporary (such as an event of the month) and which will be permanent?
9. What are your expectations for this site? What are your expectations for our involvement in developing the site, both during the semester and beyond?

10 How complex does the site need to be? What functionality do you want it to have? (For example, enabling supporters to donate online, to volunteer online, etc.)

11 What tone, mood or attitude should the site project? What tone, mood or attitude should be avoided?

12 Do you have examples of sites you like, sites similar in approach or philosophy to what you want?

13 What are your plans for usability testing?

14 Who is going to maintain and update the site?

The class attempted to design a site for the chapter that is easy to navigate, one with an obvious design structure. Habitat wanted site visitors to be able to "get it" without having to ask, "Where do I start?" or "Can I click on that?" so the class aimed to eliminate or otherwise anticipate user questions. (The Habitat site the class designed is located on the Web at http://www.habitatrome.com/.)

Good Web site usability design means that visitors will not have to ask:

- Where am I?
- Where should I begin?
- Where did they put _____?
- What's most important here?
- Why did they call it that?

Users glance. They scan. They click. They do not always choose the BEST path on the page to take them where they want to go; so it is up to us to make the pathways to their destinations immediately clear.

With these priorities in mind, the Habitat design team's goals included:

- Creating a clear visual hierarchy on each page.
- Taking advantage of conventions.
- Breaking up pages into clearly defined areas.
- Making it obvious what is and what is not clickable on each page.
- Minimizing noise and distractions.

In addition, the design team sought to make sure that the elements users see on the page—search boxes, links, buttons, etc.—accurately convey their importance and utility. The more important the content, the more **prominently** it should be placed.

Good navigation is one of the highest priorities in making a good Web site. Navigation must be clear, consistent and simple. As Web usability expert Steve Krug says, navigation is not just a feature of the Web site, it *is* the Web site. There are two types of users—hunters and gatherers—according to Krug. The search-dominant hunters ask, "Where's the search box?" while the information-gatherers ask, "Where are the links?" Excellent layouts and designs should help both types of users get from one place to another on the site and help orient them within the site, tell them what is available and reveal the content. Think of the map you typically find in a shopping mall that clearly shows "YOU ARE HERE." The map shows how big the place is and situates you in relationship to everything within the space.

One good model of a clear navigation design can be found at the *New York Times* Web site at www.nytimes.com. Finding a box score on the site for the latest Yankees game, for example, is relatively simple, and the path clearly displayed: Home >> Sports >>Major League Baseball >>Yankees v. Orioles >> Box Score. The reader knows precisely where he or she is in the site in relationship to the rest of the site and is able to return to any previous part of the site with just one click.

At a glance, a home page should be able to quickly and clearly:

- Establish identity and mission.
- Show site hierarchy.
- Show where to start.
- Show what's here.
- Indicate shortcuts to main, most desired pages, sections.
- Convey the big picture.
- Avoid clutter.

Several institutions have conducted comprehensive usability studies that inform other, more local usability evaluations. The Yale University Library, for example, completed two usability studies of what it calls the Research Workstation Web site, which serves as the primary gateway for researchers and is the default home page on most public workstations in Yale's main library. In its report, the library describes the methods used to plan and conduct the studies and provides several ways of evaluating the data for long- and short-term Web site planning. Though a bit dated, the studies are carefully documented. See: http://www.library.yale.edu/~prowns/nebic/nebictalk.html.

Another aid is the National Cancer Institute's Usability Guidelines, a document describing what the National Cancer Institute has learned about its own usability, which is quite a bit. The Institute's site is quite sophisticated. The development phases that this site recommends also are helpful: Plan, Analyze, Develop, Test and Refine. Other topics covered in this comprehensive usability help site include:

- What Is Usability?
- Why Is It Important?
- How Much Does It Cost?
- Can Usability Be Measured?

The Institute offers research-based guidelines for the home page, page layout, navigation, links, text appearance, graphic design, accessibility and search, as well as providing a toolbox of templates and examples. Available: http://www.usability.gov/.

● Plan	● Analyze	● Design
● Think About the Process ● Develop a Plan ● Assemble a Project Team ● And more...	● Learn About Your Users ● Conduct Task Analysis ● Develop Personas ● And more...	● Determine Site Requirements ● Write for the Web ● Use Parallel Design ● And more...

Usability Topics

● **Usability & Government**
- Usability in Government
- Lessons Learned
- Requirements & Best Practices
- And more...

● **Usability Basics**
- What Is Usability?
- Why Is It Important?
- How Much Does It Cost?
- Can Usability Be Measured?
- And more...

● **Research-Based Guidelines**
- Home Page
- Page Layout
- Navigation
- Links
- Text Appearance
- Graphic Design
- Accessibility
- Search
- Software/Hardware
- And more...

● **Templates & Examples**
- Usability Test Reports
- Online Surveys
- Usability Testing Forms
- And more...

● **Usability Methods**
- Card Sorting
- Personas
- Task Analysis
- Usability Testing
- And more...

Chapter Assignment

1 Choose a Web site you visit regularly, one where you read a lot of the content. Imagine that you have been hired as the site's new editor-in-chief. Make specific recommendations to improve the presentation of content at the site, integrating and referencing the chapter as much as possible. What elements or features promote use of the site? Again, think of all the elements described in this chapter. How are graphics and visuals incorporated, and do they encourage or discourage use? How do they do this? How much thought was given to navigation throughout the site? Are the elements—graphical, navigational and metaphorical—consistently applied throughout the site? Is the tone or rhythm of the site consistent throughout? Do these dimensions match the audience(s) for the site? Here is a categorical checklist of site dimensions to critique:

   1 Navigation
   2 Page layouts (balance | contrast | unity)
   3 Consistency
   4 Tone and voice
   5 Writing quality
   6 Site organization.

   Length: Approximately 800–1,000 words.

Online Resources

The GNOME Usability Study Report from Sun Microsystems and the GNOME Open Source Project
http://developer.gnome.org/projects/gup/ut1_report/report_main.html
Report includes a set of user testing studies from March 2001 and 32 design and development suggestions based on those studies.

International Journal of Human Computer Studies **Usability Special Issue**
http://ijhcs.open.ac.uk/index.html
Provides eight Adobe Acrobat .pdf versions of reprints of several usability
articles, which are a bit dated but still useful.

Steve Krug's usability Web site
http://www.sensible.com
Krug takes the individual user's perspective and is sensitive to small
business and small publication owners.

Patrick J. Lynch and Sarah Horton, *Web Style Guide*, 3rd ed.
http://www.webstyleguide.com/
Companion site to *Web Style Guide: Basic Design Principles for Creating
Web Sites* by Patrick J. Lynch and Sarah Horton.

**David M. Nichols and Michael B. Twidale, "The Usability of Open Source
Software"**
http://www.cs.waikato.ac.nz/~daven/docs/oss-wp.html
A peer-reviewed paper that "reviews the existing evidence of the usability
of open source software and discusses how the characteristics of open
source development influence usability."

Jakob Nielsen, "Writing for the Web"
http://www.sun.com/980713/webwriting
This booklet, created primarily for commercial sites, contains some of
Nielsen's instructions on maximizing readership.

Sources

Carolyn Dowling, *Writing and Learning with Computers* (Camberwell, Vic., Australia:
Acer Press, 1999).

Anders Fagerjord, "Rhetorical Convergence: Studying Web Media," in *Digital
Media Revisited*, Gunnar Liestol, Andrew Morrison, and Terje Rasmussen, eds.
(Cambridge, MA: MIT, 2003): 293–326.

Steve Krug, *Don't Make Me Think* (Upper Saddle River, NJ: New Riders Press, 2000).

Patrick Lynch and Sarah Horton, *Web Style Guide 2* (New Haven, CT: Yale University
Press, 2001); also available: http://info.med.yale.edu/caim/manual/contents.html.

Rachel McAlpine, *Web Word Wizardry: A Guide to Writing for the Web and Intranet*
(Berkeley, CA: Ten Speed Press, 2001).

Jakob Nielsen, *Designing Web Usability* (Indianapolis, IN: New Riders, 2000).

Anthony Tedesco, "Adapt Your Writing to the Web," *The Writer*, 114, no. 5 (May
2001): 16.

Nathan Wallace, "Web Writing for Many Interest Levels" (1999), available: http://
www.e-gineer.com/articles/web-writing-for-many-interest-levels.phtml.

4 HEADLINES AND HYPERTEXT

Everything that is needless gives Offense.
Benjamin Franklin

We must abandon conceptual systems found upon ideas of center, margin, hierarchy, and linearity, and replace them with ones of multilinearity, nodes, links, and networks.
George Landow, educator and author of *Hypertext 2.0*

Each of us literally chooses, by his way of attending to things, what sort of universe he shall appear to himself to inhabit.
William James, psychologist

Chapter Objectives

After studying this chapter, you will be able to:

- write effective headlines, deckheads, subheads and sub-subheads;
- use hyperlinks correctly to organize information, facilitate navigation and help users access information;
- organize information in lists, both ordered and unordered, and better understand what kinds of information lend themselves to lists;
- understand how essays, long writing and text-intensive stories and articles should be presented online.

Introduction

In the last chapter, we explored online style, writing style and visual style. We drill down further in this chapter by discussing in the context of style some specific writing techniques such as hyperlinks and headlines, and how these techniques can help readers navigate in and through our content. Other tools to facilitate scanning and surfing include "chunking" text—breaking text down into smaller, usually paragraph-sized chunks—and presenting subheads, deckheads and lists. Also considered is how to break up and present longer writing pieces.

Hypertext

In Chapter 1 the book and the process of printing are described as technologies that have shaped our understanding of scholarship and of composition. Hypertext, or computer text capable of taking the reader somewhere else on the Web with the click of a mouse, is changing this understanding. "Hyper" comes from the Greek root meaning "beyond" or "over"; when clicked, hypertext takes a reader beyond the page he or she is visiting to somewhere or something else.

Hyperlinks, or links, are the most common form of hypertext. Because links change the direction of the reader's experience in or through a page or document, as opposed to the linear activity of reading promoted by books, a new rhetorical style is needed that recognizes this non-linearity. This new style must acknowledge that the user, not the author or producer, dictates the order in which the information is read or accessed. Navigational hyperlinks take visitors to other pages or sections within the site. Content hyperlinks take visitors to other sources of information, as addenda to what is being read.

The question becomes: To what kinds of information should a Web writer link? The sea of information available to a user can easily lead to confusion, so the Web writer should very carefully consider his or her links. Some of the more common destinations for links in journalistic writing include primary sources and public records, interview notes and excerpts, related or archival stories and information, definitions of terms and brief explanations, and multimedia. Many if not most of these forms of links can be conceptualized as footnotes, or the kinds of information footnotes have traditionally contained, only with the new benefit of proximity. To access resources footnoted in print, you would have to, say, visit a library and check the resource out on loan. In online environments, these resources are proximous. The once solitary main text has a potentially infinite number of neighbors.

[68] Davis, 153.

[69] *Chicago American*, Editorial, 8.

[70] In the Davis article, Elston Howard is quoted telling the *St. Petersburg Times* that white players could make all their arrangements in advance through an agent. Howard, however, had to wait to see what living conditions he could secure before bringing his family down. And Robinson, in *Baseball has done it*, tells the story of another player whose wife left because of her fear of going into town and facing discrimination (115). "Most black players kept their families isolated from these problems by simply leaving them at home," Davis wrote (156).

[71] Baseball historian Bill James conducted a fascinating statistical study in 1987 comparing 54 black rookies with 54 white rookies, expecting to find "nothing in particular or nothing beyond the outside range of chance," (in Jon Entine, *Taboo: Why black athletes dominate sports and why we are afraid to talk about it* [New York: Public Affairs, 2000]: 23). James found that the black players went on to have better playing careers in 44 of the 54 cases, played 48% more games, had 66% more hits and clubbed 66% more home runs. "Nobody likes to write about race," he said, but "the results were astonishing."

[72] Leo W. Banks, "An oasis for some pioneers; Lucille and Chester Willis put up black ballplayers when Tucson's hotels wouldn't," *Sports Illustrated* 70, no. 116 [8 May 1989]: 116-117.

Hyperlinked footnotes in an online document, demonstrating the proximity of resources online.

How to Hyperlink

Hyperlinks should be obvious and unambiguous; readers should know exactly what they will find by clicking, enabling them to decide whether to click now, later or not at all. The links themselves should be explicit about the type of content to which they lead, and they should be consistent in appearance. (Repetition was discussed in the previous chapter.) Conventions online call for hyperlinks to be approximately the same size as the main body text.

Hyperlinks should not appear merely as labels or pointers to content: they should be regarded as content themselves, much as headlines are. "Click here" is the equivalent to a headline in print that states, "Important story below." Such a pointer does not provide enough helpful information; it merely points to content. Here are a few examples:

Bad: For more information on the Boeing 777, <u>click here</u>.
Good: The company has more than a dozen <u>Boeing 777s</u> in its fleet.

Bad: The commission's report is available, <u>click here</u>.
Better: The commission's report is available: <u>www.report.com</u>.
Best: Read the commission's <u>report</u>.

Let's look at another example of good hyperlinking, from an undergraduate student's blog:

> The news media, including journalists, editors and executives, largely agree that the core principles of journalism are getting the facts right, getting both sides of the story and not publishing rumors. According to the <u>Pew Research Center for the People and the Press</u>, journalists increasingly agree with public criticism of their profession and the quality of their work. About half of news media executives and journalists rank *lack of credibility* with the public as a major reason for declining audiences. In 1989, only one-third of the press said this. Americans' evaluations of the news media's credibility have declined since the mid-1980s.
>
> <u>The poll</u> was conducted in coordination with the <u>Committee of Concerned Journalists</u> from November 20, 1998 to February 11, 1999. Lack of credibility is the single issue most often cited by the news media as the most important problem facing journalism today.

Note a few attributes of the student's hyperlinks:

- They take readers to the supporting evidence and primary source material in such a way that they do not interrupt the flow of main body of text.
- They help readers predict at least generally where the link will take them.
- They each are only a few words, or the shortest possible amount of text. Long, hyperlinked phrases are difficult to read, and likely will not get read. They also clutter the Web page.

The student's links also make use of two common Web conventions for links—blue text color and underlining. Although still in currency, however, these conventions are in flux. The explosion of blogs and the increased style capacities of CSS relative to HTML have fueled a move away from underlining and from blue link text. Underlining has given way on many sites to same-sized text presented in a secondary color, one typically lighter than the main body text color. An example, with links in a lighter tint:

 Comments   Trackbacks

Tactics of the Adept Practitioner in Modern IP Mediation

Posted on June 28, 2009 by Victoria Pynchon

I'm sharing today a power point presentation that was the basis of an ALI–ABA IP Mediation seminar conducted by me and David Donoghue of Holland + Knight. The course outline with bios is here. The course itself can be found here. This presentation is modified from one I presented with the Hon. John Leo Wagner of Judicate West at an ABA conference. Many thanks to Judge Wagner for his insights, many of which are captured here.

The specific text and link color choices are not that important (provided they are legible, of course), but consistency and repetition are important. If one hyperlink is deep green, all of the hyperlinks should be in deep green.

Hyperlinking should be viewed as the quickest way to get a reader to the most relevant information that reader might be interested in. In an online presentation about the hazards of childhood smoking, for example, appropriate would be links to clinical studies, to resource centers and to related articles on smoking among children. Readers do not have to rely solely on the one story, but neither are they likely to be distracted by the links to the supporting information. To this same end, where possible the Web writer should state or summarize the conclusions of a clinical study or supporting details and source information.

Because they typically are a different color, links are similar to words in boldface. They promote scanning, then, which Web writers should consider when composing them. An example from the home page of the Association of Lighthouse Keepers (www.lighthouse.fsnet.co.uk/) below demonstrates links' function as guideposts in surfing and scanning.

The **Association of Lighthouse Keepers** was formed in 1988 by a group of serving and **retired keepers**, with the aim of maintaining contact between its members and enthusiasts throughout the world who share an interest in lighthouses and other **coastal** and **inland** aids to **navigation**. Our aims are to forge links with other **lighthouse associations**, to act as an information exchange, to expand our growing **archive** on lighthouse-related material, and in the long term, to establish a museum/study centre to promote the growing interest in **pharology**.

Readers can, and likely will, scan the boldface words quickly to discern the purpose of the site and its organization. Hyperlinks should be handled in much the same way. Linking entire sentences or long phrases, then, is verboten. A scanning eye can only pick up two or three words at a time, and readers' habits and tendencies should not be ignored.

In summary, ask the following questions when developing hyperlinks and presenting them in online environments:

- How can I assure and orient readers when they first arrive on or at the page?
- How can I help them read efficiently and with pleasure?
- How can I help readers to retrace the steps they have taken in their reading paths, or to return to any one step or level in any one of those paths?
- How can I describe or signal the destinations for the links in the document?

Types of Links

Embedded links and, as sub-sets, inline links and anchors are the main kinds of hyperlinks you will find on the Web. Each type operates a little differently, but all will determine where a reader goes when clicking—whether to a point within the same Web page or site on which the link appears (an anchor link) or off to a new page or site.

Embedded links are by far the most common type of link, and they are usually placed behind a word, a selection of words, an object (image, button, icon) or a "hot area." If the word or object is clicked, the visitor will be redirected somewhere else. And though most embedded links you encounter are embedded in text with HTML, other elements can include embedded links, such as buttons and icons, navigation bars and image maps.

> **In a big departure from the hands-off approach to market regulation of the last two decades, the chairman of the** Commodity Futures Trading Commission, Gary Gensler, **said his agency would consider new limits on the volume of energy futures contracts that purely financial investors would be allowed to hold.**

Embedded links, "Commodity Futures Trading Commission" and "Gary Gensler."

A **hot area** typically is found in or on an image, diagram or other graphical object in which an HTML image map has been placed. Moving the cursor over the hot area activates one or more embedded links. Below, HTML code is shown that embeds individual African country links into a larger map of eastern Africa, a graphical file named "navbar":

```
<P>
<OBJECT data="navbar.png" type="image/png" usemap="#mapA">
  <OBJECT data="navbar.gif" type="image/gif" usemap="#mapA">
    <MAP name="mapA">
    <P>Navigate the map:
      <A href="sudan.html" shape="poly" coords="0,0,118,28">Sudan</a> |
      <A href="chad.html" shape="poly" coords="118,0,184,28">Chad</A> |
      <A href="ethiopia.html" shape="poly" coords="184,200,60">Ethiopia</A> |
      <A href="uganda.html" shape="poly" coords=
            "276,0,276,28,100,200,50,50,276,0">Uganda</A>
    </MAP>
</OBJECT>
```

Moving a mouse cursor over the section of the map labeled "Sudan," which is pinpointed on the graphic using coordinates, then clicking, would take a site visitor to an HTML page file named "sudan.html," or a Web page with more information on or about Sudan.

Inline links, by contrast, do not send the visitor somewhere else, but bring content from somewhere else to the page being viewed. There is no need, therefore, to embed the link or the content. Images and graphics are the most common inline link content. The link typically shows part of the larger content, like a thumbnail or a preview at lower resolution of what could be seen enlarged when clicked. Or, the image can appear in its entirety, but is actually located somewhere else, owned by someone else. Images appearing in blogs frequently appear using inline links, meaning that the blogger is merely linking to the graphic elsewhere on the Web with HTML that makes it appear as if it is part of the blog page being viewed.

Anchors are in-page or within-document navigational links, redirecting a visitor to another part of the same document or page. They are commonly used to create top-of-page navigation to sections below, often in text-intensive or lengthy Web pages to avoid excessive scrolling.

As a set or sub-set, links also can serve different purposes. The home page of Arts & Letters Daily (www.aldaily.com), for example, is an aggregator, or an intersection or navigational point from which to decide where to travel next. The links all are outbound, re-directing readers to the artifacts and sources being abstracted. By contrast, at Wikipedia, the hyperlinked terms and words typically lead only to other Wikipedia content. (See page 37.)

There is considerable debate among Web designers about whether hyper-links should open in new windows or not, and whether they should link to outside sites, even a rival's site. If linked material opens up in a new, separate window, the original window and story are still there, so the reader can resume reading the main narrative after accessing the sidebar or background

information. But, new windows can quickly clutter up a desktop, which of course readers do not appreciate. Links that open up content by creating a new tab on the browser might be a good compromise, leaving the original story but providing access to sidebar information within the same browser window.

The hyperlinking ethos online has changed in the past few years from one resistant to jettisoning readers from a news organization's Web site to one that acknowledges that readers want this kind of universal access. News organizations have begun linking even to competitors, making them aggregators as well as content producers. The philosophy, learned from Google, seems to be that if a news site does a good enough job sending people away, they will come back for more. In distilling this new ethos, journalism professor Jeff Jarvis has proposed linking's golden rule: "Link unto others' good stuff as you would have them link unto your good stuff."

Good hyperlinking, like writing in general, is about clarity and consistency. Readers should not have to hunt through links, confused about what they might do for them. It is about providing content. It is about telling them that the content they need is there. And it is about clearly displaying that content. You cannot control for every possible user experience. Some people might be confused or follow a link and not return. You can be clear and consistent and therefore minimize the confusion.

Hyperlinking's History

Given how important hyperlinks are in the way we read text online today, it is difficult to believe that they were controversial when they were first introduced in 1989. Critics in English departments throughout the United States believed that hyperlinking interferes with reading comprehension and understanding. Researchers ultimately found, however, that hyperlinks do not "slow down the reading process [and] do not affect text comprehension" (De Ridder 2002). One might argue that links can actually enhance comprehension of Web pages because a quick look at the links can give the reader a general sense of what the page is about.

Hypertext, along with the ease of copying, erasing, rearranging and otherwise manipulating text, is breaking down the linear model of the book. How scholarship, information and content are delivered is changing at a fundamental level. Hypertext is helping to put authors' and researchers' notes and original data in "experientially closer proximity," as Landow writes, placing a premium on these combinations and rewarding transparency and citation of sources. Blogging is a contemporary example of exactly what Landow describes, connecting the speaker directly in touch with his or her audience and placing the content in proximity to its source material or related material—typically via links on the Web page.

Interestingly, though hypertext can produce completely non-linear or multi-linear texts, which can be read or accessed through multiple pathways, Web readers still seem to prefer material on the Web that follows a traditional narrative format. While many authors have experimented with producing elaborate, narratively complex, multi-layered writings in hypertext, there apparently are limits to how many directions readers are willing to travel.

Another problem or consideration in using hyperlinks is their care. Not surprisingly, broken hyperlinks are a common and recurring problem for any site with large collections of links. Broken links chip away at a page's credibility, and they are a sign of age, so hyperlinks must be periodically checked to make sure they are still active. Most Web authoring software does this automatically. Additionally, if the link is still active but the URL owner has changed, the original purpose for the link may be subverted.

Read All About It! Headlines and Subheads

One of the fundamental realities emphasized in this book is that Web users skim, surf, scroll and scan. They do not read word by word by word. Headlines, headings and headers are essential, therefore, because they stand a better chance as a set of being read than does body copy. If handled properly, headlines can halt the "scanner" and mark the way. They can predict for the reader what content will follow, allowing the reader to decide whether to pause to read that content or to keep moving. We mentioned headlines in the previous chapter; here we zero in on how to write good ones.

Headlines and headers should be organized on several levels: Individual pages might have their own headings to introduce them, then subheads throughout the pages and possibly sub-subheads if the text is particularly dense. If an article or story is longer than 350 words, Web writers should employ subheads to help readers scan and to organize the presentation.

Like headlines, subheads should be brief, straightforward, active and useful, adding another layer of information rather than merely repeating something said somewhere else. Web writers should consider headings and subheads in sets or groups, distinct from the text, to make sure that readers can see why they have been arranged in the order in which they are presented, and why some have been grouped and not others.

Across media, print and online, headlines serve several functions. In *The Art of Editing,* Brian S. Brooks and Jack Z. Sissors (2000) give headlines at least six tasks. Well-written headlines will:

- attract the reader's attention;
- summarize content;
- help reader index that content;
- depict mood and tone;
- help set the tone;
- provide typographic relief.

Headlines also help readers determine *what not to read*, and this is every bit as important as helping readers decide to what they will attend. Good headlines attract attention to content that otherwise may be ignored. But headline writers should resist the sometimes overwhelming temptation to be cute. Headlines first and foremost should inform rather than entertain, particularly because the audience online is potentially a global one. Conciseness and accuracy should not be sacrificed for personality, therefore. For the same reason, abbreviations, slang, idioms, colloquialisms and puns generally should be avoided. The "just the facts" style of most headlines doesn't win prizes for originality, but it does help a reader make an intelligent decision about whether to stop and read or to keep moving.

For similar reasons, think carefully about tone in headlines and subheads, as well. Cute and clever headlines are tempting to write, but they are difficult to pull off in print, and even more problematic online. The reference or pun that might make your headline seem so clever to you may be lost on a global audience. Sexual innuendo, too, is often lurking just around the semantic corner, so headlines and subheads should be more descriptive in tone and aim to convey useful information about the text. Remember that users scan to headings to navigate the Web page or site and to get the meaning of the text, so straightforward headings will help them. Headlines and subheads also are used by search engines to rank pages, so the more direct the descriptions, the better the page's fortunes in search findings.

A page from the National Cancer Institute illustrates many of these points:

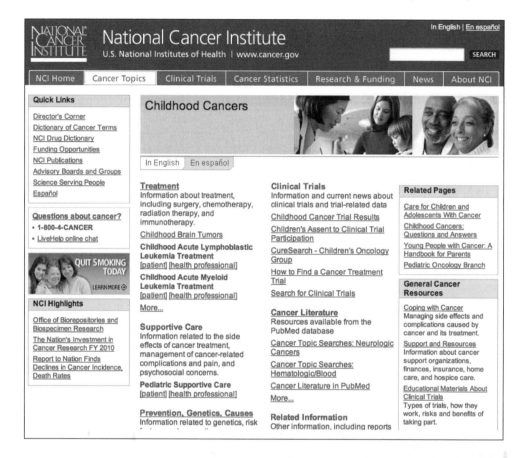

Note the easy navigation to supporting information positioned in an offset left panel. The page also employs a **straightforward headline**, "Childhood Cancers." Sectional navigation is positioned on the right side in a legible type style and contrasting color. The borders and colors clearly organize the content. This is a strong layout for a text-intensive page, and its serious tone is appropriate to the subject matter.

Keep It Simple

When the actor Heath Ledger died in January 2008, the online version of the *Sydney Morning Herald* in Australia posted the following headline: "Heath Ledger Dies." Dull? Perhaps. But this headline generated traffic because people using search engines could easily find the story. Compare the headline to the *Herald*'s competition, from *The Age*: "Dead in Bed." Cute? Clever? You be the judge, but search engines judged it obtuse.

Though lacking in glamour, search engine optimization is a multi-billion-dollar business that is fueling how content is found or lost online; at a time when news organizations are struggling to develop long-term business models for online news, dull and well read beats clever but lost every time.

There are two steps in composing a headline:

- Determine what to highlight.
- Decide how to phrase it in the given space limitations.

To determine content, Brooks and Sissors recommend "the key-word method." Select the key words that convey the meaning of the content. Think about how the content would be indexed in a book or found by Google, or WWGD: What Would Google Do? Online headlines, therefore, should be intuitive, not cryptic, vague or leading. Simply by reading a headline the reader should be able to grasp what the story's about, as he or she can with "Heath Ledger Dies."

A well-crafted online headline provides the reader with sufficient information and incentive to decide whether to click a link to read the story. "Panel Re-visits Damage Plan" and "Congress Passes Bill" fail to say what their respective stories are about with any meaningful degree of specificity.

Following up the general steps for writing headlines above, here are more specific directions when it is time to write a headline:

- Explain what the article or story is about in the simplest of terms. The headline should make absolutely clear what the story concerns.
- Skip articles such as "a," "an" and "the," especially when starting the headline.
- Make the first word important.
- Do not start all page titles or headlines with the same word. The same word repeated would confuse.
- Use clear type and legible colors, and make the text big enough to read.

If a headline was submitted with the document that is being adapted for online presentation, a new headline should be written because of the different roles that headlines serve online versus in print. Again, the "Heath Ledger Dies" case study is useful. "Dead in Bed" might work well in print, where the story could be accompanied by a photo of the actor, a deckhead providing another layer of information and other visual cues as to what happened, what the story is about. (A deckhead is a small headline under the main headline that provides a next-layer level of information about the story. Deckheads are also called drop heads.) This context is more difficult to provide in the smaller spaces online, comparing a single screen's worth of information to, say, a newspaper spread, and because visitors are interacting with the information differently online, in a different order or sequence.

In presenting its headlines, the Web site Arts & Letters Daily (www.aldaily. com) employs all of the tools discussed in this module. The use of headers, including "Articles of Note," "New Books" and "Essays and Opinion," helps

JULY 7, 2009

Telecoms Face Antitrust Threat

Wireless Market, Generic Drugs Reviewed as Justice Department Steps Up Enforcement

| **Article** | Comments |

A headline and deckhead combination from the *Wall Street Journal*.

to map the home page's content and cue readers on a text-intensive Web page. To conserve space, the page eschews formal headlines for bolded words within text "chunks," tipping readers to the hyperlinked article's main topic. The site also lists third-party resources down the left side of the page.

Prominent and abundant use of headlines would be expected at a newspaper site like *The New York Times*, which employs some of the planet's most able editors to write the headlines, editors who typically accomplish most and sometimes all of Brooks's and Sissors's purposes in a single headline. (See page 85.)

These *Times* headlines help readers **skim**. They provide **structure** and **organization** to the page, in this case hierarchically according to news value. Compare the *Times*'s business page with that of the Arts & Letters Daily page. Which is easier to skim? Headlines are a good first cue. Subheads, too, help organize content.

A Word about Type

The type choices we make for print often do not work as well online. When printed on paper, type can handle ornamentation, serifs, ascenders and descenders, and embellishments. Online, however, fewer typefaces read or render well. Computer monitors have trouble displaying fonts with serifs—the curved embellishments on letters—because monitors use tiny squares called pixels to build each letter.

Therefore, every letter's "curve" on screen is really a collection of tiny squares that actually follow a tiny jagged line, not a truly smooth curve (magnify the letter S in a serif typeface like Times New Roman to 400 percent or so, for example, and you will see the squares, even in the letter's "curves").

Type magnified online to reveal square pixels, the building blocks of all content online.

U.S. Considers Curbs on Speculative Trading of Oil

By EDMUND L. ANDREWS
1:40 PM ET

Reacting to recent swings in oil prices, federal regulators said on Tuesday that they were considering limits on "speculative" traders in markets for oil and other energy products.

In Russia Speech, Obama Emphasizes Shared Interests

By PETER BAKER and CLIFFORD J. LEVY 8:28 AM ET

President Obama made the case for joint action on global security, but rejected complaints about U.S. support for missile defense and the expansion of NATO.

· Text: Obama's Speech

Saul Loeb/AFP — Getty

· Obama Dines In, to Some Russians' Distaste 1:30 PM ET
· Room for Debate: Russia and the Perils of Personal Diplomacy

LIVE VIDEO

At Jackson Service, Dancing and Mourning

By RANDAL C. ARCHIBOLD and MARIA NEWMAN 54 minutes ago

Michael Jackson, whose life was a complicated tale of celebrity, is being honored at a memorial service in Los Angeles as millions watch live broadcasts.

· Slide Show: Fans Around The World Celebrate Michael Jackson

ARTSBEAT BLOG

Latest Updates From the Jackson Memorial

By DAVE ITZKOFF and JON PARELES 3 minutes ago

Martin Luther King III and Bernice A. King offered condolences after a song by Jermaine Jackson.

MORE ON JACKSON

· Send Us Your Memorial Photos

· Video: Mourning Public Figures

· Your Favorite Jackson Song?

· Global Reaction

Iran's President Calls Disputed Elections 'Beautiful'

By MICHAEL SLACKMAN
11 minutes ago

President Mahmoud Ahmadinejad tried to put the disputed presidential elections behind him in his first speech since the vote.

TOUR DE FRANCE

Armstrong in 2nd as Astana Wins Time Trial

By JULIET MACUR 14 minutes ago

Lance Armstrong has moved into second place at

Therefore, sans serif fonts like Arial or Helvetica perform better on pixilated displays because they feature more straight lines and fewer curved embellishments.

serif   sans-serif

Perhaps the most famous of sans serif types is Helvetica. Note the lack of ornamentation and how one letter flows into the next for a wonderful push and pull within the type:

Aa Bb Cc Dd Ee

Compare Helvetica's clean look, which makes it ideal for online use, with a highly ornamented serif typeface such as

Snell Roundhand

Snell Roundhand's ascenders and descenders would pixilate at even a relatively small size online, and it is more difficult to read, in any medium, compared to sans serif typefaces.

Italics do not work well online, either, for the same reasons. Some type choices, in fact, are futile, depending on the monitors and browsers being used by your readers. Some monitors have only a narrow band of type sets that they will support, so choosing the perfect type on the production side does not ensure that the user will see your choice. A proprietary type choice such as Gotham might be translated to Times New Roman, a common type supported nearly universally.

In general, most monitors do support Web-safe sans serifs such as Verdana and Georgia, which were developed specifically for use on computers by type designer Matthew Carter, or Trebuchet, Helvetica and Arial. There are several reasons these type choices work online, in addition to the absence of serifs, or embellishments. Their lowercase characters are larger than the average typeface, if only slightly, so by rendering larger, the letters' open spaces do not seem to fill in or collapse online like most of the serif types.

HTML code poses other challenges for type online because it has many rules controlling line spacing, hyphenation, column and table cell widths, and line leading. The Web uses far more defaults and lowest-common-denominator rules than does print. Because monitor sizes vary from user to user, Web designers cannot lock into dimensions for display in the same way that print designers can be certain that their newspaper page, for example, has very specific page measurements. Design specifications will simply change from browser to browser, giving Web designers another significant challenge or barrier. Not only will Web pages look different on differently sized monitors, they may also display differently on different Web browsers. For example, a site developed on or for Mozilla Firefox might yet render dramatically differently in Explorer or Safari.

Chunking Text

Another way to recognize that visitors are scanning is to "chunk" content, or to think of content in discrete, short, paragraph-sized elements. Few Web users will read long articles online and will instead either save them to a file or print them out for more comfortable reading later. Web editors, then, should look for opportunities to break up text into discrete, digestible chunks. Long Web documents or pages also are disorienting because so little text is viewable on the screen at any one time.

The size of a chunk of text should vary according to the nature of the content, which will provide cues as to how it should be sub-divided and organized, but think in terms of short paragraphs. Paragraphs of even 100 words online can seem pretty long. The shorter the paragraph, the less intimidating it is to readers. A paragraph that's too big will make the text unwieldy, while a text divided into too many short paragraphs might make the text read too choppily and frustrate readers. The three case studies shown here illustrate some best practices for chunking text in different scenarios.

Case Study 1: *The New Yorker* (www.newyorker.com): Rating—Good

The article presented here is a long feature written for the magazine's print version. Online, the article looks as though it has been simply dumped into the *New Yorker*'s Web site, showing no attempt to break up the text with graphics, subheads or hyperlinks. Therefore, there is little relief for the reader and no help for the scanner. Failing to use hyperlinks is poor stewardship of an online resource, particularly in a piece as ripe for linking to supplementary material as a personality profile. Also note the poor headline, "Trust." Search engines will be hard pressed to turn this article up on any search for the subject, Joe Torre.

- The site does some things well, however. Easy-to-find, easy-to-use navigation of the *New Yorker*'s departments is listed in the left panel, navigation that mirrors the print product.

- The type choices and graphics boost the print edition's brand by being consistent with the printed product, and they are relatively easy to read.
- The main content is in the middle, where it belongs.

The use of headers ("Arts & Culture") cues the reader to the section. The headline and descriptive subhead are hierarchically presented.

Case Study 2: *The Atlantic Monthly* (www.theatlantic.com): Rating—Better

The Atlantic Monthly, one of the country's oldest periodicals, completed a major site redesign in January 2008, overhauling every aspect of its site. The new look puts graphical content front and center, making it much easier to navigate than the site's previous version. These enhancements, along with additions such as video and blogs, quickly quadrupled traffic to the site, according to *The New York Times*. First the old design, then the new, see p. 89 (top):

The Atlantic online

Go

Home
Current Issue
Back Issues
Premium Archive
Forum
Site Guide
Feedback
Search

Subscribe
Renew
Gift Subscription
Subscriber Help

Browse >>
  Books & Critics
  Fiction & Poetry
  Foreign Affairs
  Politics & Society
  Pursuits & Retreats

Subscribe to our free
e-mail newsletters

SHOP THE
ATLANTIC
MARKETPLACE

More on Foreign Affairs from
The Atlantic Monthly.

User ID   Password   LOGIN

The Atlantic Monthly | July/August 2006

The Short, Violent Life of Abu Musab al-Zarqawi

(page 1 of 4)

How a video-store clerk and small-time crook reinvented himself as America's nemesis in Iraq

by Mary Anne Weaver

• • • • •

[Edited for the Web, June 8, 2006]

On a cold and blustery evening in December 1989, Huthaifa Azzam, the teenage son of the legendary Jordanian-Palestinian mujahideen leader Sheikh Abdullah Azzam, went to the airport in Peshawar, Pakistan, to welcome a group of young men. All were new recruits, largely from Jordan, and they had come to fight in a fratricidal civil war in neighboring Afghanistan—an outgrowth of the CIA-financed jihad of the 1980s against the Soviet occupation there.

SPECIAL REPORT
IDEAS

Our Idea of Obama
Is Barack Obama an instinctual conservative, or an ambitious progressive determined to reshape America?
READ MORE

PLUS: Our Idea of the Day and special reports from the Aspen Ideas Festival.

MAGAZINE

JULY/AUGUST 2009
TABLE OF CONTENTS

JAMES FALLOWS JULY/AUGUST 2009

Dr. Doom Has Some Good News
An international system of tradeable open-seas fishing permits would mean more fish for everyone.
READ MORE

MORE FROM THE ATLANTIC

SPOTLIGHT

CORRESPONDENTS: CHRISTINA DAVIDSON 8 JULY 2009

The Sharecroppers' Daughter
Dottie's mother was the subject of a famous Depression-era Walker Evans portrait. She was also an honest woman who helped prepare her daughter for today's hard times. READ MORE

TA-NEHISI COATES 8 JULY 2009

Who Is the "Common Man"?
When black and white Americans discuss the democratic ideal, they might as well be speaking different languages
READ MORE

IDEA OF THE DAY: CONOR CLARKE 8 JULY 2009

Get Rid of Polls
"Polls are as integral to the American political tradition as sex scandals or earmarks. Yet it's not clear that they serve any beneficial purpose." READ MORE

TODAY'S HEADLINES FROM THE ATLANTIC

POLITICS
White House Very Skeptical About "Second Stimulus"
Sarah Palin--Tweeting Up A Storm
Polling And The Herd Mentality

BUSINESS
Credit Card Companies Adjust
The Rental Market Stinks Too
Yes, Google Chrome Could Beat Microsoft Windows

FOOD
Stops Along An American Food Tour
Comfort Food with a Foreign Accent
American Mozzarella's Evolution

FROM THE MAGAZINE
IDEAS Civilize Homeland Security
If we can't eliminate it, mitigate the damage
ENERGY Greening With Envy
Save by peeking at your neighbor's electric bill
IDEAS Reengineering the Earth
Dubious new techniques can change the climate

VOICES

Andrew Sullivan
The View From Your Recession
7.8.09 3:25 P.M.

Marc Ambinder
White House Very Skeptical About "Second Stimulus"
7.8.09 3:37 P.M.

James Fallows
Cornucopia of updates #1: "regreening" 7.8.09 1:15 P.M.

Megan McArdle
Sasha Baron-Cohen Strikes Again 7.8.09 2:30 P.M.

Ta-Nehisi Coates
Advancing In A Different Direction 7.8.09 1:43 P.M.

Jeffrey Goldberg
Durango Blogging
7.8.09 11:37 A.M.

Compared to the *New Yorker* copy, the *Atlantic*'s is an easier read because of the variation in text placement, with an ebb and flow of copy going down the page, but this design still presented the reader with a lot of text. Center justification is not recommended, especially after left-justifying the magazine title and issue date. This forces readers to find the beginning of each and every new line rather than defaulting down the left side. Readers will possibly bail out, even if they are not sure why.

Compare it to the redesign (see p. 89, foot). TheAtlantic.com looks like a completely different Web site, boasting energy, variety and, also new, mostly free content, including archived content. James Bennett, the magazine's editor in chief, told *The New York Times* that finally the magazine was treating the Web site as "a publication in its own right" rather than merely an adjunct of print. This change in approach made possible the addition of photo slideshows, one of which anchors the home page seen here, and video presentations.

Case Study 3: Salon.com (www.salon.com): Rating—Best

Salon.com does many of the same things the first two sites effectively do but with some enhancements as well:

- Navigation down the left panel, differentiated by type, spacing and color
- Hierarchy of heads and subheads, with cues to the article content in the photo
- A focal or dominant graphic to pull in the reader
- Variation in the text presentation with white space and an easy-to-read font and size
- Navigation for both hunters and shoppers
- Plenty of white space or rest.

The clean logo presentation in the upper left offers a quick route back to the home page and re-emphasizes the site's Web address.

All of the copy is left-justified, making Salon's article an easier read than the *Atlantic* article. The reader wastes no time finding the next place to read or start.

Finally, the sizes of the type are all relatively small, which Eyetrack studies indicate actually promote readership, with some air (called line leading) between the lines. In the Eyetrack studies, larger headlines are seen more as graphics, and therefore are not read by as many visitors as smaller headlines like those employed by Salon. The subhead and body type, too, are relatively small.

"Safe Area"

All three case studies recognize that computer screens typically are smaller than the printed page. Web page developers should show mercy on users with only small monitor screens. If a page is designed to display in a space larger than roughly 800 x 600 pixels, then for many visitors both vertical and horizontal scrolling will be required. Most Web users simply are not willing to scroll both directions (Nielsen 2000). Many reasons a visitor might have to stop reading are beyond a content developer's control, but page sizing is not one of them.

The University of North Carolina (www.unc.edu) home page demonstrates effectively designing to the lowest common denominator, at least in terms of spatial requirements. Note how the content floats in the center, adapting to larger and smaller screen sizes; the actual content fits very neatly even in a 640 x 480 pixel space, which by today's monitor sizes and standards is small. As UNC is a public university seeking to serve all North Carolinians, this democracy in design sends an important implicit message about access, as well.

The design, which rolled out in early 2008, also facilitates both hunters (the easy-to-find, easy-to-use search box) and gatherers (the major subheads of information). (See p. 92, top.)

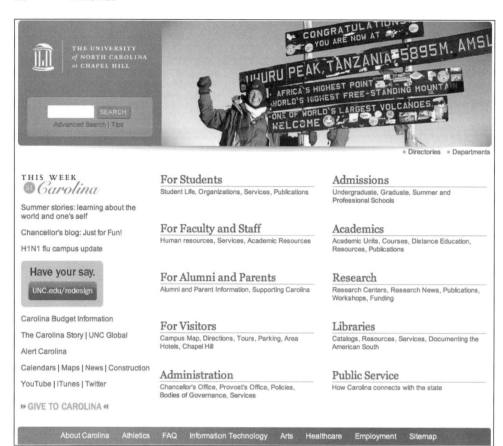

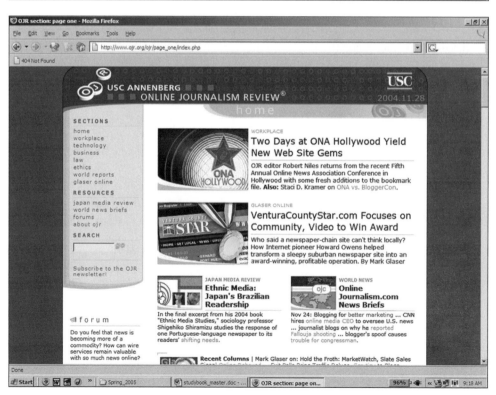

Note also that for most screen sizes, even most laptops, the UNC home page requires no vertical or horizontal scrolling. (See page 92, top.) Of course, the qualifier here is that UNC's home page is primarily for navigation, identifying the various paths available to the page's and the University's likely constituents. This places very different—and far fewer—demands on the page design than Salon.com's, for instance, or *The Atlantic*'s or *New Yorker*'s. Design is a series of choices and tradeoffs in the search for solutions.

A home page with more content but similarly designed for the safe area is the University of Southern California's *Online Journalism Review* (http://www.ojr.org) (see page 92, foot). Predictably, this site is a model in many respects, including its page layout and design, the blend of graphic and textual content, the extensive (but not over-) use of hyperlinks, and macro- and micro-site navigation. It is an exquisite, information-rich site. The site uses subtle colors to cue sectional purposes and divisions.

Moving Through Pyramids

In traditional news media, the inverted pyramid style imagines the pyramid's base at the top of the article. The most important information comes at the top of the print column, forming this base, with lesser information ordered below. As the reader goes further down the column, he or she reads increasingly less crucial information. In other words, readers travel down the pyramid.

Online, we might imagine moving into the pyramid. The pyramid's base faces the reader, meaning that all of the most important points are highlighted right there on the first view. As the reader moves deeper into the pyramid or, to borrow from Lewis Carroll, uses links to navigate through rabbit holes, the reader accesses related, sidebar information. The reader travels forward into the pyramid, or sideways through rabbit holes. As Web surfers approach the point of the pyramid, the reader isn't finished. Now facing the reader are more and more pyramids, facing him or her on their sides, their bases and their points.

Headlines, headers, hyperlinks and content chunks are ways of helping readers through these spaces, or forward through our pyramids. As Web writers and editors, then, we are architects of spaces and of navigational schemes through those spaces. It is a high calling indeed.

Chapter Assignments

1 Find three examples online of poor headlines used as hyperlinks and provide their solutions (in other words, fix the headlines). Be sure to include the source for each bad headline, including URL, where applicable.

   Example:
   Headline: Chubby Babies in Breast Cancer Link
   Problem: Awkward. Possibly offensive. No verb.

Solution: Infant Size Linked to Cancer Risk
Source: CNN.com, February 10, 2008, http://www.cnn.com/2007/HEALTH/10/17/infant.cancer/index.html.

2 Find at least one article on the Web that you think could be improved by deploying lists. Submit the "before" version and your edited "after" version of the article, or part of the article.

3 Re-write the headline for your Chapter 1 writing sample with this chapter to inform your work.

4 To practice writing to specification, write three different headlines for the following story fragment. Make the first headline eight words and the second six words. For the third headline, provide both a headline and a subhead, a headline of about six words and a subhead of about eight words. Separate the head and the subhead with a colon (example: "Dodgers Edge Braves in Second Game: Spahn's 3-hitter wasted as Atlanta bats remain silent").

The story fragment:

ACWORTH, Ga.—An Acworth man turned himself in to police Sunday night after robbing a Motel Six here and later attempting to mug a second victim on North Main Street.

Howard E. Smithton, 54, a resident of the Gazebo Park apartments on Old Cowan Street in Acworth, entered the Motel Six, also on Cowan, at 8:50 p.m. Sunday night and demanded money.

The clerk on duty, who said he knew Smithton, withheld his name for fear of his safety. He said he refused to give Smithton any money. A struggle ensued. Smithton overpowered the clerk, forced him to open the cash register and left with an undisclosed amount of cash, according to the clerk. Smithton then attempted a second burglary approximately one hour later on the 4800 block of North Main.

Smithton demanded that the victim, 59-year-old Bob Wilson, a member of Acworth's board of aldermen, give Smithton his wallet. Wilson said he refused and began beating Smithton over the head with a walking stick, which chased Smithton away.

Smithton later turned himself in at Acworth police headquarters on Industrial Drive at approximately 10:30 p.m. He is being held on a $10,000 bond at the Acworth City Jail, according to Michael Rose, Acworth's sheriff.

The money from the Motel Six has been returned, Rose said.

5 **Capstone assignment**
On the accompanying Web site is a long, 5,000-word text-only article with a sidebar (secondary story or information package). Applying the tools in this chapter, "webbify" the article and sidebar for online consumption.

Look for content to present in list format. Add a headline, subheads and, if appropriate, sub-subheads. Think about and perhaps recommend screen grabs, photography and graphical content. Indicate what text and perhaps other elements you would link, as well as to what you would hyperlink. Think through internal navigation. Divide into meaningful chunks.

Let's assume you are "webbifying" content for TravelBeat.net, a Web site devoted to "travel with a purpose," or travel and vacations that aspire to more than just tourism or sightseeing. Your audience is made up of 30-somethings and 40-somethings who are active, who are fairly savvy travelers. They are politically aware, purposeful vacationers (they do not go to DisneyWorld; they do go to Nepal, Croatia, Beijing, South Africa).

Remember to storyboard!

Online Resources

Evolution of Type
http://www.mediumbold.com/04_thinking/type/
Multimedia presentation on the development of typography.

Identifont
http://www.identifont.com/
Online directory of typefaces. Can be used to select type or to identify type.

Jeff Jarvis's Buzz Machine blog, specifically his Golden Rule of Links
http://www.buzzmachine.com/2008/06/02/the-ethic-of-the-link-layer-on-news/
Jarvis teaches journalism at City University of New York.

Time **magazine's "The Ag" blog**
http://time-blog.com/theag/
A model of how and when to hyperlink, and to what kinds of information to link.

Sources

Brian S. Brooks and Jack Z. Sissors, *The Art of Editing*, 7th ed. (Boston: Allyn & Bacon, 2000).

Isabelle De Ridder, "Visible or Invisible Links: Does the Highlighting of Hyperlinks Affect Incidental Vocabulary Learning, Text Comprehension, and the Reading Process?" *Language, Learning & Technology*, 6, no. 1 (January 2002): 123.

George P. Landow, *Hypertext 2.0* (Baltimore: Johns Hopkins Press, 1997).

Patrick Lynch and Sarah Horton, *Web Style Guide 2* (New Haven, CT: Yale University Press, 2001); also available: http://www.webstyleguide.com.

Rachel McAlpine, *Web Word Wizardry: A Guide to Writing for the Web and Intranet* (Berkeley, CA: Ten Speed Press, 2001).

Andrea Marks, "The Role of Writing in a Design Curriculum," Oregon State University, American Institute of Graphic Arts, available: http://www.aiga.org/content.cfm/the-role-of-writing-in-a-design-curriculum.

Kendra Mayfield, "Reality Check for Web Design," *Wired* magazine, October 2, 2002, available: http://www.wired.com/news/technology/0,1282,55190,00.html.

Jakob Nielsen, *Designing Web Usability* (Indianapolis, IN: New Riders, 2000).

Roger C. Parker, *Guide to Web Content and Design* (New York: MIS Press, 1997).

Richard Perez-Pena, "A Venerable Magazine Energizes Its Web Site," *New York Times*, January 21, 2008: C4.

Thomas Powell, *Web Design: The Complete Reference* (Berkeley, CA: Osborne/McGraw-Hill, 2000).

Jonathan Price and Lisa Price, *hot text: Web Writing That Works* (Indianapolis, IN: New Riders, 2002).

Jeffrey Vern, *The Art and Science of Web Design* (Indianapolis, IN: New Riders, 2001).

5 DESIGNING PLACES AND SPACES

Your audience gives you everything you need. They tell you. There is no director who can direct you like an audience.

Fanny Brice, entertainer

Chapter Objectives

After studying this chapter, you will be able to:

- participate in site and page planning;
- understand audience needs and how to satisfy them;
- plan how to attract users to a site and keep them coming back for more;
- create and use style guides;
- ensure quality control for a site.

Introduction

The best publications are those that are most relevant to the people they aim to serve. In this chapter, the focus is on audience, on learning as much as possible about the information needs, sensitivities, interests and objectives of a desired audience, and on planning and building spaces for specific audiences. Deep knowledge of our audience should inform how we build out our Web sites and fill them with content. To guide site planning, we also discuss how to develop an audience-specific style guide, adherence to which ensures a site of consistency and, for our audiences, familiarity.

Pre-planning

Before we write a word of content, we need the answers to at least two fundamental questions: Who is our audience? What is the site, blog or online publication supposed to do? The more contact we have with our users, the better the planning naturally will be. Of course, most site development projects occur in a vacuum, with little or no contact with the intended audience(s). No wonder there is so much waste in cyberspace. To the extent we can involve real users in planning, development, testing and updating, the site has a better chance of succeeding.

As a starting point for the discussion, consider what kind of site you are developing or for which you are producing content. One way to think about this is to conceptualize a spectrum of types organized from the information-rich on one end and the very sensory-oriented on the other. YouTube, for example, resides at the sensory extreme by emphasizing the visual, impressions, emotions and vicariousness. On the other end of the spectrum, we might put corporate intranets, reference sites like the Library of Congress, and sites by and for institutions of higher education. In the middle are those sites that provide some information, but also seek to provide an experience of some kind, like most e-commerce sites and news sites. Knowing where your project fits on this spectrum can inform the kinds of content that should be developed and the ways that content should be presented or delivered.

On the sensory end of the spectrum, consider an interactive feature at the *Chicago Tribune*'s Web site, a rather simple Flash movie that enables baseball fans to display their names on an online version of Wrigley Field's scoreboard: http://www.chicagotribune.com/business/chi-wrigley,0,2136131.flash.

Before adding the feature, *Chicago Tribune* site developers knew they wanted something to provide an experience, something entertaining that delivers near-instant gratification. The marquee-generator might be considered an amenity at the site not unlike a ride at a carnival or public park in town. Knowing the purpose and the audience—the newspaper's Cubs fans—informed the development of the feature, which was the subject of an alert the newspaper sent via the social networking site Facebook. (See p. 99, top.)

On the other end of the spectrum, a Web page designed to help parents diagnose cerebral palsy should be extremely high on information and very low on entertainment or emotion. (See page 99, foot.) A sober tone, a logical organization of the information and a clear demonstration of credibility and authority contrast a Web page from the Centers for Disease Control and Prevention from a fun naming game at the *Chicago Tribune*.

Write your own Wrigley sign

What would you name Wrigley Field? See how your idea would look at Clark and Addison.

▼ TYPE IN YOUR IDEA FOR A NEW WRIGLEY SIGN

| Tinker to Evers to Chance | View name | Print |

TRIBUNE GRAPHIC

CDC Centers for Disease Control and Prevention
Your Online Source for Credible Health Information

CDC Features

CDC Home › Features ›

New Data Show 1 in 278 Children Have Cerebral Palsy

Learn more about the signs and causes of cerebral palsy and what to do if you think your child might have it.

Cerebral palsy is a group of disorders that affect a person's ability to move and keep their balance and posture as a result of an injury to parts of the brain, or as a result of a problem with development. Cerebral means having to do with the brain. Palsy means weakness or problems with using the muscles. Often the problem happens before birth or soon after being born. Cerebral palsy causes different types of disabilities in each child. A child may simply be a little clumsy or awkward, or unable to walk at all.

How Common Is Cerebral Palsy?

CDC released a new study in the March 2008 issue of *Pediatrics* which shows the average prevalence of cerebral palsy (CP) as 3.6 per 1,000 children or about 1 in 278 children. This first report of the prevalence and characteristics of CP, the most common cause of motor disability in childhood, are from Georgia, Alabama and Wisconsin.

The study, "Prevalence of Cerebral Palsy in 8-year-old Children in Three Areas of the United States in 2002: A Multisite Collaboration," found the prevalence to be remarkably similar across all three sites, ranging from 3.3 in Wisconsin to 3.8 in Georgia. All sites reported the highest prevalence among boys, African-Americans and those living in low- and middle-income neighborhoods. Prevalence rates were lowest among Hispanic children.

What Are Some of the Signs of Cerebral Palsy?

The signs of cerebral palsy vary greatly because there are many different types and levels of disability. The main sign that your child might have cerebral palsy is a delay reaching the motor or movement milestones. If you see any of these signs, call your child's doctor or nurse.

A child over 2 months with cerebral palsy might:
- Have difficulty controlling head when picked up
- Have stiff legs that cross or "scissor" when picked up

A child over 6 months with cerebral palsy might:
- Continue to have a hard time controlling head when picked up
- Reach with only one hand while keeping the other in a fist

A child over 10 months with cerebral palsy might:
- Crawl by pushing off with one hand and leg while dragging the opposite hand and leg
- Not sit by himself or herself

Maximizing Content Fitness

You know how information-heavy the site should be, and how much visitors are looking for a sensory experience. Now consider your audience in terms of the kinds of information they are looking for, or how the information you present might fit into the larger puzzle that your audience is trying to fit together over time, a quality information researchers call "fitness" (Huang *et al.* 1999). Research has shown that information quality has little to do with technology and everything to do with the fitness of the information as determined by users. Information science researchers Kuan-Tsae Huang, Yang W. Lee and Richard Y. Wang found that when people visit a Web site, they base their judgments of the quality of information more on how well that information matches what they are seeking than on how sophisticated the site is in terms of technological bells and whistles. Their research suggests four dimensions of "information quality," reproduced here and adapted:

Information quality (IQ) category	IQ dimensions
Intrinsic IQ, or information that has quality for the user in its own right	• accuracy • objectivity • believability • reputation
Contextual IQ, or information that must be considered within the context of the user's tasks	• relevancy • value-added • timeliness • completeness • amount
Representational IQ, or user issues surrounding systems that provide information such as databases	• interpretability • ease of understanding • concise representation • consistent representation
Accessibility IQ, or user issues surrounding the provision of information	• access • security

Adapted from Hammerich and Harrison (2002: 280).

The IQ dimensions identified and organized in the study provide a useful checklist for evaluating the fitness of content for the audience you are trying to serve. Are they visiting your site to buy something? Access and security, or Accessibility IQ dimensions, will rank highly. Are they looking to you for information on cerebral palsy? Your Intrinsic IQ dimensions are going to rank first. A news site will need to score well on nearly all of the dimensions in the chart.

Content Development

After determining the kinds of information for which your audience is looking, the next logical step is to develop specific content that meets those type needs. Here are some questions to help you decide both what to develop or produce and how to present it.

First, think about who you hope will visit your site, and think in terms of categories. Occupational categories, demographics, gender, culture and age ranges are good places to start. Be as specific and as comprehensive as you can, which will help you determine not only the substance of your content but the degree of detail and abstraction. Think of the Web page on cerebral palsy. With a primary audience of very concerned parents, writers for this page knew the content needed enough detail and substance to truly inform but not so much that the information overwhelms. They also knew that abstraction was not an option. If your audience includes the elderly, you will want to consider larger typefaces. College students? Think visual! Graduate students? Long text articles should be no problem.

Readers with backgrounds in the professional fields of business, science or technology likely will expect a wealth of empirical data, perhaps supporting charts and graphs as well. Readers in the humanities, by contrast, tend to prefer text as the focus.

Think about where your audience lives. Are they local, national, international? Does the answer have implications for your content in terms of cultural, ethnic or linguistic considerations? If your audience includes readers in Asia, for example, you will want to avoid idioms and slang, and you will want to be careful in your color choices.

Consider the information challenges your audience might have. Information technology professionals, for example, have no shortage of information. The challenge for your site would be to stand out, to offer an expertise found nowhere else. Does your audience need how-to information? If so, you will want to develop sequential content. Does your audience need to collaborate? What social networking tools and communication environments will you offer? Are they looking for pleasure or efficiency, advice or participation in something meaningful?

Think about the kinds of sites, publications and documents your audience is accustomed to reading. Where does your audience currently go to satisfy its needs? Think of specific Web sites, newspapers or magazines, radio and television programming, and newsletters. You can learn both what to do and what not to do from these sources. What conventions, then, can your design borrow from those types of information sources? The familiarity you can offer will make your content more appealing, and you will spend less time in design and development because you need not contrive something wholly new.

A related suggestion is to think about the conversation you wish to have with your audience. Imagine what kinds of FAQ pages you might need. What recurring questions do you think your audience will have?

How often do you want or do you anticipate visitors coming to your site? Once, daily, weekly, monthly? The frequency will determine how often your site's content should be updated or refreshed.

Read everything you can about your audience, including relevant online bulletin boards, discussion and chat, and Web sites targeting the same or similar audiences. Spend time with and among the members of your audience, even online in social networking contexts such as Facebook or LinkedIn. Go native. Ask questions. Listen.

Knowing your audience's technical limitations can help determine the kind of content you develop, even the media formats you might choose. What browsers and operating systems are your visitors using? (Firefox and Explorer, for example, are very different; often what works on one will not function properly on the other, or at least not in the same way. The PC–Mac divide, too, can cause compatibility and operability issues.) What is their connection speed? Broadband? What kind of broadband? Are they accessing from home or from work? What advanced browser features do they support? JavaScript, dynamic HTML, style sheets, Java applets, third-party plug-ins like Flash and Quicktime?

Finally, consider your audience in terms of cultural contexts. A Web site's audience in most cases is potentially global, so you should be sensitive to nationalities and cultural groups in making design and content choices, including choice of color. Red, for instance, means entirely different things to different cultural and ethnic groups:

- Red is the most popular color in Thailand and is used, therefore, for all sorts of purposes.
- Red connotes prosperity in China.
- Malaysia uses red to symbolize valor and might.
- In the Ivory Coast, red is associated with mourning.
- In the United States, red is on STOP and EXIT signs.
- In many African countries, red is associated with death.

So, ask yourself about your graphical content. Can it be interpreted in ways that vary significantly from my interpretation? What are your alternatives, either textually and visually, that might be more culturally neutral?

A quick example. You are writing about the political strife that has characterized Northern Ireland for more than 40 years. When choosing photography,

One of many murals in Belfast, Northern Ireland, one celebrating Loyalist paramilitaries. Photographic content can potentially alienate or even inflame audiences, depending on the context.

you might be tempted to include, for instance, a Celtic cross, a rather stereotypical image of Ireland. The article focuses on Northern Ireland, which is mostly Protestant, loyalist, English. A Celtic cross would communicate Catholicism, the Republic, Irishness.

Others might opt to show some of the political murals found on buildings throughout Belfast and Derry/Londonderry, Northern Ireland. These murals are laden with political commentary and, in many cases, provocation. Great care, therefore, would be needed in choosing which murals to present and how to present and describe them.

Information Architecture

Once you know your audience and the types of information that they hope to find on your site or page, after you've carefully considered what this audience needs and how they are accustomed to getting it, the next question is how to present that information in a logical manner that makes it easy for users to find. Planning how information will be organized and how this organization will be revealed to users should be a first step in any Web site design.

The planning and organization of information is referred to as "information architecture," a process complex enough that there are entire academic departments dedicated to its study. At its most basic level, though, the aim of information architecture is to determine an information hierarchy for a site by grouping related information. These groupings should be presented according to some hierarchy of importance, which can then determine page layouts and site tree development. (A site tree is a graphical representation of how a site's parts relate or link to one another.) Once the hierarchy has been determined, map it out graphically on paper for the beginnings of a site tree, shown below.

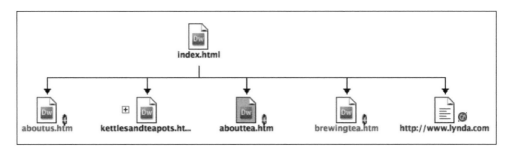

A site tree for a site with a home page, four sub-pages and a hyperlink to Lynda.com.

There are many possible models for site architecture, some linear, or sequential, and some non-linear, or webs of pages. Again, it might be helpful to conceptualize a spectrum, with a 1–2–3 or straight linear model on one end and a highly interconnected web model on the other end. Slideshows, for example, are sequential. Sites that walk users through a procedure, skill or practice are, as well. They have a predictable structure and are therefore fairly simple to plan. The VCR is a handy metaphor here—hit "play" to go forward, "rewind" to go back.

On the other extreme is a site like Wikipedia, with no discrete beginning and no determinate end. Pages interconnect and cross-reference, providing a deep, rich web of information accessible in an almost infinite number of different sequences. Wikipedia is flexible and scaleable, changing quite literally all the time. Wikipedia is therefore a very complex site, but its architecture permits and facilitates this interconnectedness and its ability to continually expand.

Some sites, like many intranets, will combine these models. In the aggregate, most corporate intranets are webs of interconnected, hyperlinked information. But you're likely to find a section or two for training, sections that will follow a sequential progression. The *New York Times* site has a clear beginning—the front page or home page—but a reader may wish to access a wide variety of different kinds of articles in any number of sequences. The *Times* site is organized into sections and areas of interest, or "neighborhoods," rather than by sequential order.

Basics of Page Layout

Let's shift our focus from the site level to that of the individual Web page, or from site architecture to designing and laying out individual pages. Many of the skills and sensibilities that produce good print pages are also valuable in Web page design. For example, a page layout, whether online or in print, should create a consistent visual rhythm or pace for the reader as he or she moves through the page. That rhythm can be established through the placement and repetition of shapes, colors, typefaces, textures and relationships. If quick and lively is the rhythm we seek, we might use lots of small, closely placed shapes. If, however, solemn and dignified is the preferred rhythm, we will likely use large, lone shapes.

Consider your favorite print publication—*The New York Times*, *Wired* magazine, *Cosmo*, *Transworld Skateboarding*—the choice is yours. What kind of rhythm or pace does it have? How is that rhythm communicated? What libraries of elements does the publication use? What kinds of layouts are common? What is consistent throughout the publication? What kind of tone does it establish? How are these choices informed by knowledge of the intended audience?

The primary tool in print page design is the grid. Whatever visual rhythm you choose, it can be plotted out on a grid, which can be indispensable in planning out *all* of the space, including the white space, the margin areas and the areas of visual rest. Text, photos, illustrations and logos also can be placed on a grid. There are a lot of grids from which to choose (see facing page).

The complexity of the grid should depend on the complexity and quantity of design elements, so determining what you have to work with—what content

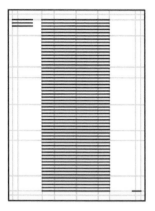
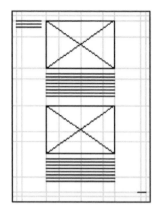
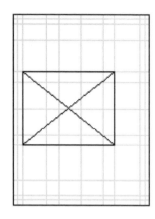

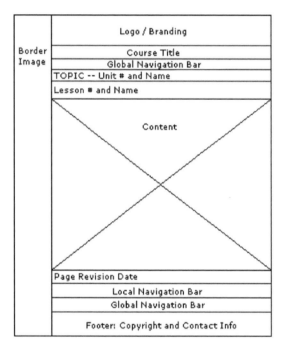

An example from Adobe of a grid-based home page layout.

elements you have—is a good place to begin thinking about what kind of grid you will need. The more elements you have, the more choices you will have to make. Keep it as simple as possible.

One of the more simple layout patterns is the "Z path" that guides the human eye through most text documents from the upper left to the right, then down diagonally, then left to right. To define a path, you need an entry point, a focal point, an obvious point of entry that inspires and motivates the reader to keep moving along the path you have charted.

This ad for the 1964 Jeep clearly uses the Z path Western readers' minds instinctively want to follow. We begin in the upper left, sweep right, down diagonally following the incline of the Jeep itself, then left to right to take in the details. This ad also uses an inverted pyramid, delivering the main message with a dominant visual and a headline first. The secondary information is at the bottom of the ad.

This 1949 magazine ad for Cunard provides another example of using a Z pattern to plot out content. The elements here: company name (Cunard White Star), headline (*Caronia*, a new ship in the fleet), dominant visual, body copy, and sidebar information. A three-column, four-row grid was used to map out these five elements.

You have a rough map or grid of where your content is going to go on the Web page. Next, apply some of the basic page design aesthetics to your design to make sure you have achieved excellence in what we could call "The Big Three," or **balance**, **contrast** and **unity**. Let's look at each one.

Balance is a state of equilibrium, or the appearance of rest. A well-balanced page will typically be easy to read because all of the elements of the layout appear to be in the right place, with no particular element competing too strongly for our attention. An imbalanced layout will present the reader with the vague feeling of uneasiness if there is too much weight in any one place within the layout. For example, a top-heavy page, achieved by placing a heavy object like a photo on top of something lighter such as the body text, will lack balance and may appear unpleasant to the eye of the reader. The Cunard ad above works because there is plenty of body copy, including a heavy back-screened box, to support a fairly small representation of the ship. Notice how little water there is, contributing to a "lightness" in the graphic.

Generally, the "weight" of design elements, from heaviest to lightest, is as follows:

- Photos
- Graphics
- Headlines
- Subheads
- Other graphic embellishments
- Main body text
- White space.

ABSOLUT ESCHER.

The well-known, seemingly ubiquitous Absolut vodka ads are models of balance, evenly distributing their elements or weight. Bottles are almost always symmetrical, so Absolut is wise in keying its layouts on the shape of its trademarked bottle.

Symmetry is proper proportion of the parts to one another and to the whole with regard to size and form. It is an excellence of proportion, in other words, and is therefore very closely related to balance. For page design, practically this means that each page has a vertical axis, which can be used to map out content either symmetrically or asymmetrically. Symmetry is most often used for traditional presentations and asymmetry for playfulness, informality and attitude. Shown here is an exquisite ad for the French Open, one that is perfectly balanced, that depends on symmetry. In fact, balance and symmetry make up the whole point of the ad, a point emphasized by a half tennis racket, like

THE FRENCH OPEN

Courtesy of Dentsu Young & Rubicam, Singapore, Patrick Low, Art Director.

an exclamation point. To achieve this, the designer started with the page's vertical axis.

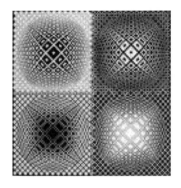

Contrast is the unlikeness or differences between two or more things. This difference is achieved in page layouts by creating variety, interest, drama and unpredictability. Any layout needs emphasis, which will then contrast with everything else on the page. Contrast's enemies are dullness, boredom and sameness, but not consistency and progression.

Your tools in achieving contrast include color, headlines, typeface, photo sizes, placements (isolation, clusters, symmetry, asymmetry), borders (uneven borders, for example) and edges (even ragged ones), shapes (including unusual ones), and congruity/incongruity. An oversized graphic, for example, can provide contrast while at the same time reinforcing the text. Like-sized photos, on the other hand, can crowd each other out of a reader's attention, like uniformed soldiers anonymously marching by. Imagine a football field full of university students walking in their graduation ceremony, all in black robes and black mortarboards. Except one. He's wearing a gorilla suit and holding a giant placard. Who do you think will be noticed in this processional? Why? It's all about contrast.

Unity is perhaps the easiest dimension to understand and the most difficult to achieve. The term refers to the sense that all the parts of the design and the layout belong together and work in harmony together. Unity requires more than balance, or how weight is distributed, although balance is an important ingredient of unity. Synthesis, cohesion and Gestalt are the hallmarks of unity, or the notion that the whole is greater than the sum of the parts. *Gestalt* is a German word that is translated as "form" or "wholeness." The term describes an early 20th-century German movement in psychology that focused on perception. In particular, these psychologists found that our perception of form depends not just on seeing individual parts but on the organization of the whole. We see the whole first, then we start breaking it down into parts. For example, what do you see in this diagram?

Do the dots suggest a square? That's Gestalt, because each dot is merely a single dot. Together, lined up as a unified group or battalion, they give the appearance of a square.

Look at the yin–yang-like logo for the Gestalt Institute of Houston from the 1970s, a logo designed to communicate the institute's *raison d'être*,

Gestalt. The logo's disparate parts flow in and out of one another to form a unified whole:

Two Web sites that immediately communicate Gestalt, or a sense of a unified whole that is greater than the sums of their parts, are those for New Mexico Museum of Art and Full Sail, an art institute, though each site achieves unity in different ways.

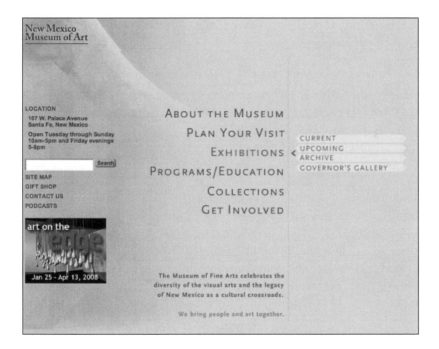

The home page for the New Mexico Museum of Art achieves unity or harmony in its choices of color scheme (all earth tones), in the contrast of a light background and dark foreground elements, and with its timeless typeface. The visual rhythm is one of rest, of contemplation, which is appropriate for an art museum. The elements are asymmetrical to emphasize the navigational sub-menus that pop up on the right.

The home page for Full Sail Real World Education, a school that specializes in computer and graphical arts, has a much busier rhythm communicated through the large number of features adorning the building's façade. A street corner under a blue sky achieves both contrast and balance, and there is symmetry—the corner of the building is in the page's center, on its vertical axis. Unity is achieved by correlating a school specializing in the visual with a montage of visual images presented in the context of display ads springing out from a building, presumably the school itself.

The grid employed by Full Sail is a simple one. Two elements: the building and the navigation menu. There is little to compete for the visitor's attention—the building will be seen first, then the navigation. Only after the visitor scans these basic content elements will he or she begin reading individual words, first with headlines, then subheads and finally body content.

Another example, from *The Economist*, demonstrates some of these same principles. Notice how the hierarchy of content from headlines to subheads to body text is quickly communicated purely by the size of the text and the use of white space separating them. The page is easily navigable, therefore, and easily scanned. Now imagine the grid behind the content that mapped out its elements.

The Economist's page organization uses ample white space or air, which facilitates more comfortable or enjoyable reading. There is contrast, both in color choices and between the visual elements and the text to the right. Readers like variety and moderate changes in pace, but they also need reassurance and familiarity. The site's ubiquitous or persistent navigation on the left provides that familiarity, freeing the mind to enjoy the content on the right. The page also achieves unity, largely through typeface choices and by proximity. Nesting the content signals that the elements belong together and were carefully placed.

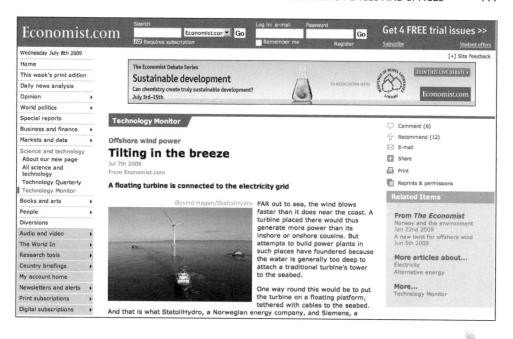

One criticism of *The Economist* might be its long lines of text that crawl across all or most of the width of the screen. The line lengths the news magazine uses are approximately twice what is recommended, or the equivalent of two print columns.

If you design well, readers likely will not consciously perceive your layouts. If you design poorly, however, they will simply stop reading. Bad design makes readers uneasy and uncomfortable.

Developing a Style Guide

For consistency and efficiency when creating, editing and displaying content, you (and your organization) will benefit greatly from a style guide, or a manual that governs how Web pages and their content should be written and presented. We are not talking about writing style or tone, as we did in earlier chapters, but about specific style guides of which the *Associated Press Stylebook* is an example. Such a manual provides guidelines on, among other things, spelling, capitalization, grammar and punctuation, and usage, and they often include special, topical sections such as those in the *AP Stylebook* on business, sports, punctuation and Internet-related terms.

In Web development, the terms "style guides" and "style sheets" also can refer to the system of HTML codes used by programmers to make sure the Web pages they are creating are consistent in behavior and appearance. The style guides discussed in this chapter refer to editorial style guides, not those used for programming and coding.

A style guide is the sourcebook and toolkit when problems are encountered with copy online, and a style guide can be used to prevent problems to the extent content producers conform to it. The goals of style guides are the goals of good writing: clarity, concision and consistency. In the *Associated Press Stylebook*, for example, "Web site" is uppercase and two words. In *Wired* magazine's style guide, however, it is "website." Which style an online publication or site employs is not important; what is important is that one is used and used consistently. Whenever publications using AP style use the term "Web site," it should be presented that way. Whenever *Wired* refers to a "website," the references should be consistent. A publication should not toggle between two or more variations or versions of the term. This is unsettling for the reader, and it suggests carelessness or, even worse, an issue of information credibility.

The description from the Associated Press (http://www.apstylebook.com) of its own style book:

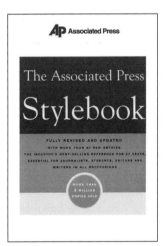

The journalist's "bible," the style manual is an essential tool for all writers, editors, students and public relations specialists. It provides guidelines on spelling, capitalization, grammar, punctuation and usage, with special sections on business and sports. Included is a guide on media law, with practical guidelines on libel law, privacy, copyright and access to places of information, and a special section on Internet and computer terms, a comprehensive effort to unify spelling and usage of computer-related terms, from Web site and email to URLs and "cyber-" prefixes. This segment also offers Internet searching tips and cautions.

Another standard style, *The Chicago Manual of Style*, began more than a century ago when one proofreader began writing down on a single sheet of paper a few basic style rules. This list became a booklet, then in 1906 the first edition of *The Chicago Manual of Style* was published. The 15th edition checked in at 925 pages. One reason this style is so strong, besides its detailed instructions, is the manual's balance between establishing rules and allowing the author or writer or publisher flexibility. Freedom and flexibility are stated goals of the manual, at the heart of which is a "respect for the author's individuality, purpose, and style, tempered though it is with a deeply felt responsibility to prune from work whatever stylistic infelicities, inconsistencies, and ambiguities might have gained stealthy entrance" (*The Chicago Manual of Style* 1993: vii). Front-end work developing a style guide will save a great deal of time later.

Creating a Style Guide

At *Wired* magazine, the style guide in force began as a single sheet of paper onto which copyeditors recorded every copy challenge they faced and the solutions to these challenges negotiated by the staff. This sheet of paper evolved into a lengthy computer file, which grew into a book, *Wired Style: Principles of English Usage in the Digital Age*. (Unfortunately, this guide is no longer available online.)

Like all style guides, the one in use at *Wired* continues to evolve. The staff wrestles with terms and words and when a new term, buzzword or acronym emerges, the publication's editors debate its style and proper usage. Somehow out of all of the email messages and debates, agreement emerges on usage and proper *Wired* style. As examples, here are two terms and their style explained from *Wired*'s usage book:

FDDI
Pronounced "fiddy" and standing in for "fiber distributed data interface," this fiberbased network architecture offers a faster and more dependable alternative to Ethernet or Token Ring. (It transmits at 100 Mbits per second over LANs and MANs.) Of course, with gigabit Ethernet on the horizon, the future of FDDI looks bleak.

file name
Two words, like "screen name" and "domain name." In the early DOS days, computers wouldn't allow spaces in names and forced users to make file names one word. But "file name" was never closed up—in DOS or in English.

Students will want to select a style and adapt it or create one of their own. It is not difficult. Even if a student chooses an existing style, such as *Associated Press* or *Chicago Manual of Style*, some adaptations and additions will need to be made because each audience and every project makes unique demands. Most conventional style guides address digital media in a less than comprehensive fashion, which can leave lingering questions, such as "Should 'Web' be capitalized?" "Should 'email' be hyphenated?" A style guide anticipates and answers these questions, and it changes over time to increasingly better anticipate questions and issues.

Embedded in any style guide are assumptions about the readers, assumptions that may include age or perhaps generation, interests, technological proficiency and expertise in the area(s) addressed by the content. Once again, primacy is placed on knowing our audiences. To illustrate this point about assumptions, here are a few examples of how a style guide might handle style and usage questions common about Web pages, and they assume a level of sophistication using and referring to multimedia:

When presenting file names, use only lowercase letters. Examples:

florence.wmv
siena.jpg
verona.pptx

On first reference, put technical terms in italics:

Viewing this movie requires a *Flash plug-in*.

Except when beginning a sentence, follow proprietary company name conventions. Examples:

amazon.com
eBay
twitter

For comparison, here are a few entries from the *AP Stylebook*, all from the "A" section at the front of the volume, entries that make far fewer assumptions about the guide's readers:

- **Academic degrees**—Put an apostrophe in bachelor's degree and master's degree. This is to show possession. The degree belongs to the bachelor or master (that's you). Even when shortened to bachelor's and master's (no "degree" afterward), you keep the apostrophe.

- **Addresses**—Abbreviate the words street, avenue and boulevard (think S–A–B), but only if they appear after a numbered address. Also abbreviate compass directions, but only if they appear with a numbered address. So, you'd write 50 S. Court St., but if you leave off the house number, you'd write South Court Street. Got it? Never abbreviate drive, highway, place, or any of the other words that might follow an actual street name such as Court, Union, Ventura, Lombard, Pennsylvania or whatever. Let's use this system for Utah addresses: 1160 E. 100 South St.

Is style a big deal? Consider this example taken from *Eats, Shoots & Leaves* (Truss 2004), a one-time bestseller in England on the subject of punctuation. The example hopefully underlines how important every jot and tittle, every comma and colon potentially can be:

A woman, without her man, is nothing.

A woman: without her, man is nothing.

The only difference in the two, besides their entire meaning, is one colon and one comma.

As with most things Web-related, keep your style guide as simple as possible, allowing it to evolve and grow over time. Including examples can help provide general parameters, as well, though no style guide is all-encompassing and all are works in progress. The *AP Stylebook* is updated with a new print edition annually, and it is updated more frequently for subscribers online.

Choosing a Style Guide

To speed development of a style guide, you might choose an existing one as a base or foundation, then add to that foundation over time. The traditional choices include the *Associated Press Stylebook and Briefing on Media Law*, *The Chicago Manual of Style*, and *The MLA Style Manual* (Washington, DC: MLA, 1985). These guides are designed almost exclusively for print. The *AP Stylebook*, for example, does not address issues such as displaying links, writing link text and writing page titles. *E-What: A Guide to the Quirks of New Media Style and Usage* (Alexandria, VA: EEI Press, 2000) is a more forward-thinking style guide. This book, for example, relies on *AP* for text and Lynch's and Horton's *Web Style Guide 2* for design and visual elements, or visual style. Using a traditional style guide and supplementing it with other resources and personal experience can direct students in developing a customized guide that addresses both the big picture *and* the little details.

Details a style guide should cover include, among other elements:

- Vocabulary
- Abbreviations and acronyms
- Italics, bolds, quotation marks and parentheses
- Hyphens and dashes
- Punctuation
- Capitalization
- Headlines and subheads, including colors and font types and sizes
- Hyperlinking protocols (active, visited, etc.)
- Ordered and unordered lists
- Graphic design issues
- Photo captions
- Numbers
- Spacing
- Logos, slogans, etc.

Web writers' style guides will vary. Every type of Web page is unique in terms of terminology used and text elements employed. A site with medical information, for example, is going to be very different than one providing help in real estate. Terminology; graphics, photography, and diagrams; tables and charts; and level of formality in writing all will be very different. The style should depend on the site's audience.

Chapter Assignments

1 Identify a publication, company or organization for or about which you will create online content. This entity can be real or imagined, corporate or non-profit, local or national or international. Suggestions? *Outside Magazine*, *The New York Times*, *Coin Collector's Digest*, Coca-Cola, Habitat for

Humanity, International Association of Business Communicators, the Miami Dolphins. The entity you choose should be a publication or organization with which you have or want to have some connection or affiliation, one with which you are already familiar. It can be the one for which you already work, or one for which you want to work in the future.

Prepare a two-page summary of the audience needs for the publication or organization for which you will be writing content. Do research. Your summary should include:

- **Audience profile**—Who will be reading the content?
- **Purpose of publication**—Is it for entertainment, for news, for both?
- **Frequency of publication**—Is it a monthly magazine or an hourly-updated blog?
- List of **the competition**—What are the other publications competing for the same audience?
- **Style issues**—Will you maintain the current style guide of the publication or organization, or is there need for a new one?
- **Information challenges**—What does the audience need to know, or what information does the organization need to broadcast? Do any special obstacles stand in the way of communicating that information quickly and clearly?
- **Your response to the information challenges**—How will you overcome any barriers and get your content out there?

2 Detail the online content you will create for your organization or publication. What you write and develop is up to you, so you have the flexibility to do what makes sense and to write what can best serve you where they are now—school, on the job or on the job hunt. Possibilities for this assignment include:

- A news story or series of news stories
- A feature story
- Criticism (such as restaurant review, play or movie review, book review)
- A press release
- A how-to feature.

These are just a few of the possibilities. Keep your publication's audience first and foremost in your mind. Identify the topic or angle of your proposed piece, making sure the topic is relevant and timely. This is a story or piece you will actually write, develop and produce. You will gather the information, do the reporting, conduct the interviews, see the play—whatever is necessary to produce the copy.

Online Resources

American Copy Editors Society
http://www.copydesk.org
Resources at the site include reference materials, quizzes and help in discussion.

Dictionary.com—Style Guides
http://www.dictionary.com/Dir/Arts/Writers_Resources/Style_Guides/
Online listing of style guides and manuals, including a handful of guides specifically for online usage.

"Guide to Grammar and Style"
http://andromeda.rutgers.edu/~jlynch/Writing/
Online guide to grammar, style, and usage by Jack Lynch, Associate Professor of English at Rutgers University.

InfoDesign
http://www.bogieland.com/infodesign
Articles about information design.

Poynter Institute, online section
http://www.poynter.org/subject.asp?id=26
Poynter offers some of the richest information for journalists anywhere. This section of Poynter's vast site is dedicated to online and technology.

SiteNavigation.net
http://www.SiteNavigation.net/snguide.html
Links to sources and resources about site navigation.

The Slot: A Spot for Copy Editors
http://www.theslot.com
Site of Bill Walsh, long-time copyeditor and author of several books on editing.

Society of News Design
http://www.snd.org
The society is for designers in journalism, and the site offers resources selected for this group.

W3's "Web Style Guide for Online Hypertext"
http://www.w3.org/Provider/Style/
This document was written in the early days of the Web, defining such terms as "Webmaster," the "www.name.com" convention, and a few basic points which are just as valid today. Readers should note that the site has not been updated to discuss recent developments in HTML, and it is out of date in many places.

Sources

Associated Press Stylebook and Briefing on Media Law (New York: Associated Press, 1977 and updated annually).

Michael Butzgy, *Writing for Multimedia*, available: http://home.earthlink.net/~atomic_rom/contents.htm.

The Chicago Manual of Style, 14th ed. (London: University of Chicago Press, 1993).

Constance Hale, ed., *Wired Style: Principles of English Usage in the Digital Age* (San Francisco: Hardwired, 2002).

Irene Hammerich and Claire Harrison, *Developing Online Content: The Principles of Writing and Editing for the Web* (New York: John Wiley, 2002).

Susan Hilligloss and Tharon Howard, *Visual Communication: A Writer's Guide* (New York: Longman, 2002).

Kuan-Tsae Huang, Yang W. Lee, and Richard Y. Wang, *Quality Information and Knowledge* (Upper Saddle River, NJ: Prentice Hall, 1999).

Steve Krug, *Don't Make Me Think: A Common Sense Approach to Web Usability* (Indianapolis, IN: Macmillan, 2000).

Patrick Lynch and Sarah Horton, *Web Style Guide 2* (New Haven, CT: Yale University Press, 2001); also available: http://info.med.yale.edu/caim/manual/contents.html.

Roger C. Parker, *Guide to Web Content and Design* (New York: MIS Press, 1997).

Thomas A. Powell, *Web Design: The Complete Reference* (New York: McGraw Hill, 2000).

Lynne Truss, *Eats, Shoots & Leaves* (New York: Gotham Books, 2004).

6 GETTING IT RIGHT
Online Editing, Designing and Publishing

I revise a great deal. I know when something is right because bells begin ringing and lights flash.

E.B. White, novelist and poet

An editor should tell the author his writing is better than it is. Not a lot better, a little better.

T.S. Eliot, poet and playwright

An editor doesn't count spelling errors and judge the writer accordingly; the editor is a reader, user advocate, and writing consultant.

Judith Tarutz, author of *Technical Editing*

Chapter Objectives

After studying this chapter, you will be able to:

- explain the fundamentals of online editing and publishing;
- understand the responsibilities of the editor;
- understand the process of publishing online;
- begin editing online content.

Introduction

The theory of Gestalt holds that the whole is different from the sum of its parts. To ensure the quality of the whole online, we have to inspect and evaluate all of the parts. Each and every element on a Web page should be scrutinized, from the dominant graphic to the text in navigational icons, bars and buttons. Headers and hyperlinks have to be checked, as do copyright notices, words in graphics and illustrations, photo credit lines and all headlines and subheads. The immediacy of online might lead us to assume that editing for the Web means less attention to detail, less time spent checking, re-checking, verifying and vetting, when in fact the complexity of online media means that there has never been more to inspect.

Multi-tasking, Cross-training, Silo-busting

Online publishing is not at all like editing for print, at least in terms of job responsibilities. In print, there are clear distinctions between roles and duties among writers, designers, editors and copyeditors. Media convergence online is blurring and blending the job descriptions and responsibilities traditionally assigned to writers and editors. Even hotshot page designers need to know how to write a declarative sentence; writing skills are not optional. Web newsrooms are filled with content producers, not specifically writers or specifically editors, and this relatively new breed of newsroom worker is above all flexible and adaptable.

Because of their many job duties, online editors and content producers typically are organized, self-directed and versatile. They are ethical and persistent, and often they have a pretty good sense of humor. These attributes point to the very stark differences between the processes of writing and editing, though of course writing and editing are complementary and interdependent. Many of the editor's traits are required for the arduous processes of proofreading and copyediting, which require an eye for detail and a reservoir of patience. Editing is mostly about making choices. Editing well means being able to attend to several different levels at the same time, from where commas do and do not belong to whether or not a navigation scheme is accommodating users.

Ideally, an online editor is involved in page or site development even in the earliest stages of planning. As an advocate for readers, online editors should influence if not direct information design and planning rather than merely fixing or correcting problems like typographical errors later in the process. In fact, when or at what stage editors are integrated into a Web site's or publication's design and operation can say much about that site's or publication's estimation of editors' importance or value.

With these roles in mind, some of the responsibilities common for online editors are presented here. They have been adapted from Carolyn Rude's *Technical Editing* (2005), and they appear in Alysson Troffer's tutorial on creating online documents.

Online Editing: Step-by-Step

- **First, identify the readers and the purpose of the content**. It is important to think, and to think a great deal, about readers' needs, which was the focus of the previous chapter. Knowing readers also means knowing what hardware and software they may be using (and conversely, knowing what they probably are not using).
- **Define document structure and links**. Develop a document structure (or organization) that is suited to the content's purpose and that is obvious and easy to navigate. Sections and pages should be largely independent, with associative and navigational links serving as transitions or linkages.

Web pages should support non-sequential and incomplete reading, and the content on those pages should be broken up into coherent, self-contained chunks that are understandable even if read out of sequence. A reader's path may be unpredictable, but the structure of the document should not be. Readers require a clear sense of how the document is organized so they can easily move through it. Troffer writes that the goal of an online editor is to reduce the risk of disorientation. Readers should not become "lost in cyberspace"—having to retrace their steps or move forward with no clear idea of where they are going.

An effective hypertext structure is organized according to a simple and meaningful pattern. It offers links that anticipate readers' needs. And such a structure features consistent visual design, such as the consistent placement of navigation links and the use of color and icons to identify different sections.

Main structural divisions should be obvious. The home page or opening screen, for example, could identify these main structural divisions and function as a table of contents. If this page establishes a consistent visual design, it teaches readers where to look for various types of information such as navigational links. Keep in mind, however, that readers can enter at points other than the home page. The page or site should identify and link to the main structural divisions and home page from every page.

- **Define the style.** A site needs guidelines for style and for creating the screens that users will see. Use templates to save time and reduce inconsistencies. (Much more on style in the previous chapter.)

- **Edit.** Review and edit content, structure and navigation, links, writing style and visual design. Begin early and repeat throughout. Check colors, graphics, headlines, subheads, paragraph lengths and consistency of all elements. Troffer suggests editing content chunks in random order rather than in sequence. This basic trick helps ensure a suitable and accessible organization for readers.

Here is a short example of how to edit a text chunk for online presentation:

Before (for print):

> Tokyo is filled with internationally recognized attractions that draw large crowds of people every year without fail. During the first six months of 2009, some of the most popular places were the Imperial Palace (1.2 million visitors), Tokyo Disneyland (1.1 million), Ueno Park Zoo (678,000), Toshugu Shrine (386,598), Tokyo Science Museum (360,000), and Yasukuni Shrine (228,446).

After (for Web), hyperlinking each bullet item to a site or source, or to richer presentations on each of the tourist sites:

> In the first six months of 2009, six of the most-visited places in Tokyo were:

- Imperial Palace
- Tokyo Disneyland
- Ueno Park Zoo
- Toshugu Shrine
- Tokyo Science Museum
- Yasukuni Shrine

- **Copyedit.** Online copyediting also involves checking consistency in visual design, testing links and ensuring accurate reading. Because the organization of a site is translated into file names according to certain conventions, this copyediting function should include inspecting naming conventions for individual pages, folders and sections. Also check pages in different browsers, using different monitors and connection speeds.

  Misspelled words are an embarrassment, and they detract from credibility, so multiple copyediting processes should be in place. Reviewing hard copy printouts, for example, can be a useful process, as can reading many times, even backwards, to catch mistakes and typos.

- **Copyedit II.** Good editors read on many different levels at the same time. An article or piece of content should be read first for understanding. Is the information complete? Does it make sense? Is it logical?

  Editors read content for organization and focus. Does each paragraph focus on a single idea? Are transitions clearly and simply made?

  Editors read for accuracy. Names, places, figures—facts need to be checked. Are the facts consistent with each other? Have counter-intuitive assertions been corroborated?

  Editors read for grammar, spelling, punctuation and style, or the kinds of things covered in Chapter 1. Is the language clear and precise? Does it flow? Is there too much jargon?

  For this second category of copyediting, editors will want several reliable sources close by, in print and/or online, including:

  — Stylebook
  — Dictionary
  — Writing and usage handbook
  — Thesaurus
  — Maps, an atlas and a general information almanac
  — Directories, biographical information (depending on topics and categories)
  — Encyclopedia
  — Archives of the publication, site or blog.

- **Write headlines.** As was discussed in Chapter 4, headlines online serve different purposes than do their print counterparts, so they should be written differently. Headlines online are often displayed out of context, alone or as part of a list of articles, such as in a listing of findings for an online search query. Users don't have the benefit of background information and context to interpret the headline's meaning, so headlines should be written in a very direct style. While scanning a list of stories, people often look only at the highlighted headlines, skipping summaries and other information, so the headline also must be able to stand alone.

- **Test usability.** Test the tasks that readers probably will want to perform. Check that navigation is easy and intuitive. Evaluate reading comprehension.

As is indicated by the list above, an online editor must be part content developer, content strategist, producer, manager, managing editor and project manager. Online editors might also end up producing multimedia, moderating a chat room or social network, or going into the field to do the heavy lifting of original reporting.

Case Study 1: Checking Copy

Demonstrating the processes that an organization can put in place to check copy and find error, an editor for a large custom publishing company described how she edits copy, identifying a multiplicity of hiding places for error and oversight:

> When I proof a layout, I use "the ten steps to perfect proofing." These steps include checking:
>
> - photo credits;
> - the folios (or four-page groupings of pages);
> - throw lines (or 'see p. x' lines) to other pages or sidebars;
> - grammar and orthography in all display copy;
> - byline name spelling and matching name in the biography;
> - every single line for correct/best hyphenation;
> - every line that wraps around a photo, photo captions, pull quotes matching body copy appearance of that text;
> - consistency of spelling of all names;
> - bad breaks, widows and orphans.

On my publication, our copyeditor has a baseline list that she always [checks], including running a spell check, cross-checking any mention of a page number, spacing around em-dashes, city/state style, split infinitives, checking that the table of contents entries match every layout. But she adds on items each issue based on recent experience. For instance, she is known as the "hyphenated adjective ninja" these days. (Or is that "hyphenated-adjective ninja"?) Once a client complained about our splitting his company name over a line, so now she checks for that in the magazine, as well.

If a piece is intensive with service information, one round may be devoted only to phoning all numbers and testing every Web link published. This may also be the time to check the spellings of proper names, places and the like.

Most of our publications have a separate, fairly early fact-checking phase for all copy. Some editors' checklists for this simply state "check all facts." I issue a two-page instruction memo that goes into much more detail.

And before all of this happens, the story undergoes content editing—from structure and length to identifying information to put higher in the story and smoothing out awkward language. The writer may have conducted additional reporting to fill information gaps. And another editor has written a headline, deck and subheads.

By the time I'm looking at bluelines (the last phase before press time), I'm hopefully confident enough to have my checklist down to less than five items: looking at the display copy, quadruple checking the page numbers/folios and reviewing the changes requested at the proof stage prior.

Another revising strategy: setting a word limit, or at least a target. I generally write long, particularly when I am quoting sources. Cutting a story down to the right length is an important part of my revising process. Why is this useful? Making a story shorter can't be done with only one method. I find it has to be a combination of line edits, substitutions of long phrases for short adjectives and removal of entire blocks of text. I found I did this with the [Chapter 1] writing sample, despite the fact that I didn't have an exact layout, with the critique feedback I composed and even with a fundraising letter I wrote this week for a charity event.

This hints a bit at my pre-writing process. I have a rough outline of topics, work a lot of composing in my head but also let myself free-write at points, which then needs to be reined in.

This editor describes a process and a culture of editing and of careful attention to detail. She lays out a process of established routines shared by several people in her company. The immediacy of online is forcing changes in these print-based processes, but not in the importance of and premium on a discipline of verification. The writer makes another critical point, that no one method can substantially edit down a story or article or check that article for errors of fact or of writing. Both require multi-step processes.

When editing text, here are a few tried-and-true methods:

• Print the story out on hard copy. For reasons discussed in Chapter 2, the human brain sees more words and therefore reads more of the story in print than it does online, where it likes to scan and surf.

- Read once quickly, to get a sense of what the story is about and to identify the flow or the arc of the narrative.
- Look for weaknesses, for holes in the story, and for problems of flow and organization. Think of the article as a building, with each paragraph serving as a floor or story. Is there a better order? If you moved the 13th floor to the 4th, would the story make more sense? If a floor was removed, would the building be better off?
- Read the copy aloud. This method reveals problems of word choice and flow, among other things. It also serves to slow the mind down enough to truly "hear" the text.
- Read the copy backwards, either word by word or sentence by sentence. This prevents the brain from skipping words and/or phrases by focusing it, and it is perhaps the best method for spotting typographical and spelling errors.
- When you think you are finished, go get a cup of coffee. Take a nap. Go for a run. Do something different. Then come back and give the piece one more read, especially the headline.

Case Study 2: *The Washington Post*

In 2008, the *Post* announced changes in how its editorial team would edit copy in an effort to more quickly get news onto its Web site. From an assembly-line approach, a model that has been the norm in newspapering for decades, the *Post* announced moving toward more of a network editing structure in which different editors perform varying roles depending on the news needs. A memo from then Executive Editor Leonard Downie recommended removing layers from the editing process to increase flexibility and to promote "thinking Web first."

"We will create truer alignment of editing for the web and for the paper, recognizing that deadlines for many pieces are defined as the earliest moment they can be edited and published online," Downie wrote, describing several specific changes. They included:

- *New assistant editors*, who will begin their work earlier in the day. These editors will "have broad responsibilities for moving early copy to the web and for the next day's paper." Describing the network approach, Downie wrote that these new editors "will provide the first read on some stories and the final edit on others."
- A *new night desk* with responsibility and flexibility across the news enterprise, for speed. The paper planned to establish new copy flows to allow for, among other things, continuous editing during the day, an acknowledgment that pre-determined deadlines are increasingly a luxury of the print-based past.
- *Earlier decisions*: "Editors of words, photos, graphics and layout will collaborate more closely," Downie wrote. Another luxury from print's

past is specialization. Rather than working in silos, content producers move throughout the network, sometimes writing, sometimes editing, sometimes gathering information. And the new context for this flexibility is collaboration and teamwork. "We will deepen collaboration among editors on assignment desks, copy desks, photo and the news desk to change how a story, graphic or photograph goes into the newspaper," Downie wrote in his memo to *Post* staff.

- *Fewer "touches" on some stories*: This is where the layers come out. Downie described front section stories as being edited by a half-dozen different editors. "Under the new model, many stories will be handled under a 'two touch' rule; they will have a first editor and a second editor," he wrote, describing the elimination of four layers.

Eliminating "meddlesome editing," as Slate's Jack Shafer referred to the *Post*'s streamlining, is of course a good idea. The concern, however, is compromising the discipline of verification, the key differentiator between credible news-gathering and reporting organizations and most of the derivative blogosphere. This is one of the more intriguing online riddles: how to accelerate processes and yet assure quality in editing and fact-checking, while still participating in the breakneck, never-ending 24/7 news cycle of online. In other words, how does an online publication retain those aspects of first-order journalism that truly inform a self-governing democracy, while at the same time acknowledging the tremendous time pressures and seemingly overwhelming competition on any one story? "We believe this evolution is possible while ensuring the quality of our editing and the quality of life of editors," Downie wrote, acknowledging the riddle.

In reacting to the *Post*'s changes, Shafer wrote that one reason many newspapers rely so heavily on editors is that some reporters cannot write, and he is absolutely correct. The reporters' copy often has to be re-written. Taking layers out of the process will reveal these poor writers, who likely will get weeded out of journalism's garden. Writing well has never been more important.

(Downie stepped down as executive editor in June 2008. At the time, the *Post* reported more than 9 million Internet readers each month, according to Nielsen online, trailing only *The New York Times* and *USA Today*.)

Case Study 3: Error Prevention Project (Brazil)

A group of eight newspapers in southern Brazil also is changing its editorial processes in response to the new demands of online news, and the group also is removing layers or "touches" in editing.

Called the Error Prevention Project, the collaboration is an effort to reduce error and to be more transparent to readers about error when and where it occurs. All part of the RBS Group, the eight newspapers are working together to, according to one assistant editor in the group, "identify and avoid their most common errors" (Lorea 2008). Among the Project's initiatives, according to Eduardo Lorea, an editor with *Zero Hora* (Zero Hour), one of the eight newspapers, are:

- An online database of all of the corrections published in the eight newspapers.
- An internal campaign throughout the group to encourage checking for the five most frequent types of errors:

  — Names
  — Professions/positions/ages/political parties
  — Dates/numbers
  — Geography
  — Emails/addresses/Web sites/telephones.

- A "Manual of Procedures and Error Prevention" of procedures for writing, reporting and editing. Writing an obituary, for example, is covered by guidelines for what must be checked and what sources are considered reliable when writing obits.

According to Lorea, Zerohora.com publishes reporters' stories "minutes after reporters hang up the phone, with almost no formal editing. For this reason we felt that it was even more important to make sure journalists use proper reporting techniques to ensure accuracy." This type of editorial process puts more of the burden of accuracy on the reporters, and it acknowledges that a lot of error is caught not by editors but by readers. Cataloging, classifying and explaining the errors in a publicly accessible database produces transparency

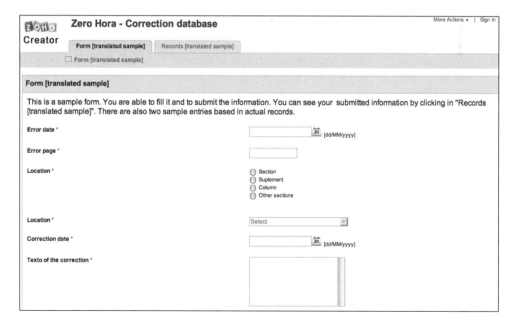

The online database application for submitting errors to RBS newspaper, *Zero Hora*.

and communicates credibility to a readership being acknowledged as part of the discipline of verification. Though not the right model for every news organization, and admittedly very new and therefore largely untested, the RBS initiative does force a revisiting of long-held routines and practices in newsrooms.

Multimedia Storytelling

Because the online environment must accommodate scanning and non-linear information retrieval, the job of an online editor is a bit different than that of his or her counterpart in print. An online editor needs to be more than familiar with several of the skill sets and knowledge bases covered in previous chapters, including online writing (style, organization, presentation, etc.); use of links (how many, what to link to, style, etc.); and design.

Two skill sets previously mentioned are **XHTML coding** and working with **multimedia**, including sound and video. Online editors should be able to create a simple Web page and have a basic understanding of XHTML and CSS, particularly of the coding languages' unique limitations. Increasingly, XML also is being used for sites that solicit information from users, rely on databases and/or transact e-commerce.

One of the more important decisions an online editor makes is the medium or media through which to tell a story. Knowing the possibilities and limitations of different publishing environments can inform these choices. When, for example, is a multimedia approach to online storytelling better than a text-based approach? When is it better to combine still photo and audio? What kinds of media do viewers want, and how much control do they want over those media?

Consider as an example a story package on the sub-prime mortgage crisis of 2008–9 and its effects on mortgage lending rates. Television news might interview a banker and a heart-broken homeowner (or former homeowner), then perhaps show a visual of an empty subdivision. Is there a better way? Multimedia could, by contrast:

- Provide a short list of the problems in the mortgage markets illustrated with a large photo of someone at a foreclosure auction.
- Offer a short video and/or audio clips of the voices of the housing market, presenting people telling their stories of foreclosure or being stuck in a slow market. The same person in the foreclosure photo could be featured in one of the videos. In fact, the photo could link to the video.
- Create interactive maps that show where problems are the worst in a particular state or the nation.
- Provide a "rate your mortgage savvy" interactive quiz or test to illustrate to readers problems they might run into securing a home loan.
- Link to resources, such as banks and the U.S. Federal Reserve.
- Provide a narrative tying all of these elements together.

The key distinction here is the value that each of these dimensions or layers adds to the story. If the use of multimedia does not add to what another medium, such as television, can do, there is no need for it. A slideshow of photos with audio interviews is no better than a TV presentation of those interviews; in fact, the slideshow would be rather dull by comparison.

Stories and packages that call for multimedia are not traditional, linear experiences. Linear stories are those that do not need multimedia, or incorporation into multimedia presentations. Planning, therefore, is essential. Other stories need to be seen to be fully appreciated, or experienced. Think, for example, of a presentation on vibrant sea life. A straight narrative would work, but a video clip of underwater sea life, with fish, a coral reef, movement and color could be quite compelling. A story on New York City's street musicians? A straight narrative could tell the story. Now imagine adding audio clips and photography of the musicians, which could be sampled before, during or after reading the narrative. Multimedia should offer an experience, in other words, not merely a download.

The Poynter Institute's Eyetrack studies reveal some truths common to successful multimedia presentations:

- Short is better.
- Interactive is better.
- Personal (or local or hyperlocal) is preferred.
- Navigability is central (the better the interface, the better the experience).

Demonstrating the last point, *End of the Road* (endoftheroad.org), a multimedia package detailing life at the end of Peru's road to Patagonia, offers an example of one of the Web's better multimedia interfaces. Developed by undergraduate students at UNC Chapel Hill, the interface is intuitive, easy to use, and makes a strong graphical impression. (See p. 130.)

Content Management Systems

How an editor does his or her job is in important ways influenced if not dictated by the organization's computer network system or, in the absence of a network, the hardware and software the company uses. Most online newspapers deploy a content management system (CMS) to run their Web sites and network the various parts of the production process.

A CMS is a sophisticated software package that automates many of the processes or functions of moving copy and content to the Web. A CMS also helps online publications achieve and maintain a consistency in look while constantly updating the site's content from any number of sources from within the organization and from without, including wire news services. The software makes it easier to publish, removing the need for writers and editors to learn or to know XHTML or CSS. Relying on templates, a good content

The News & Observer's section scrolls. The newspaper's CMS automates its presentation; RSS feeds push them out to readers who subscribe to the feeds.

management system makes it fairly simple for almost anyone to learn how to upload content to the publication's site and to format that content using simple tags.

These CMS software packages also automate how a Web site interfaces or otherwise links up with databases. For example, if an online newspaper wants to allow site visitors to search and view its database of real estate listings, a CMS can provide an easy-to-use drop-down menu or sequence of drop-down menus enabling that database to be searched by price or location or any other field of the database.

A CMS might also be used, for example, to automate the placement of headlines and first paragraphs of new news stories onto the home page after uploading to interior pages. The CMS can be set up, in other words, to grab headlines and lede graphs of stories submitted via the CMS to the site, then to place them onto the home page, then to shift older stories down the page or to onto other, interior pages. A good CMS can do many of the functions of print editors, freeing up human resources for the more important tasks of fact-checking and copyediting.

The next two screen grabs demonstrate how a CMS typically works. First, a list of content blocks an editor could install in the CMS and, therefore, present on the Web site. Shown are Quicktime movies and jpeg images, all on the CMS dashboard, or the back end of the CMS.

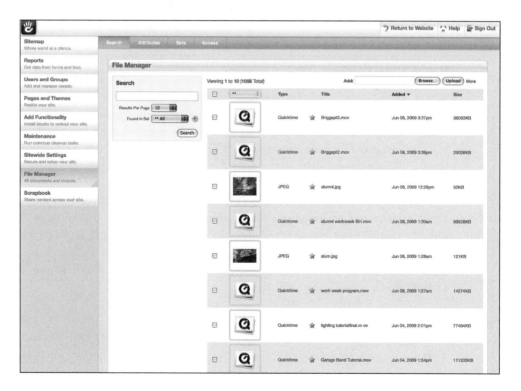

When you want to add a block to the page, the Concrete 5 CMS displays this pop-up window. Editors choose a block, modify it by adding display text or perhaps a hyperlink, then save the changes to the site. Done! Oh, except for editing and proofing.

Rapid Adaptability

Given the multiplicity of places errors can appear, and because knowing and using technology has become such an integral part of the editing process, editors are more important than ever, although their roles, as we have seen in this chapter, are fundamentally changing. This chapter identified and explored the multi-dimensional roles of the online editor and some of the processes of publishing online.

Hallmarks of this new breed of online journalist include rapid adaptability, cross-training and preparedness for anything, for everything. (Technology is a fickle friend, behaving in unpredictable ways.) These writers and editors think in layers, both to provide an experience and to leverage online media, thinking of stories as multi-dimensional and multi-directional. There are a variety of ways to tell any one story.

Chapter Assignment

1 Develop and complete the content piece you detailed in the previous chapter's assignments. Develop and present the piece for online readership by using the techniques and tools discussed in Chapters 2–6. Do not merely post a large block of text or cut-and-paste from Word. This assignment asks

you to apply what you have been learning. Be sure to spend plenty of time editing, including fact-checking, spell-checking and editing for grammar, punctuation and organization.

Length: At least 700 words.

Online Resources

Alysson Troffer's "Writing Effectively Online"
http://homepage.mac.com/alysson/httoc.html
Troffer's research on hypertext and strategies for writing online.

"Ode to a Copyeditor"
http://query.nytimes.com/gst/fullpage.html?res=9F06EED6123AF935A2
5751C0A9639C8B63
A tribute to the behind-the-scenes valor and importance of an editor, from *The New York Times*, February 16, 2005.

Wandering Rocks blog
wanderingrocks.wordpress.com
The author's blog on writing and editing for digital media, and other topics.

Sources

Irene Hammerich and Claire Harrison, *Developing Online Content: The Principles of Writing and Editing for the Web* (New York: John Wiley, 2002).

Eduardo Lorea, "Improving Accuracy: Creating a Newsroom System," Poynter Institute, March 10, 2008.

Patrick Lynch and Sarah Horton, *Web Style Guide 2* (New Haven, CT: Yale University Press, 2001); also available: http://www.webstyleguide.com.

Jakob Nielsen, *Designing Web Usability* (Indianapolis, IN: New Riders, 2000).

Roger C. Parker, *Guide to Web Content and Design* (New York: MIS Press, 1997).

Jonathan Price and Lisa Price, *hot text: Web Writing That Works* (Indianapolis, IN: New Riders, 2002).

Carolyn D. Rude, *Technical Editing*, 4th ed. (New York: Longman, 2005).

Judith Tarutz, *Technical Editing* (Chelmsford, MA: Hewlett-Packard Press, 1992).

Alysson Troffer, *Editing Online Documents: Strategies and Tips* (August 1999), available: http://www.contentious.com/.

PART III
CONTEXTS

7 BLOGITO, ERGO SUM
Trends in Personal Publishing

*It's easy to write poorly, but it's hard to write poorly every day . . . It's hard
to write every day.*

Rebecca Blood, pioneering blogger

When in doubt, tell the truth.

Mark Twain

Chapter Objectives

After studying this chapter, you will be able to:

- identify the principles of personal publishing;
- understand the blog format and why it has proliferated;
- describe blogging's roles in journalism;
- harness good blog-writing practices.

Introduction

The democratization of the tools of publishing by the Web has been nothing
less than revolutionary in terms of its effects on and implications for society,
culture and mass media. "Citizen journalism," personal publishing, including
blogging, and desktop publishing are re-shaping media and re-defining roles
and job descriptions throughout journalism and communication. This chapter
focuses especially on blogs, the most popular format or dimension of personal
publishing, a format that has brought the cost of writing for the Web to the
vanishing point. As part of the broader trend toward participatory, networked
grass roots journalism, blogs are influencing how products are introduced, how
political campaigns are run and even how wars are fought.

Weblogging and Webloggers: A Brief History

Because of the many ways blogs are employed, there is a great deal of confusion about the term and just what it is supposed to mean. A **weblog** or **blog**
is simply a Web page or site for frequently updated posts, or entries, that

Graphic for a conference on blogging at Yale University, November 2002.

typically are arranged or presented in reverse chronological order, so that new entries always appear on top. Other common attributes of blogs include archives, permalinks (or hyperlinks to specific posts, which, when clicked, usually present accompanying comments beneath the post), time stamps and date headers, tags (key word identification), and blogrolls (hyperlinked lists of and to other blogs, usually presented as a sidebar to the blog's main content). Blog posts typically connect their readers with source materials that were used to write or that are referenced in the post, a connective tissue that also serves to provide layers of information and to build credibility. If, for example, a blogger is commenting on a speech, it would be customary to provide or link to a complete transcript of the speech or to an audio recording or podcast of the event, making it transparent to the reader where fact leaves off and where opinion begins.

The term "blog," however clunky and unfortunate, means nothing more than the collection of the few attributes described above. As such, the "blog" is a value-neutral medium or media format for publishing online. A blog is not necessarily a personal diary, though many blogs are used for this purpose. Most blogs are single-voice narratives made up of mostly brief posts that blend fact with personal opinion, but there is nothing about the form that predicates these norms.

Perhaps the easiest way to conceptualize blogging is to think of the activity as nothing more (or less) than writing. Ink pens are used for all sorts of purposes, from signing checks to journaling to drafting manuscripts for the next great novel. As a technology, there is nothing about the ink pen that makes it more or less capable of producing exquisite literature or pure drivel. A blog is no different.

The content and purposes of blogs vary greatly—from links and commentary about other Web sites, to news about companies, people and ideas, to diaries, photos, poetry, mini-essays, project updates and even fiction. In this chapter we are more interested in those blogs that are dedicated to news, information and issues rather than those deployed to relate personal events and private thoughts. In other words, we will focus more on blogs like

What qualifies as true innovation?

April 3, 2008

The article, "Diffusion of Innovations" (Rogers and Singhal), began with these words: "What is diffusion?" I would like to start instead with the question, "What is innovation?" I ask because I think many of us are a bit quick to confer such high status to mere evolutionary progress, to incremental advances, to mostly consumer products that, in fact, fall far short of being truly innovative.

 Is the iPhone, for example, truly an innovation? Does it, or has it, in fact transformed the way we communicate? Who we are? Our understanding of telecommunications and Web use? (Hint: No, no and no.)

The hybrid corn seed was truly an innovation. What about Facebook? The bionic eye?

In communication, as the article pointed out, we are interested in diffusion as a "communication *process*, independent of the type of innovations that are diffused." This is why, just for funsies, that we are the department of communication and not the department of communicationS, because it is a process.

Think through, then, what has to be true for some thing, some new device or method or process, to be innovative. Next, think about how that device or method or technological innovation has changed how we communicate, the *process* of communication, perhaps even who we are.

Next, as you think about where you are on the adoption curve, consider the article's valuable point about adoption (or diffusion) as at least partly a social process, something we've really keyed on in Intro to Digital Communication. Think about how much social interaction, peer groups and influencers have impacted how and when you adopt a new way of doing something, especially online. In other words, how do your interpersonal networks influence what you buy, what you adopt, when to change how you do something? (These are rich questions given the fact that the Internet has become such a thoroughly social tool or enabler.)

Now the most difficult question and, therefore, the most important: So what? Are these innovations in the end progress? Are these new devices, methods and technologies taking us all to a better place, or merely to a different place? To prompt us: In the 1950s, it was wholeheartedly believed that technology would produce the three- or four-day workweek, that increases in productivity would yield vast amounts of found leisure time. We're working harder — and longer — than ever.

(My apologies for the difficulties most had in commenting to last week's post. I've checked around at WordPress.com and cannot find a systemic reason. Perhaps Berry's IT quirks have struck again. It does appear that changing your posting name and/or email however slightly does the trick.)

🗨 17 Comments | 🖉 Uncategorized | 🖥 Permalink
👤 Posted by brian carroll

Typical blog post, with blue hyperlinks, indicated in this screen grab with a lighter tint; a link to comments below; a permalink to this particular post; and an authorship line identifying who posted.

> 🗨 16 Comments | 🗂 Uncategorized | Tagged: COM 329, journalism, revenue models | 🖶 Permalink
> 👤 Posted by brian carroll

Tags help blog readers and search engines find particular posts; they also help blog authors organize their content. The tags for this post are "facebook," "me media," "social networking" and "swarm behavior."

The Politico (http://www.politico.com/) and PressThink (http://journalism.nyu.edu/pubzone/weblogs/pressthink/) than on personal diary blogs like Supermatt at LiveJournal (http://supermatt41.livejournal.com/).

The best blogs create for their readers a sort of "targeted serendipity," as pioneering blogger Rebecca Blood has called it, or a shared point of view and information and sources a reader perhaps did not even know he or she wanted to see. At the very least, blogging is an exercise of expression, making one's views public. Increasingly, though, blogging is also an expression of community, allowing individuals to communicate and congregate.

The (Blog) Major Leagues: A Quick Overview

Talking Points Memo

In December 2002, Joshua Micah Marshall's "The Talking Points Memo" got a great deal of attention for raising questions about then Senate majority leader

Trent Lott's views on race. In doing so, TPM (http://www.talkingpointsmemo.com/) legitimized blogging as journalism, or at least established that blogging and the mission of journalism are not necessarily at odds or mutually exclusive. Both bloggers and traditional journalists have debated since whether or when and under what circumstances blogging can be considered journalism.

In the wake of Lott's statement on national cable television that the United States would have been better off had Strom Thurmond been elected president in 1948—Thurmond ran on a segregationist platform—Marshall revealed a history of what could be described as racist statements made by Lott. The Mississippi senator previously compared court rulings in 1981 upholding affirmative action programs at colleges to the dating ban between black and white students at Bob Jones University, according to TPM.

After a full weekend of silence, during which only TPM blogged on the subject, mainstream news media picked up on Marshall's analysis, piecing together Lott's record. The media coverage fueled a national debate that ultimately led to Lott's removal as majority leader, but not before the surreal: Lott appearing on BET to apologize to the nation's black community. Lott's capitulation or, more accurately, Marshall's attention to an overlooked political story, proved a watershed moment for blogs, which were still considered by many at the time as a minor league publishing option.

It is important to note that Marshall politically is on the left, and that he is candid and transparent about this political orientation. He began publishing TPM in November 2000 during the Florida presidential election vote recount. He also is dedicated to a form of watchdog investigative journalism that is vanishing as ever-larger media companies stress entertainment and the sale of advertising over service to the public interest.

Josh Micah Marshall

TPM has found a loyal audience—in fact, several loyal audiences. TPM launched its second site, TPMCafe.com, in 2005 and TPMMuckraker.com and TPM Election Central in 2006.

Though Marshall is proud to be a blogger, he also believes that what he and his dozen or so reporters do is journalism. TPM, after all, is credited with investigative reporting on the firing of eight U.S. attorneys, reporting for which TPM received the Polk Award for Reporting. Importantly, TPM's coverage of the U.S. attorney scandal utilized crowdsourcing, or the wisdom of the crowds. TPM pursued tips from readers, synthesized the work of other news outlets, provided its own original reporting and solicited and received the help of thousands of readers in sifting through piles of documents released by the Bush administration. "There are thousands who have contributed some information over the last year," Marshall told *The New York Times* of TPM's crowdsourced U.S. attorney coverage.

In 2006, when watchdog groups that monitor federal spending wanted more information on nearly 2,000 pork barrel projects buried in a Congressional spending bill, they listed the projects on the Web and asked readers to do some research. Readers did, and information began pouring in. Similarly, also in 2006, Porkbusters.org enlisted readers to find out which senator had blocked legislation that would create an online database of federal grants and contracts. Ted Stevens, R-Alaska, and Robert Byrd, D-W.Va., were uncovered in a matter of days. The wisdom of the crowds was leveraged to shine more light into the dark places of government.

Memogate

On the political right, it was self-avowed conservative bloggers that first called into question the authenticity of four documents presented by Dan Rather of CBS News on *60 Minutes* purporting to be from President Bush's commanding officer in the Texas National Guard. The documents described efforts to get preferential treatment for the future president. Bloggers pointed out that, given the equipment on which the memos were composed, they couldn't possibly have been written in the early 1970s, as alleged on the news show.

Just hours after *60 Minutes* aired, a man with the user name Buckhead posted a comment on Free Republic (www.freerepublic.com). The poster observed that the CBS memos, which had been posted online, had been typed in a proportionally spaced font that was unlikely to be found on or from a 1972-era typewriter. A blog called Power Line (www.powerlineblog.com) and written by three lawyers reprinted Buckhead's speculations, along with comments from readers who claimed knowledge of IBM typewriters, fonts and superscripting. A reader who had been a Navy clerk/typist and another who had been an Air Force personnel manager weighed in on military typewriters, paper sizes and procedures. Power Line's initial post quickly listed 605 trackbacks, meaning that 605 other online sites linked to the blog's analysis. Again, crowdsourcing generated smarter coverage than any one reporter likely could have produced.

CBS News and Dan Rather stuck to their story. Rather stated on air:

> The story is true. The story is true. I appreciate the sources who took risks to authenticate our story. So, one, there is no internal investigation. Two, somebody may be shell-shocked, but it is not I, and it is not anybody at CBS News. Now, you can tell who is shell-shocked by the ferocity of the people who are spreading these rumors.
>
> (September 10, 2004)

The story was not true as reported, and CBS News ultimately admitted this, making the episode an important point on the timeline of blogs. For one, the episode pitted traditional or mainstream news media against new media, specifically blogs, and blogs won the day. A few days after *60 Minutes* made its claims, a former CBS executive vice president, Jonathan Klein, sneered at CBS's critics who claimed the old memos had to be modern forgeries written on a computer: "You couldn't have a starker contrast between the multiple layers of check and balances [of professional journalists] and a guy sitting in his living room in his pajamas writing," Klein told Fox News on September 10, 2004.

Bloggers became reporters of a kind. Thousands of blogs picked up the story. Type designers, computer workers and former military clerks joined the debate. Mainstream news media other than CBS News joined in as well. Professional journalists interviewed document experts, who raised the same questions as the bloggers. Then CBS's own experts revealed that they had never bothered to authenticate the memos. As the *San Francisco Chronicle* noted, many mainstream journalists were reading the blogs to track the discussion and find sources.

"The Internet has empowered ordinary citizens to become fact-checkers and analysts. People with a wide range of experiences can collaborate online, sharing knowledge, sources and ideas, and challenging each others' facts," wrote the *Chronicle*'s Joanne Jacobs ("The Way It Is Today Isn't How It Was: If the Facts Aren't Right Bloggers Are All Over It," *San Francisco Chronicle*, September 26, 2004, available: http://www.sfgate.com/cgi-bin/article.cgi?file=/chronicle/archive/2004/09/26/INGAG8T2FT1.DTL).

Bloggers as Journalists

In the first decade of the 21st century, blogging as a journalistic form caught on. Traditional media's big newspapers, including *The New York Times*, *The Washington Post*, *Los Angeles Times*, *Wall Street Journal*, and *USA Today*, all have blogs. The Associated Press and CNN launched their first blogs for the Democratic National Convention in July 2004. *The New York Times* prominently used live blogging during the presidential primary season in 2008.

MSNBC's "Hardball" with Chris Matthews uses the blog format for a star-studded group blog, Hardblogger, that includes posts from NBC News' Andrea Mitchell, former San Francisco mayor Willie Brown, former Howard Dean campaign manager Joe Trippi, and conservative pundit Pat Buchanan (http://hardblogger.msnbc.msn.com). One of the blogosphere's most read group blogs is *The Huffington Post*, launched by former California politician Arianna Huffington (http://www.huffingtonpost.com/theblog/). From beginnings in celebrity news, the blog has evolved and matured into a sort of online newspaper specializing in politics and political commentary, boasting as of mid-2008 approximately 1,500 bloggers and 4 million visitors per month.

The Caucus

The New York Times Politics Blog

Back to front page »

February 19, 2008, 11:37 pm

Hello Wisconsin!

By KATHARINE Q. SEELYE

Barack Obama in Houston. (Photo: Richard Carson/Reuters)

Wrapup | 11:40 p.m.: Wrapup: Mrs. Clinton heads back to New York tonight and there probably aren't too many people who want to be on that plane ride, unless they are the Houdinis of politics. Her presidential bid is handcuffed, in a locked treasure chest, under the ice. Will Ohio and Texas let Mrs. Clinton come up for air?

Those states just got harder tonight. Mr. Obama has now won nine states in a row, by impressive margins. The Clinton campaign may have planned it this way (right), but could they really have thought they could absorb nine consecutive losses? Were they in any way prepared for Mr. Obama to cut into her base, particularly with blue-collar workers and women?

Negative attacks against Mr. Obama so far have not worked. Is there more of that to come? Will Mr. Obama stumble? Will Mr. McCain's portrayal of him as an empty vessel end up helping Mrs. Clinton? It's hard to imagine a thematic overhaul for Mrs. Clinton or the emergence of a new and different person, but at this point, everything has to be on the table.

The next two weeks may reveal more about Mrs. Clinton than we have seen during her 15 years on the national stage.

11:33 p.m. | More From Ohio: Our colleague John Broder reports from Mrs. Clinton's event in Youngstown, Ohio.

11:03 p.m. | Mighty Fine Place to Be: Our colleague Jeff Zeleny reports on the scene from the Toyota Center in Houston.

Meanwhile, the networks are calling the Washington primary for John McCain.

Live blogging at NYTimes.com.

The most popular group blog as of mid-2009 was Engadget (www. engadget.com), a blog focused on the latest gadgets in technology.

Blogging Software

Behind the fast growth of blogging has been easy-to-use software that makes becoming a blogger a low- or no-cost exercise in a matter of a few minutes. One of the leaders of the blogging movement, Meg Hourihan, co-founded Pyra Labs to develop a blogging software now known as Blogger.com, which Google acquired along with the rest of Pyra in May 2003.

Blogger.com's software is one of a number that automate the blog publishing process and therefore eliminate the need for users to write any code or install any sort of server-side software or scripting. Once launched, Blogger.com's blogs use forms and a Word-like toolbar to make writing and submitting posts a simple exercise.

That anyone with a Google username and password can begin writing and publishing to the world from his or her own URL in a matter of minutes at no cost is momentous, on a scale similar to Gutenberg's liberating of knowledge with moveable type. While Web site publishing has long been available

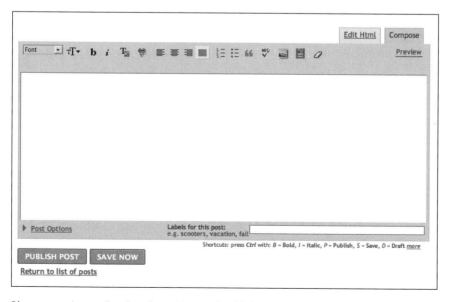

Blogger.com's template box for writing and publishing blog posts.

to anyone willing to learn HTML coding or WYSIWYG design, the advent of blogging software has given tens of millions of individuals a simpler way to maintain Web pages.

Blogger.com, TypePad, LiveJournal, Greymatter, WordPress and Movable Type are some of the more popular blogging software tools. Some, like Blogger, are remotely hosted, while others, such as MovableType, are installed on the user's own computer. Those who become bloggers can be HTML novices or experienced Web designers, first-time writers or professional authors.

The Blogger v. Journalist Debate

Is anyone with a blog a journalist? Is anyone with a camera a photographer? What happens to journalism when every reader can also be a writer, editor and producer? These are but some of the questions long debated in both the blogosphere and in journalism, and still no clear consensus has emerged. The blogger–journalist dichotomy clearly is a false one. Many journalists blog; many bloggers do journalism. Key distinctions, then, include the methods or processes employed and the purpose or goal of the content.

Where an information-gathering process includes what Kovach and Rosenstiel (2007) call "the discipline of verification," and where the purpose is service to the public interest, then blogging could be said to be journalism. Where one or both of these is absent, the blogger would be hard pressed to claim to be doing real journalism. Original reporting that has been corroborated, fact-checked and verified, reporting that seeks to inform a self-governing electorate, be it on a blog or anywhere else, must be called journalism.

Most blogs have a different mandate than does journalism, however. Most blogs are dedicated to some form of commentary or opinion. To the extent a blog lacks original reporting, it is removed from the primary enterprise of journalism. For most bloggers, a high value is placed on the act of expression, on providing in the aggregate a diversity of voices. Also important in the blogosphere are writing or publishing with speed, offering transparency of sourcing and of the opinions that influenced the writing, and decentralizing information and knowledge. For journalism, by contrast, great value is placed on providing a filter for information, editing the content, fact-checking, ensuring accuracy and fairness, setting the agenda and centralizing news dissemination. In some cases, then, the value sets of the blogosphere and of journalism are in tension, if not conflict. The vetting and editing process typically used in print, for example, comes at the expense of speed and of single-voice authenticity, hallmarks of the blogosphere.

Blogging's priority usually is to publish, then to begin filtering; journalism's priority is to filter, then after and only after to publish. Blogging, then, can be seen as a thoroughly postmodern form of expression and pursuit, and post-modernism rejects objectivity as a goal or ideal. This rejection pits many bloggers against the guild of journalism, which still strives for objectivity, at least in its methods, if not in its products.

The filtering and editing in journalism is possible because of daily printing cycles and large editorial and production staffs. With large, capital-intensive printing presses and a prohibitively expensive distribution system, newspapers in fact require large staffs. Organized hierarchically, these staffs funnel the information out from a center. With the imperative to publish, then to filter, bloggers are as concerned with *unmaking* and testing public opinion as forming it. The ethos for news and information blogs, then, is based more on values such as immediacy, transparency, interconnectivity, and proximity to the events. As a heterarchy, diverse bloggers post, cross-link, blogroll, and track back to interact in a network pulling ideas and knowledge from the edges. This *networkedness* and resulting proximity to news are among the reasons U.S. intelligence and law enforcement officials are tracking blogs and why China is looking for ways to block them.

An incident from the 2008 presidential primary might illustrate some of the tensions between the imperatives of most bloggers as contrasted with the mission of the professional guild of journalism. A supporter of Barack Obama attending one of his rallies in California, a rally not open to the public or to the media, found herself witness to what she immediately recognized as newsworthy commentary from the candidate. Obama referred to Pennsylvania's small-town voters as "bitter," as clinging to guns and religion, and as having antipathy to people "who aren't like them." The blogger deliberated for four days whether or not to publish what she had heard.

Declaring herself to be a "citizen journalist," 61-year-old Mayhill Fowler determined to publish the news, which she did on OffTheBus.Net, a cooperative news blog launched by Arianna Huffington of *The Huffington Post* and Jay Rosen, a journalism professor at New York University. Fowler's decision underlines how digital communication has changed campaign coverage in unpredictable ways. But it should not surprise. The democratization of publishing inevitably alters our political process. Obama perhaps did not think his remarks would reach beyond the ballroom; he did not know he was being blogged.

Fowler's claims to journalism notwithstanding, does her campaign rally post represent journalism? As an eyewitness account of remarks at a campaign event that most would agree was important to the race for the party nomination, Fowler's post must be considered an act of journalism. Does this make Fowler a journalist? As an avowed contributor to Obama's campaign (and Clinton's and even Fred Thompson's, as well), Fowler's standing at the rally presents some real problems were she to claim to be a journalist. Most journalists would never make public their political cleavages, nor would they attend as a supporter a political event that had been closed to the media. Fowler's four-day delay before publishing points to these problems or conflicts. A journalist would not have to weigh the pros and cons of publishing news in the public's interest, at least not in the circumstances the California fundraiser presented.

Objectivity as a Process Goal (Not a Product Goal)

Most journalists and journalism professors would agree that pure objectivity is impossible, at least as an attribute of journalism's products, the news. Striving for as objective a news-gathering process as possible, however, still is widely regarded as noble and good. Contributing to candidates clearly threatens and even mocks that objective process. The fact that Fowler has been criticized both by media and by her fellow Obama supporters points to this inherent conflict, bringing to life the biblical paradox of trying to serve two masters and, as a result, loving one and hating the other. As Rosen (2008) commented on the episode, "journalists, the pro kind, aren't allowed to be loyalists. But loyalists . . . may find that loyalty to what really happened trumps all. And that's when they start to commit journalism." This doesn't make loyalists journalists, however.

According to Friend and Singer based on the research of others, a journalist in American society is someone

> whose primary purpose is to provide the information the citizens of a democracy need to be free and self-governing; someone who acts in accordance with a firm commitment to balance, fairness, restraint, and service; someone whom members of the public can trust to help them make sense of the world and to make sound decisions about the things that matter.
>
> (Friend and Singer 2007: xvi)

Journalists, including online journalists, then do perform this *sensemaking* role. David Simon, a former reporter and a producer of HBO's *The Wire*, asked in *The Washington Post*: "In any format, through any medium—isn't an understanding of the events of the day still a salable commodity?" He asks if the Internet is so profound a change in the delivery model that "high-end news," or journalism that really matters, will become increasingly scarce, rare, exotic.

An operative term in this definition is "trust." To instill trust, traditional journalists agree to a code of ethics, however tacitly, typically one similar or identical to the Society for Professional Journalists' (SPJ's) Code of Ethics. The Online News Association also has a code, which was modified from SPJ's version for online, specifically for bloggers. As Friend and Singer write, "a code of ethics does not create ethical behavior" (2007: xx). Such a code can provide a compass, or a map of orienting philosophy to govern or guide behavior.

Where these codes of ethics have failed to prevent lapses in journalism, bloggers have brought checks and balances of their own, serving as a sort of watchdog of the watchdogs, a Fifth Estate to journalism's Fourth Estate. Bloggers routinely criticize journalism and mainstream news media for what they see as sloppy, erroneous and incomplete coverage and reporting. Journalism, therefore, provides these blogs with most of the fodder for the blogs' posts. One 2006 study found, for example, that more than 95 percent of blogs are derivative, or are dependent on journalism's original reporting. Less than 5 percent, therefore, are involved in doing the legwork of journalism, the heavy lifting required of the discipline of verification.

Most blogs are utterly dependent on journalism. They react, in other words, comment on issues, events and people in coverage, and provide context and elaboration. These distinctions are not to belittle blogging; on the contrary, blogging has assumed important roles in building a vibrant, well-informed democracy. The distinctions are made to help us understand how the information landscape is changing, and how interdependent are the new media and traditional mass media ecosystems.

Corporate Blogging

The cover story for *BusinessWeek* magazine on May 2, 2005, read: "Blogs Will Change Your Business." Blogs indeed have changed business, and years after that article corporate America's embrace of them continues. According to the ePolicy Institute, 81 percent of corporations reported in late 2006 that they were either blogging or planning to blog. At about the same time, in the United States there were more than 5,000 corporate bloggers and about 10 percent of small businesses had already incorporated blogs into their marketing plans.

Two *BusinessWeek* covers, the one on the left from May 2008, the other from May 2005.

Blogs offer businesses the opportunity to build informal, lasting relationships with customers. As a new media academic told *The New York Times*, "There's a conversation going on out there about every company and every brand, and talking with people engenders better relationships." A quick search in November 2007 on the blog search engine Technorati for mentions of "Ikea," for example, turned up nearly a half-million blogs, and that was for instances in the previous 24 hours.

Tech specialists can make a Web site more visible, but bloggers can generate buzz. Ikea, again, is a good example, daily garnering hundreds of positive blog mentions. For small businesses, blogs can be particularly powerful in shining a spotlight on a product or aspect of the business that deserves the attention. As a side benefit, the corporate blog creates additional inbound and outbound hyperlinks that in their aggregate also serve to raise a company's search profile with the big search engines.

Of course, it helps if you have something to say. This is the hard part. Anyone can start up a blog technically, but few can write well enough, with enough substance, to make it a worthwhile read over a sustained period of time. For a model of how to do it, how to say something worth reading, see Robert Scoble's Scobleizer blog (http://scobleizer.com/). He is a software engineer at Microsoft who blogs about technology, including Apple products, even admitting when the Mac folks do it better. General Motors vice chairman Robert A. Lutz has a blog, as does Jonathan Schwartz, chief executive officer at Sun Microsystems, and billionaire Mark Cuban (blogmaverick.com).

---

1. On my Qik channel. I'll do frequent live Qik videos. I'll try to Twitter when interesting ones are about to start.

2. On my Twitter feed. I frequently Twitter from the road about what we're doing and experiencing, plus I can answer your questions there.

3. On my FriendFeed. Even better place to talk with me. My Twitters, photos, and other things, show up on FriendFeed within minutes of me doing them and this is the best place to talk with me. I probably spend 80% of my time there, so watch this to see the best stuff.

4. Another important feed to watch is my "Likes" feed on FriendFeed. This is totally different than #3 and is YOUR stuff that I've "Liked." If you want to see if there's some value to FriendFeed this is a good place to lurk and it's where I track the top news items.

5. On my Flickr feed I'll post photos. My Nokia phones can get photos up within seconds of me taking them.

6. I'll be participating in the chat room on my Kyte.tv channel — the chat room there is better because it stays up permanently and I can participate in it via text, audio, or video.

Part of a post on Robert Scoble's blog, scobleizer, showing the myriad ways Scoble keeps in touch with his readers—Qik videos, twitter posts, Friendfeed updates, Flickr photo sharing and Kyte.tv channel chat. Other ways he pushes content include Google's "Shared Items," a FastCompany.com social network and an RSS feed (see below).

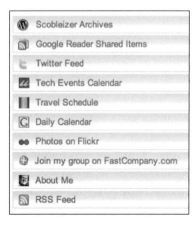

As an unfiltered, conversational, personal, transparent and interactive media format, blogs are powerful tools in establishing a dialogue with customers and clients. Blogs are humanizing, which remedies one of the chief problems of businesses, bureaucracies and organizations in projecting any sort of humanity. The corporate blogs mentioned above do a good job creating a dialogue by providing writing that is candid, simple, concise and often amusing. Humor and wit are important arrows in the blogger's quiver. Successful corporate blogs do not try to sell anything, at least not overtly, and they don't preach or teach. They speak plainly and transparently, and therefore build trust.

Media's Embrace of Blogs

In addition to the reasons businesses are utilizing blogs, news organizations are looking to them to accomplish what is more difficult in print or broadcast. These news organizations have deployed blogs in order to:

- **Connect with audiences, and therefore build trust.** News organizations like MSNBC, *The Dallas Morning News*, the *Seattle Post-Intelligencer*, the *Houston Chronicle* and others are using blogging as one of many channels through which to flow editorial content. Blogs help to make these organizations more accessible, answerable and transparent.
- **Provide context, notes and content that cannot make it into the publication or onto the broadcast.** Blogs make room for content that does not neatly fit into traditional media.
- **Follow up on ideas and opinions that emerge first in the blogosphere.** Blogs are a way of tapping into this new, networked media eco-system.
- **Build community.** Readers become active partners rather than passive consumers. Blogs can give readers a stake in the process and its product, increasing loyalty and understanding along the way. News organizations underestimate word-of-mouth referral power in the new media eco-system at their own peril. Hyperlocal newspaper and Web site *Chi-Town Daily News*, for example, aims to have a citizen journalist/blogger in each and every Chicago neighborhood, or 75 in all. The newspaper wants to combine community activism with the journalistic prin-ciples of accuracy and objectivity to more deeply connect people to neighborhoods.
- **Give reporters and writers, who by nature love to write and to express themselves, another avenue for that expression.** The challenge in this area has been to find ways to incent and reward this expression at a time when newspapers and local TV news stations are in fiscal crisis.

Certainly blogging is here to stay, and traditional media are being forced to respond, to adapt and to co-opt. Blogging is emblematic of broader trends

---

Journal: Muhammad trial journal

John Allen Muhammad stood trial in Virginia Beach in the sniper spree that terrorized the D.C. area last fall. Kerry Sipe, online news coordinator for The Virginian-Pilot, reported live from the Beach courts complex, through Muhammad's conviction and death sentence. E-mail Sipe at kerry.sipe@pilotonline.com
>> Full sniper trials section

Muhammad after verdict

Read the journal forward starting at ... Day 1 | Day 2 | Day 3 | Day 4 | Day 5 | Day 6 | Day 7 | Day 8 | Day 9 | Day 10 | Day 11 | Day 12 | Day 13 | Day 14 | Day 15 | Day 16 | Day 17 | Day 18 | Day 19 | Day 20 | Day 21 | Day 22, Verdict | Day 23 | Day 24 | Day 25 | Day 26 | Day 27, Sentence

Entries 1 - 10 of 609 | Next

See Sipe's blog at http://home.hamptonroads.com/guestbook/journal.cfm?id=53.

toward participatory, grass roots media and personal publishing. Not surprisingly, journalists see opportunities in blogging for a type of commentary, immediacy and intimacy impossible with or through other forms. Two examples of this adoption trend are a blog by *The Virginian-Pilot* covering the Malvo–Muhammad sniper trials in Virginia and a blog at the *Seattle Post-Intelligencer* written by the reporter who covers Microsoft for the newspaper.

The Virginian-Pilot's Kerry Sipe blogged throughout the sniper trials from the media room in the Virginia Beach municipal center. He tracked everything from jury instructions and testimony to John Allen Muhammad's mood. Connected to the courtroom through closed-circuit video and the rest of the world through a wireless Internet connection, he published posts that went immediately online via his newspaper's Web site. The judge barred video coverage of the proceedings, so Sipe's minute-by-minute updates gave readers the closest thing they had to real-time news.

Sipe is the *Virginian-Pilot*'s online news coordinator and one of a number of writers using a blog to report the news. Along with Sipe's unfiltered copy came an unfiltered experience, which raised the "Is it journalism?" question early on. This kind of reporting leaves the burden of assessing the news to readers, a job many say they would prefer to take on.

It is also important to note that Sipe's blog was just one part of the *Virginian-Pilot*'s trial coverage. Blogs are not necessarily replacing other forms of journalism, but they are adding a new, unique layer of coverage. Other *Virginian-Pilot* writers covered the story in more traditional ways.

A blog launched by the *Seattle Post-Intelligencer* in 2003 accomplishes a very different purpose. Written by Todd Bishop, the blog is a daily extension of an important Seattle beat covering software giant Microsoft.

The print edition and traditional Web site are still the proper places to break news, according to Bishop, but he says the blog gives him space to follow up on print stories with information that perhaps does not require a full story. His blog also has become a place to give readers valuable context. "After writing a story about liability for software flaws," he said, "I posted an entry

See Bishop's blog at http://blog.seattlepi.nwsource.com/microsoft/.

that gave readers access to a lot of the material that helped me understand the issue and put the story together."

Bishop's posts have helped him collect sources for future stories, people he says he would not have found without the blog. One reader emailed him in response to a post about Microsoft's software patching strategy; that reader turned out to be the person responsible for patching his own company's PCs. The next time Bishop covered the issue in print, he contacted his new source for comment.

How to Write for Blogs

Bishop's blog provides a good example of how blogs can be employed effectively by journalists. First, note that he does not use the blog to merely dump onto the Web what has already appeared in print. Instead, Bishop uses his blog to post new, complementary content that expands on or builds off his stories for the print edition. In his role as a reporter on the Microsoft beat, Bishop may come across new insights or angles on previously published stories or brief news items that don't necessarily warrant a full story in print. Bishop can post that information on his blog, instead, to provide continued coverage of a running story or issue and to invite comment from his readers.

A journalist's blog also is an ideal repository for information that has been edited or cut out of a story to fit the available space in the newspaper or on the broadcast. An observation, an anecdote or extended quoted material from that edited version can be posted on the blog, which should be a relatively simple exercise because the writing has already been done. This is not to say, however, that long, unexpurgated interview notes should be dumped online; blog writing typically is brief. By linking to the printed or aired story, addenda on the blog can extend the coverage.

In addition, writing in a conversational tone, one not unlike that used for email, leverages online's capacity for interpersonal communication, or communication very different and much more personal than mass media deliver. Most blogs are by a single author, so tone becomes all-important. As Bishop demonstrates, a blog allows the writer's individual voice to come through unfiltered.

A journalist's blog can be used to aid reporting by soliciting information. If you cannot make it to a public meeting or event, for example, posting can notify your readership community of the event and let them know why you think it might matter. Perhaps someone in your readership can attend the meeting, ask questions and even provide some reporting on what happens. Asking readers to post their reactions to the event or meeting gives readers ownership of the coverage and can strengthen the bonds of the community. Of course, the obligation to check facts remains for the journalist, even when presenting news gathered by blog readers.

A journalist's blog also can be used to pose questions to the readership. Open questions that identify concerns about a particular issue or event can build community and inform reporting over the long term. Using a blog in this manner can also help the journalist to gauge the readers' interest in certain issues and to determine which stories to continue reporting on, resisting the daily print impulse to write and publish a story and then move on without following up.

Community-building is an essential element of successful blogging that represents a tremendous opportunity for journalism. Bloggers should actively think of ways to engage readers, to begin and continue conversations, and to create and sustain loyal audiences. One of the most powerful ways to build community is to foster communication and interaction between readers themselves. Some of the best conversations can be started with very brief blog entries that ask for input and reactions. Of course, starting the conversation is only half the battle; a good blogger will also continue to facilitate the conversation by getting involved, steering the line of inquiry, responding to posts and participating. This level of involvement is alien to print journalists, who are accustomed to reporting, publishing, then moving on to the next story without much, if any, interaction with readers.

Applying the Blogging Basics

Three hallmarks of most good blogs: First, they are updated frequently, at least once every day or every other day, depending on the audience and the nature of the subject. A fast-moving story, like the sniper trials, might lend itself to several updates per day, as information comes in. Regardless of the topic, however, the blog should be frequently, regularly updated, which is the reason for the simplicity of blogging software in the first place. Second, most blogging software automatically puts the most recent post at the top, or in reverse chronological order, so readers do not have to scroll or hunt for the latest information. Last, good blogs tag posts, or identify them with key words that can be used to find related posts. A post on blogging, for example, might be tagged with the key words "blogging," "writing" and "personal publishing." For similar reasons, the post's headline should spur interest and invite reaction. Particularly with RSS (Really Simple Syndication) feeds delivering your headlines in competition with a host of others, the headline should arrest and inspire.

For blog posts, think about the key words that convey the meaning of your content. Consider how the content might be indexed in a book or found by Google. As Chapter 4 discusses, headlines online should be intuitive, not cryptic, vague or leading. Simply by reading a headline the reader should be able to grasp what the post is about. However, writing plainly or directly does not mean producing the merely banal or simple labels: "Baby Pandas! Baby Pandas!" Leave these banalities to CNN.com.

Online readers do not like to read long columns of text unless the content is extremely compelling. A better way to get a series of complex points across is to create a list of key points that readers can scan, along with a description of each point. This will also help you structure your thoughts in a way that seems more lucid.

---

1. Avocado
Misconception: I shouldn't eat avocados because they're high in fat.
Why They're Good for You

2. Coffee
Misconception: The only thing you get from drinking coffee is being awake.
Why It's Good for You

3. Mushrooms
Misconception: Mushrooms are a low-calorie food with little nutritional benefit.
Why They're Good for You

4. Peanut butter
Misconception: This creamy spread is an indulgence best enjoyed occasionally because it's high in fat and calories.
Why It's Good For You

5. Eggs
Misconception: Eggs are high in dietary cholesterol, so they don't belong in my diet.
Why They're Good for You

Each item in the list links to explanatory text, "Why They're Good for You." This list is easily scanned, placing the explanations just a click away.

As these tips on headlines and lists demonstrate, the principles of good Web writing discussed in the preceding chapters apply when writing for blogs, too. Layering content, making it scan-able and breaking information up into easily read chunks, and linking to relevant material elsewhere on the Web are things for which blogs were designed. For blogs, layers can include headlines and subheads, links to source material and, as is shown above, to related posts both internal and external to the blog.

If you are thinking about presenting something in long form, consider summarizing it on the blog instead, then linking to the longer piece in .pdf or .doc form for those readers who wish to read more. This both promotes scanning and provides layers for drill-down. A few ideas or examples of list-worthy information:

- Components of a bill or law
- Requirements for submitting or applying for something
- Aspects of a candidate's background
- Details of a legal decision
- Supplies needed for a project
- Ingredients for a recipe
- Product features
- Sub-sections of a long or multi-page article
- Directions on how to create or complete something.

Live Blogging

The simplicity and low or no cost of blogging, as well as the spread of wireless Internet connectivity in many cities, have fueled an interest in live blogging, or blogging while a news event is taking place. Live blogging provides a near real-time and, therefore, visceral account of the event, usually from a single point of view, that of the individual blogger. Because it is "live," this exercise in blogging adds to the already difficult enterprises of reporting and writing the pressures of immediacy.

Here are some tips for successful live blogging an event, conference or convention:

- First, relax. Take a deep breath. Write a short post that introduces the event and identifies who you are and why you are writing.
- Key in your notes as unfinished sentence fragments, then go back when you have time and flesh out the narrative.
- If you are covering a speech or panel discussion, provide the transcript if possible. It's tedious, but the transcript provides a great resource for those who could not attend.
- Write a short blurb about a part of the event you couldn't get to and link to someone who did. This leverages the wisdom of the crowds.
- Once the event is over, post a retrospective, a more comprehensive commentary on what you saw and heard. Put the event, or your take on the event, in context.
- Post your blurbs just to get them online, then go back and clean up your copy. Live blog readers understand the nature of posting quickly.
- Know that the biggest challenge is paying attention to the event while writing at the same time. You can take advantage of this challenge by focusing your writing and your attention, placing you in the middle of

the stream of events washing over you. What you live blog today can become the basis for a more analytical piece tomorrow.

- Know up front that you will probably annoy someone near you. Clacking away on a keyboard really can be obnoxious. Planning where you sit can help, as can congregating with other bloggers and keyboard clackers.
- Consider special tools for live blogging, including the CoverItLive blog software (www.coveritlive.com) or twitter (www.twitter.com), which breaks up blogging into 140-character bursts.

Corrections

Mistakes are an unfortunate fact of life, whether your writing is appearing in print or online. Print journalists typically don't have the option to make a correction directly in the article they've published. Instead, they make their corrections in subsequent issues of the newspaper or magazine, often in a small "Corrections" box toward the front of the publication. Online, however, a writer has the option to make a correction or a change directly to the story they have posted. The option to erase mistakes in the entries has caused some concern for blog writers about how corrections or changes should be handled. In the blogosphere, it is considered bad form to delete anything, including and especially reader comments.

  With the premium that is placed on transparency online, deleting posts or reader comments erodes credibility. In certain cases, for example, when statements or comments that are libelous or invade privacy are posted, they should and must be taken down from the site. In most cases, however, striking through the old or incorrect information, and then providing the correction next to it, perhaps in a different font, is the best practice. This method offers maximum transparency, clearly showing readers what has been changed in post. If necessary, you can add a note to the bottom of the post or in parentheses to explain why the change was made and perhaps credit the person who pointed out the error.

I found something on one of the new Microsoft blogs that raised a question. This what I read: Pitchfork is looking for some new ~~lackeys~~ interns. Was that a real correction? Or was the blogger sharing a little joke, telling us that he considers interns to be lackeys, even though it's not right to call them that? It's like the teenager who says: "Hi loser, um, I mean, Dad."

An example of strikethrough correction.

If something has to be corrected, a blogger has several options:

- Include a note at the bottom of the original post with the new information.

- Include the new information in the post while striking through the old or incorrect information (and displaying the strikethrough).
- Write a new post with the updated or corrected information, a post that links to and refers to the original post.
- Delete the problematic post and replace it with the updated, corrected information.

Internet users have shown that they will reward a willingness to be transparent, to be forthcoming, candid and open. They seem to place more trust in those they perceive as having nothing to hide. Bloggers have taken the lead in capitalizing on transparency by disclosing their personal politics and biases, regularly providing links to original source material to allow readers to judge the material for themselves, engaging in public conversations with readers that invite critique, and admitting and correcting errors quickly when they make them. All of these transparent activities help build trust.

Blogging Ethics

Most print journalists follow the Society of Professional Journalists' Code of Ethics, which communicates certain professional, widely shared ethical standards. Some critics of blogging, including those from the journalistic community, often point to the fact that bloggers do not share such a set of professional, standardized ethics. This critique has inspired some bloggers to develop sets of ethics that build upon the SPJ code, but that also recognize some things unique to blogs, recognizing that bloggers are proudly individualistic. Rebecca Blood codified her relatively short list of good blogger behavior in her book, *The Weblog Handbook* (2002: 114–20):

1 Publish as fact only that which you believe to be true. If a statement is merely speculation, it should be so stated.
2 If material exists online, link to it when you reference it. Readers can judge for themselves, and a founding principle of blogging is exercising freedom of expression and the marketplace of ideas. Online readers "deserve, as much as possible, access to all of the facts," Blood writes.
3 Publicly correct any misinformation. Typically entries are not re-written or corrected, but later entries should correct inaccurate information in those earlier posts. Inaccurate and erroneous information on other blogs also should be corrected in the spirit of the greater blogging community's responsibility to one another and to its readers.
4 Write each entry as if it could not be changed; add to, but do not re-write or delete any entry. "Post deliberately," Blood advises.
5 Disclose any conflict of interest.
6 Note questionable or biased sources.

A reading of Blood's list and of the Society of Professional Journalists' code reveals more similarities than differences (see: Society of Professional Journalists Code of Ethics, http://www.spj.org/ethics_code.asp). Excerpted, the SPJ code calls journalists to:

- **Seek Truth and Report It**: Journalists should be honest, fair and courageous in gathering, reporting and interpreting information.
- **Minimize Harm**: Ethical journalists treat sources, subjects and colleagues as human beings deserving of respect.
- **Act Independently**: Journalists should be free of obligation to any interest other than the public's right to know.
- **Be Accountable**: Journalists are accountable to their readers, listeners, viewers and each other.

Both Blood's and the SPJ's codes espouse:

- publishing the truth;
- supporting arguments with credible sources;
- being accountable;
- spending time writing as though changes could not be made;
- disclosing conflicts of interests, articulated by the SPJ as acting independently.

While a graduate student at the University of North Carolina, Martin Kuhn devised a widely distributed code of ethics for bloggers that is general enough to encompass most forms of blogging. His code seeks to:

- Promote interactivity:
  - Post to your blog on a regular basis.
  - Visit and post on other blogs.
  - Respect blog etiquette.
  - Attempt to be entertaining, interesting, and/or relevant.

- Promote free expression:
  - Do not restrict access to your blog by specific individuals or groups.
  - Do not self-censor by removing posts or comments once they are published.
  - Allow and encourage comments on your blog.

- Strive for factual truth:
  - Never intentionally deceive others.
  - Be accountable for what you post.

- Be as transparent as possible:
  - Reveal your identity as much as possible (name, photo, background information, etc.).

— Reveal your personal affiliations and conflicts of interest.

— Cite and link to all sources referenced in each post.

• Promote the human element in blogging:

— Minimize harm to others when posting information.

— Promote community by linking to other blogs and keeping a blogroll.

— Build relationships by responding to emails and comments regularly.

Of course, problems will persist. Anonymous comments, particularly those that threaten or that include potentially libelous information, are of grave concern, in part because they invite censorship and regulation. And any code of ethics is voluntary, as much a distillation of existing organizational values as a prescription for behavior. Lawyers who violate their profession's ethics can be disbarred. Physicians can be prohibited from practicing medicine. But journalists? Writers? Bloggers? Except where a job is at stake, shame is really the only punishment for an ethical breach.

Jimmy Wales, founder of Wikipedia, began soliciting recommendations for blog behavior at http://en.wikinews.org/wiki/Jimbo_Wales_to_lead_development_of_%27code_of_conduct%27_for_bloggers, while *Web 2.0*'s Tim O'Reilly did the same at http://radar.oreilly.com/archives/2007/04/draft_bloggers_1.html. Here is Wales's start (he is still developing and refining his list):

1 Responsibility for our own words

2 Nothing we wouldn't say in person

3 Connect privately first

4 Take action against attacks

5 (a) No anonymous comments OR (b) No pseudonymous comments

6 Ignore the trolls (or those wishing harm)

7 Encourage enforcement of terms of service

8 Keep our sources private

9 Discretion to delete comments

10 Do no harm.

These ethics codes are not trivial. Cyberbullying is a growing problem, as *The New York Times* reported in April 2007. "Menacing behavior is certainly not unique to the Internet. But since the Web offers the option of anonymity with no accountability, online conversations are often more prone to decay into ugliness than those in other media," according to the article (Brad Stone, "A Call for Manners in the World of Nasty Blogs," *New York Times*, April 9, 2007). Anonymous speech has become such a problem online that Congress has considered amending Section 230 of the Communications Decency Act, which gives ISPs and newspaper Web sites immunity for non-moderated discussion and chat.

The "Tagosphere" and Really Simple Syndication (RSS)

Blogs and Web sites have multiplied so quickly that tools to track, search and identify (or tag) them have proliferated, as well. These tools and sites, known collectively as the "Tagosphere," help users find, retrieve, save, share and otherwise organize the Web. Examples include Technorati, which tags and compiles taxonomies of the blogosphere, and Furl.net, which enables users to save and retrieve Web pages and makes recommendations on what other pages a user might want to visit. A few others:

- Kaboodle.com: for shopping sites
- Reddit.com: where users can post any Web link and other users can vote on its value
- Wink.com: for links that other users have identified as useful or interesting
- Stumbleupon.com: for saving and searching users' favorite Web pages; users can join groups to discuss and share pages by topic or interest.

NewsTrust (www.newstrust.net) asks readers to evaluate news stories using traditional principles of journalistic quality; the evaluations are published on the site.

Bloggers can also use RSS (automatic news) feeds to follow new developments on a beat or issue without having to visit a hundred different Web sites. NewsGator, Newstrust and other aggregators pull together RSS findings, meaning you only have to look in one place to see all the latest updates on your issue or area of interest. Aggregators bring you these feeds virtually as soon as they are published.

It is easy to generate RSS feeds from the sites you want based on your search criteria. First, set up your search feeds, using a feed reader such as Newsfire or Google Reader. Create a folder for your issue or area, such as "data privacy." At Technorati, enter the search query "data privacy" to get a series of results. In the top right corner of the Technorati results page you will see a "subscribe" button. Once that is clicked, you are sent to a feed page displaying the latest blog posts that match the search query. Copy the URL of that page from your Web browser's location bar. Switch back to your feed reader, tell it you want to add a new feed, and paste in the URL, saving the feed in the folder named "data privacy." Duplicate this process for other online resources for fresh content on that topic. The result might still be a lot of content to scan, but scanning a feed reader is faster than searching site by site by site.

Some feed reader options (all of them free):

- Bloglines (www.bloglines.com)
- NewsGator (www.newsgator.com)
- Sage (sage.mozdev.org), for the Firefox Web browser
- Safari: The default Mac OS X web browser comes with a built-in feed reader
- Icerocket (www.icerocket.com)
- BlogPulse (www.blogpulse.com).

Feed search engines, such as Technorati (www.technorati.com), are the best way to quickly learn what's new online, as opposed to what's available. They help you stay abreast of blogs and niche news sites, breaking news, and any online resource that publishes feeds, aggregating millions of feeds.

For blog readers who like to access content via their mobile phones, there are services that will convert blog posts into mp3 audio files. BuzzVoice.com is one example, a service that also converts news stories to audio files.

The Top Ten Steps to Better Blogging

Last, here are ten practical steps or good habits that can produce a good blog.

Step 1: Write every day. In arguing for frequent, regular blogging, Rebecca Blood wrote that "it's easy to write poorly, but it's hard to write poorly every day . . . It's hard to write every day" (Blood 2002: 28). Write frequently and regularly, and your writing will surely grow stronger from the practice.

Step 2: Schedule your blogging time. Like the formation of any new habit, blogging requires planning. Determine when in the day or night you can consistently blog, and then stick to that time. Some prefer to write early in the morning, coffee in hand, with energy reservoirs at their maximum. Others prefer the reflection of late evenings, after the day's events have played out. The point isn't when, but to have a scheduled time to write each and every day.

Step 3: Be authentic. A jazz music deejay in Greensboro, NC, daily signed off his broadcasts with the call to, "Be yourself so you won't be by yourself." The best blogs have an authentically human voice that is distinctive, even idiosyncratic. Don't worry about pleasing everyone from the start. Instead, start blogging by writing for an audience of one (yourself), which will help you cultivate this authenticity, transparency and voice. The networked and Google-searched nature of the Web will connect your area of interest or expertise with readers who share a similar point of view and/or interest. Sites like Google, Technorati, Digg, Reddit, Del.icio.us, Stumbleupon and Slashdot will pick up on what you are posting and make your writing known to larger and wider audiences.

Step 4: Carve out a niche. The best bloggers focus on specific interests—the narrower the topic, the better—leveraging their own expertise and experience in the area. Larry Lessig, for example, is a Stanford law professor specializing in intellectual property law. His widely read blog, Lessig 2.0, at www.lessig.org/blog, focuses on IP law and the open source movement, though he comments on other subjects, such as pop music and technology. Readers can count on his blog to keep up with the major news and events in intellectual property law as it relates to digital media and digital content.

Step 5: Be curious and take lots of notes. Not every thought is blog-worthy, so keep a notebook or temporary file of your musings, thoughts, ideas, links and articles of interest—anything that might inform your blogging. When you keep your daily appointment to write, you can relax knowing you have a file or folder of goodies to get you going rather than having to stare at an empty template post box and write from scratch a pithy and provocative post.

Step 6: Engage. When you get comments, react to them. Encourage them. Affirm your readers and continue the conversations your posts have begun. This is about community-building, which was discussed in the previous section.

Participate on other people's blogs, include their blogs on your blogroll, and link to others' posts when appropriate. The blogosphere operates on the principle of reciprocity, so make sure you are creating plenty of social capital by being interested and engaged with the ideas of others in your blog circle or community. If you are not prepared to engage at this level, there really is no point to starting up a blog.

Step 7: Learn the software. You don't need to become an expert or a coder, but you can devote an "upgrade day" every few weeks or so to learning more about the software you're using to power your blog. Look into features like RSS feeds, spam filters, YouTube video hosting and photo hosting to upgrade your blog. On upgrade day, you could also spend some time tagging or re-tagging posts to better organize your content and to make it easier for others and for you yourself to find specific posts. This is a good time to check for broken links, too.

Step 8: Promote yourself. Don't be shy. Market your blog. Simple steps to reach more readers include registering your blog with Technorati, which indexes and provides blog search; registering with the major search engines, including Google; and setting up RSS feeds of your site to have your content delivered to anyone who wants to subscribe. Google Analytics is a free tool any blogger can use to see how people are finding you and what terms they used to locate your blog, which can inform how you tag content and what headlines you write.

Step 9: Break up the text. Your writing may be Pulitzer-worthy, but your readers will still need some visual relief. Make sure you follow the basic graphic design and layout principles covered in previous chapters. Boldface, lists, photos, graphics, cartoons, breakout diagrams and illustrations can elaborate your post and break up what otherwise might be an overwhelming storm of words. Most blogging software packages make it easy to add a photo or graphic to your post.

Step 10: Be ethical. Hold to a code of ethics. An old adage advises that the best time to plan what you would do with a lot of money is when you don't have any money, because when you are flush with cash your values can quickly change, based on your appetites. Similarly, planning ahead for ethical challenges by adopting a code of ethics will allow you to have a set of a carefully deliberated priorities, goals and values to turn to in times of crisis, when decisions about content need to be made quickly and resolutely.

Chapter Assignment

1   Live blog something—an event, a trip, a conference or a meeting. Take your readers there. We are looking here for immediacy, vicariousness, texture, reflection, a sense of what happened and what you thought about it. Think of this assignment as visceral, immediate, on-site reporting from a particular point of view—your point of view.

Live blogging means merely blogging while the event is happening, using multiple brief posts to give your readers an account of that event. Hyperlink where appropriate. There is no minimum or maximum for the number of posts; you likely will find a rhythm.

Length: minimum of approximately 700 words, but feel free to blog on.

Real world example 1: *USA Today*'s entertainment reporter, César Soriano, attended Star Wars Celebration III in Indianapolis April 21–24, 2005 and blogged about it: http://www.usatoday.com/life/movies/2005-04-20-star-wars-blog_x.htm.

Real world example 2: ESPN's live blogging of Roger Clemens's testimony before Congress on steroid use in baseball: http://sports.espn.go.com/espn/blog/index?entryID=3243182&name=congressional_hearings.

Online Resources

Weblog Communities, Software, and Platforms

Blogger
http://www.blogger.com/

Greymatter
http://www.noahgrey.com/greysoft/

Ikonboard
http://www.ikonboard.com

Movable Type
http://www.movabletype.org/

WordPress
http://www.wordpress.org

A Few Good Blogs

The Committee to Protect Bloggers
http://committeetoprotectbloggers.blogspot.com
Developed by Curt Hopkins, director.

Consensus at Lawyerpoint
http://bpdg.blogs.eff.org/
Blog by Seth Schoen, connected to the Broadcast Protection Discussion Group.

Jonathan Dube at the Media Center
http://www.cyberjournalist.net/the_weblog_blog/

E-Media Tidbits

http://www.poynter.org/tidbits

Group-authored blog through the Web site of the professional journalism education organization the Poynter Institute.

Romenesko

http://www.poynter.org/column.asp?id=45

Commentary by Jim Romenesko of the Poynter Institute.

Scobleizer

http://scobleizer.com

Technology-focused blog by Robert Scoble.

The Shifted Librarian

www.theshiftedlibrarian.com

Librarian and information science blog by Jenny Levine.

Social Media.Biz

http://www.socialmedia.biz/

J.D. Lasica's social media blog.

Talking Points Memo

www.talkingpointsmemo.com

Political commentary by Joshua Micah Marshall.

The Volokh Conspiracy

http://volokh.com/

Law blog by Eric Volokh.

Sources

Paul Bausch, Matthew Haughey, and Meg Hourihan, *We Blog: Publishing Online with Weblogs* (New York: Hungry Minds, Inc., 2002), especially Chapter 3; available: http://www.blogroots.com/chapters.blog/id/8.

Rebecca Blood, "Weblogs: A History and Perspective," available: http://www.rebeccablood.net/essays/weblog_history.html.

—— *The Weblog Handbook* (Cambridge, MA: Perseus Publishing, 2002).

John Cassidy, "The Online Life: Me Media. How Hanging Out on the Internet Became Big Business," *New Yorker* magazine, May 15, 2006.

Trevor Cook, "The Death of Quality Journalism," *Unleashed* (March 12, 2008), available: http://www.abc.net.au/unleashed/stories/s2186777.htm.

Daniel W. Drezner and Henry Farrell, "Web of Influence," *Foreign Policy* (November/December 2004), available: http://www.foreignpolicy.com/story/cms.php?story_id=2707&page=0.

Cecilia Friend and Jane B. Singer, *Online Journalism Ethics: Traditions and Transitions* (Armonk, NY: M.E. Sharpe, 2007).

Bill Kovach and Tom Rosenstiel, *The Elements of Journalism: What Newspeople Should Know and the Public Should Expect* (New York: Three Rivers Press, 2007).

Staci Kramer, "Journos and Bloggers: Can Both Survive?," *Online Journalism Review* (November 12, 2004), available: http://ojr.org/ojr/workplace/1100245630.php.

Nicholas Lemann, "Amateur Hour, Journalism Without Journalists," *New Yorker* magazine, August 7, 2006.

Jay Rosen, "The Uncharted: From Off the Bus to Meet the Press," *The Huffington Post*, April 14, 2008, available: http://www.huffingtonpost.com/jay-rosen/the-uncharted-from-off-th_b_96575.html.

Chuck Salter, "Hyperlocal Hero," *Fast Company* (November 2006), available: http://www.fastcompany.com/magazine/110/open_hyper-local-hero.html.

Cass R. Sunstein, "Fragmentation and Cybercascades," in *Living in the Information Age*, Erik P. Bucy, ed. (Belmont, CA: Wadsworth Publishing, 2005): 244–54.

Jessica Wapner, "Blogging—It's Good for You. The Therapeutic Value of Blogging Becomes a Focus of Study, *Scientific American* (May 2008), available: http://www.sciam.com/article.cfm?id=the-healthy-type.

8 WE THE PEOPLE
Part I: Citizen Journalism

Change starts at the edges.

Francis Pisani, in *Nieman Reports*

Never before have so many passionate outsiders—hundreds of thousands, at minimum—stormed the ramparts of professional journalism.

Matt Welch, *Columbia Journalism Review*

Chapter Objectives

After studying this chapter, you will be able to:

- recognize the new, communal ethos of social networking and its implications for news-gathering and publishing;
- describe what news organizations are doing to leverage participatory journalism;
- explain the ethics of "citizen" or crowd-sourced journalism;
- discuss the future of networked information sharing, including the spread of mobile Web access and information delivery and of "cloud-based" software.

Introduction

Beginning with this chapter we will embark on an exploration of some of the important issues that underlie writing for digital media. We shift our attention from the skills and techniques of writing and editing for online environments to look at some specific contexts in which our content might appear. These contexts pose unique challenges for us as content developers, as the trend of citizen journalism demonstrates. How does the professional journalist stand out when anyone can do journalism, when seemingly everyone is doing journalism?

More broadly, this chapter explores the trends of and toward social networking via the Internet, which as a collection of technologies is in many ways ideally suited to facilitate social networking and the creation and exchange of social capital. Important in this examination are the potential effects on and ethical considerations for journalism.

Understanding "We" Media

So-called "we" media are reshaping the journalistic landscape. The ease and low cost of personal publishing via the Web and the very human impulse to network socially explain why Google acquired Blogger.com in 2003, then the video-sharing site YouTube in 2006. The seemingly irrepressible need for Internet users to express themselves and to share these expressions with one another also explains why in 2005 News Corp acquired social network MySpace for $580 million, and why in the same year Yahoo snapped up the photo-sharing site Flickr. What began as an internetworked computer system for national defense, the Internet, has become a thoroughly social phenomenon.

Natural disasters such as Hurricane Katrina in Louisiana and Mississippi in 2005, the Myanmar uprising in 2007 and a catastrophic earthquake in southwest China in 2008 spawned several citizen journalism initiatives that have shown us how social the news can be. In the aftermath of Katrina, CNN.com launched iReport that solicited and published on the news Web site's home page photos and video captured by ordinary citizens. The New Orleans *Times-Picayune*, which had to go completely digital during and after the storm, also very aggressively sought contributions, reports, video and photography from Louisiana residents, contributions that helped the newspaper (and Web site) win a Pulitzer Prize for hurricane coverage.

Who takes on this role? [handwritten annotation in margin]

KATRINA: THE STORM WE ALWAYS FEARED

With **The Times-Picayune**

Ted Jackson/Times-Picayune

Remembering Katrina

The floodwaters rushed in, putting thousands in a struggle for life | Slideshow: Storm and struggle 📷 🔊
Slideshow: Then and now 📷 🔊

Hurricane Katrina struck

the New Orleans area early morning August 29, 2005. The storm surge breached the city's levees at multiple points, leaving 80 percent of the city submerged, tens of thousands of victims clinging to rooftops, and hundreds of thousands scattered to shelters around the country. Three weeks later, Hurricane Rita reflooded much of the area. The devastation to the Gulf Coast by these two hurricanes has been called the greatest disaster in our nation's history.
» **See the original reporting**

KATRINA ANNIVERSARY: DAY NINE

• Mississippi's recovery effort seems to be leaving Louisiana's behind. Why? | Audio-slideshow 📷 🔊
• Paw-abiding Bandit is home, a refugee no longer

KATRINA ANNIVERSARY: DAY EIGHT

The New Orleans *Times-Picayune* sought reader-generated content to supplement its Pulitzer Prize-winning Katrina coverage.

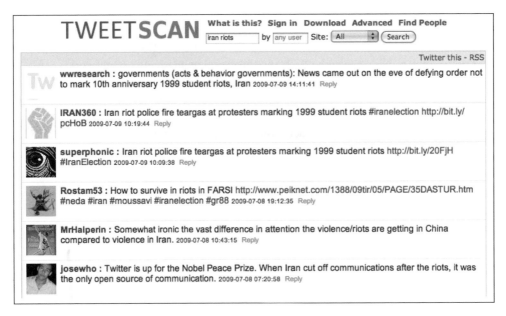

Search findings of twitter for coverage of Iran's political protests in 2009.

People globally relied on participatory journalism to follow China's earthquake and rescue efforts in May 2008, disaster "coverage" that included widespread use of the microblogging software twitter to produce a steady stream of on-the-ground reporting from the affected areas. Text messages, instant messages, microblogs and blogs provided a visceral source of first-hand accounts of the disaster in what was a remarkable development for a country known for its censorship of media and of news reporting.

What Journalists Do

Journalists gather and share information, applying a discipline of verification in order to maximize truth, minimize harm and provide a fair and comprehensive account, as we discussed in the last chapter. By this definition, a great number of people who would not necessarily self-identify as journalists are, in fact, doing journalism. Technology-driven changes, including the near-zero cost of publishing via the Internet, are democratizing the profession, expanding the nature of civic discourse and putting the tools of the craft into the hands of everyday people.

So if the key differentiator isn't what a person is doing, perhaps it is how or why. How a person goes about gathering and sharing information and why someone writes and publishes remain key distinctions online, just as they have always been for older, traditional media. Professional journalists, for example, are called upon to act independently, according to the Society for Professional Journalists' Code of Ethics. They are to be accountable for what they write and publish. They are supposed to provide readers with the information needed to

has this changed? will it?

be free and self-governing. People have always craved news. As journalism experts Bill Kovach and Tom Rosenstiel wrote, people

> need to know what's going on over the next hill, to be aware of events beyond their direct experience. Knowledge of the unknown gives them security; it allows them to plan and negotiate their lives. Exchanging this information becomes the basis for creating community.
>
> (Kovach and Rosenstiel 2007: 15)

[handwritten note: patch/ local journa.]

Jacks of Many Trades

Today's journalists are being asked to be jacks of many trades rather than masters of any one. Online journalists are almost invariably more than merely writers or photographers or graphic designers. They are content producers and as such are being asked to learn XHTML, RSS, XML, FTP, Flash, video editing software, SoundSlides and a grab bag of other software tools and computer languages and protocols. They are being asked to deliver content to socially networked mobile devices, which place an ever higher priority on concise writing. The display spaces continue to shrink. As Eric Hoffer (2006) wrote, "In a time of drastic change it is the learners who inherit the future."

Despite the new egalitarianism of Web publishing, the skills that have characterized the guild of journalism remain valuable and important. The inverted pyramid style of presenting information, for example, a style that has so dominated newspaper reporting and that is partially credited with producing objectivity as a goal or news value, remains useful in ordering information for online presentation. The pyramid style is one of several reasons journalists are perhaps best equipped to make the transition to online from other media.

Story Structures

The inverted pyramid orders information from most important to least, making stories easier to produce, easier to edit or cut to fit or fill a space, and it emphasizes the "who, what, when, where" fact-based approach to presenting information. As such, the inverted pyramid often is appropriate online, where information should be structured to facilitate scanning or drilling down. (The inverted pyramid also accommodated wire service feeds, which came into the newsroom much as blog posts are published, in reverse chronological order. The style has been common because it also helps to satisfy the print requirement that stories jump or continue from one page to another.) Already notoriously short, reader attention spans are even shorter online, so providing the key information immediately, up top, will be rewarded.

CNN.com's custom of providing story highlights is another way of layering information, making obvious how the story is ordered. (See p. 172.) CNN's articles most often employ the inverted pyramid, interspersing multimedia options and presenting similar content around the main story.

> **STORY HIGHLIGHTS**
> - Federal judge sentenced Bernard Madoff to 150-year prison term last month
> - Judge: "Fraud was staggering" and "breach of trust was massive"
> - Madoff's attorney says his client won't appeal prison sentence
> - Madoff, 71, awaits decision on where he'll be imprisoned
>
> **Next Article in Crime »**

The inverted pyramid also facilitates frequent updating because the top of an article can be replaced, with older information pushed deeper into the article. Readers can get what they want and bail out, or keep drilling and reading deeper into the coverage. CNN.com is also a model for the way it uses headers and visuals to break up the pages. At many news organizations, through staffing problems or simply a lack of motivation, too often articles are not treated as specifically online content or content that should change and develop over time, but rather as merely print poured into a new container. Articles are dumped onto the Web site and ignored until the next day's dump.

Other common story structures in print and online are chronological, narrative and thematic.

- **Chronological stories** are perhaps the easiest to write because they follow a timeline, or chronology. This structure makes sense when the story being told takes place over time, though often the climax or point of the story is presented first. Live blogging uses this structure, for example, a structure that is perfect for continuing or breaking stories.
- **Narratives**, by contrast, set the scene, then draw readers into that scene. Narratives follow a story arc that unifies a discrete beginning, middle and end. Inverted pyramid stories do not, necessarily. Narratives rely on vivid description and detail common to the novelistic style. These characteristics make the narrative style problematic online unless sparingly and expertly employed.
- **The thematic approach** organizes a complex story by theme or topic, dividing up the story into discrete pieces. For example, in a preview story leading up to the National Football League's Super Bowl, the thematic approach might first compare the two football teams' offenses, then the defenses, then the kicking games, and so on. This sort of chunking makes the thematic approach a useful one online.

Crowd-sourced Journalism

Just prior to Katrina, in London, the Underground and bus bombings served as powerful catalysts for what has since become known as the "citizen journalism* movement," if we can call it a movement. For hours after the explosions, photos taken by passengers using their mobile phones were the only pictures the world could get of the scenes inside the subway system. The first-hand accounts by passengers, and the prominent placement of the video, audio and photography from passengers on the world's news sites, boosted the profile of participatory journalism certainly in the United States and in Europe, but elsewhere in the world, as well. (*The term "citizen journalism" is problematic. Most U.S. journalists are also U.S. citizens; many "citizen journalists" are not. "Doing" journalism does not necessarily make someone a journalist any more than writing a letter or postcard makes someone a writer. Both terms, then, are imprecise. Participatory journalism and pro-am journalism are more accurate terms in their reluctance to label individuals while still describing the activity.)

In the same year as both the bombings and Katrina, riots on the outskirts of Paris in Fall 2005 boosted blog-driven journalism. With reporters struggling to find a way to tell the story of Paris's immigrant-crowded industrial suburbs, a Swiss magazine sent a squad of bloggers to one of these suburbs, Bondy. Working in shifts, the reporter-bloggers reported, wrote and posted photography from a local soccer club (http://www.hebdo.ch/bondyblog.cfm). The Swiss blog team stayed months, long after the riots calmed down and the network news cameras moved out. For magazine writers used to writing, revising, polishing, and writing some more, the new format gave them the chance to provide a visceral, albeit tentative narrative of life in the suburb during the chaotic fight for control with French police. The writers also engaged readers in live discussion online, and they used reader feedback and readers' posts to the blogs to inform and shape their writing and coverage.

newer examples?

Les blogueurs

	Nordine Nabili		Antoine Menusier
	Serge Michel		Mohamed Hamidi
	Badroudine Saïd Abdallah		Mehdi Meklat
	Widad Kefti		Ndembo Boueya
	Stéphanie Varet		Romain Santamaria
	Chou Sin		Zineb Mirad
	Ines El laboudy		Axelle Adjanohoun
	Bouchra Zeroual		Idir Hocini

Some of Hebdo's Bondy bloggers.

The shootings at Virginia Tech in April 2007, too, showed the power of crowd-sourcing, albeit in an unlikely place for original reporting. Wikipedia's entry on the shootings was immediate, and the entry grew exponentially in the days and weeks following the horrific day in May. In this event, crowd-sourced, distributed, networked journalism had another defining event, and the Wikipedia entry reflected it, with more than 2,100 contributors to the post as of late May and 119 footnotes. As an artifact of journalism, the online encyclopedia entry succeeds in providing a useful account of what happened at the university and how people were reacting to those events, and in the days just after the shooting modeled for the world how crowd-sourced reporting *and editing* can produce smart journalism. The more people contributed, the smarter the entry got, generating yet better contributions and links from those who followed. The entry became its own filter, or in some ways its own editor, as contributors self-screened and added yet more nuance, layers of information and perspectives on the events and on coverage of the events.

To call the entry its own filter is not to discount, however, the heroic efforts of the many editors that rode herd on the information as it flowed in, editing for content, tone and taste. It is a bit like taking a standard newsroom model and expanding it out until the reporters number in the thousands and the editors in the hundreds, all disparately located, all working on no deadline, on all deadlines, on one story.

An ongoing question for journalists is whether participatory journalism is part of the problem of the decline of traditional news media or part of the solution. It is probably both. User-generated content raises questions of libel liability, quality standards, and accuracy and fairness, among others. But pro-am marriages of professional journalists and regular folks with blogs, video cameras and recorders can produce involvement and participation that get more people interested in the news. "The more that citizens participate in the news, the more

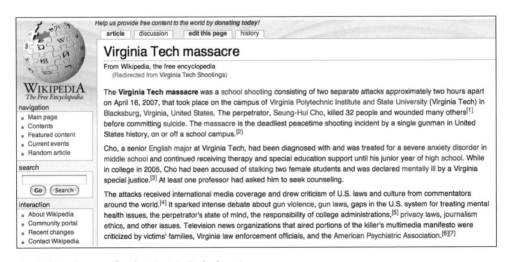

The Wikipedia entry for the Virginia Tech shootings.

deeply engaged they tend to become in the democratic process," wrote communication researchers Cecilia Friend and Jane Singer (2007: 153).

Partnering with the Crowds

Traditional news media are still figuring out how to leverage participatory journalism. How to encourage and facilitate this human impulse to share news and information but still protect the professional news brand is one of the industry's riddles. (How to pay for it is the other.) There are already several emergent models of pro-am journalism, however.

CNN's approach, for example, is to completely segregate user-generated content into a separate site with little to tether it to the CNN newsroom or brand. The separation is clearly meant to assure site visitors that there is no "pollution" of CNN content with the contributions of regular "Joes," while

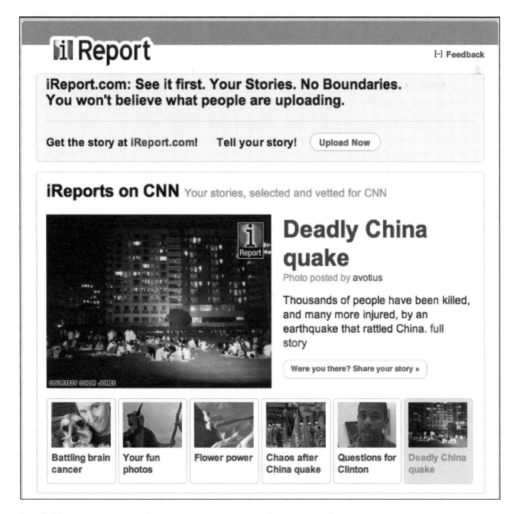

CNN's iReport.com, a site devoted to user-generated content and news coverage.

iReport provides several ways of orienting the news, including several recommendation systems ("Most Viewed," "Most Commented," "Most Shared").

still allowing a range and depth of participatory or distributed journalism and collective intelligence. A disclaimer on the separate site, www.ireport.com, states: "The views and content on this site are solely those of the iReport.com contributors. CNN makes no guarantees about the content or the coverage on iReport.com!" Note the exclamation point.

CNN is attempting to build an "iReport community" around populist notions of news and how to gather and present it. In this crowd-sourced model, CNN offers to air "the most compelling, important, and urgent ones" on the network, incenting contributors with publicity rather than money.

Another model is Korea's OhMyNews, perhaps the world's largest pro-am news site, with tens of thousands of "citizen" reporters who are paid for their stories. This model layers on top of and around the user-generated content the discipline of verification of professional journalists—editors who read, fact-check, filter and publish. From a base of 727 citizen reporters when it began in 2000, OhMyNews's network has grown to more than 50,000 with a coverage area of 100 countries, driven by its motto, "Every citizen is a reporter."

Importantly, OhMyNews publisher Oh Yeon-ho proposed "Ten Preconditions for the Value of UGC" (user-generated content) during a speech at a UNESCO conference in February 2007. These preconditions coalesced around four points or values: credibility, responsibility, influence and sustainability; and as a set provide a sense of how OhMyNews vets and checks the tidal waves of information supplied it by "citizen reporters" throughout the world.

With the sustained success of OhMyNews, it is somewhat surprising that this model has not been attempted in the United States. Backfence.com ambitiously sought 160 sites in 16 metro markets, attempting a network of participatory journalism sites. Backfence churned through its startup capital and had to shut down, providing no definitive lessons for American news media. But Backfence focused on hyperlocal news, whereas OhMyNews covers the world.

A third model is being tried by a number of sites throughout the United States, including the New West Network (http://www.newwest.net/) based in Montana. New West collects contributions from its "citizens" in several cities and towns in eight states. In addition, each day, the site features a new, contributed photo that typically is a breathtaking shot of a western landscape.

Launched in 2005, New West states that its mission is to "serve the Rockies with innovative, participatory journalism and to promote conversation that

OhmyNews INTERNATIONAL

KOREA | WORLD | SCI&TECH | ART&LIFE | ENTERTAINMENT | SPORTS | G

What Does OhmyNews Mean to You?

A call for 100,000 strong OhmyNews member club

Oh Yeon-ho writes an open letter to readers and contributors about OhmyNews' new membership subscription strategy.... (OhmyNews)

National Identities Complicate Pyongyang Policy

North Korea tests who its neighbors are

Pyongyang's nuclear and missile tests reveal not only North Korea's nationalism, but they also test how changing national identities in South Korea and China shape strategic interests and ultimately security policies.... (Leif-Eric Easley)

[Interview] Iran's Bestselling Author on Ahmadinejad

Farhad Jafari says Ahmadinejad may be Iran's best hope for reform

Jafari considers himself a liberal democrat and says there are misunderstandings about President Ahmadinejad and the "Reform Movement".... (Weiai Xu)

OhMyNews launched in 2000.

Tipis in Wind River Canyon, Wyoming. Photo by Mary Gordon

A "photo of the day" on the New West Network.

helps us understand and make the most of the dramatic changes sweeping our region." The site publishes between 10 and 15 new stories a day, in addition to photography, video, commentary and "conversation," or feedback via a number of reader forums.

Anyone is free to share his or her thoughts on any New West story via a "comment" button at the bottom of every story. Readers can also register with New West to be able to contribute ideas and opinions through its "Unfiltered" section. Guest columns are also solicited, as is freelance reporting. With a large and growing reader base, the site has a healthy revenue stream in display advertising, which also appears in a print periodical published by New West.

Which model holds the most promise? How are these models supposed to make money, at least enough to pay the Internet hosting bills? How do these sites ensure that their reporters achieve the purpose of journalism? These are as yet unanswered questions.

The Power of Folksonomies

If the definition or understanding of citizen journalism is expanded to include sites like Slashdot, we might just be able to call it a movement. For more than a decade, Slashdot has facilitated user-submitted and editor-evaluated technology news, providing each story with a forum for comments. Slashdot was one of the first popular Web sites to include a commentary section in such a prominent manner.

Another site, digg (digg.com/), is a variation on the Slashdot theme. A news aggregator, digg allows its users and readers to vote on the most interesting stories in what is a never-ending election. This continuous vote determines

Comment section on a lead story at Slashdot, on the use of twitter in political campaigns.

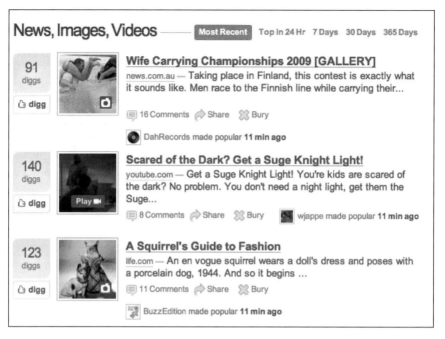

Digg.com's dynamic ranking of news.

placement of stories on the digg home page. Stories with the most votes, or "diggs," move onto the front page. The site's stated goal is to give every story, whether it is from a professional journalist or a random blogger, the same chance of making it onto the front page.

Sites like digg, as well as Reddit (www.reddit.com), Del.icio.us (http://del.icio.us/) and MySpace News (news.myspace.com) are giving readers the ability to shape a very different news agenda than that of professional news editors. Traditional agenda-setting theory holds that news media can't tell us what to think, but they can influence what we think about. News media traditionally have set the agenda for a national news conversation. These user-news sites point to a future in which readers increasingly set the news agenda and define the news in addition to news professionals, and research shows that readers have very different definitions and priorities than does the guild of journalism.

A report from the Project for Excellence in Journalism compared the news agenda of the mainstream media for one week with the news agenda found on a host of user-news sites for the same period. While the mainstream press focused on Iraq and the debate over immigration, the three leading user-news sites—Reddit, digg and Del.icio.us—were more focused on stories like the release of Apple's new iPhone and that Nintendo had surpassed Sony in net worth, according to the study. Many of the stories users selected did not appear anywhere among the top stories in the mainstream media coverage studied. In addition, the sources user-news sites draw on are strikingly different from the mainstream media. Seven in ten stories on the user sites come from either

MySpace's user-news page, in beta for more than a year.

blogs or Web sites such as YouTube and WebMd that do not focus mostly on news.

The study's findings are troubling. The user-news sites are in the dissemination business, not the reporting business. They offer ways of re-orienting news coverage, but contribute little to it. The voting systems seem to preclude follow-ups on major stories as the public's attention is competed for by such a fragmented, variable menu of news. Clearly, however, readers are no longer merely passive receivers; they are actively involved in shaping the news agenda, and in sharing and commenting on the news. Journalism professor Jay Rosen (2006) refers to this new readership as "The People Formerly Known as the Audience," or the "writer-readers." Jeff Jarvis, also a professor of journalism, instructed the guild to "give the people control of media; they will use it. The corollary: Don't give the people control of media, and you will lose. Whenever citizens can exercise control, they will" (2004).

Making News Fun

Newspapers and other print publications with a presence online are looking for ways to better capitalize on the interactive capabilities of the Internet, or inter-activity beyond open-discussion formats and forums such as discussion boards and blogs. Representative of this other category are features such as tax calculators and interactive puzzles and challenges. Minnesota Public Radio, for example, included a "Budget Balancer" to allow users to try to balance the Minnesota state budget. Players could raise taxes, make cuts and withhold payments, among other things (available: http://news.mpr.org/features2003/02/10_newsroom_budgetsim). And *USA Today* attracted more than 2.5 million

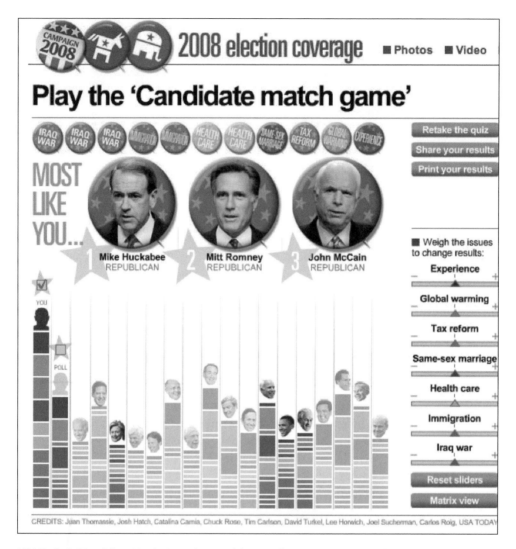

USA Today's "Candidate Match Game," a visual feast and an interactive powerhouse, available at http://www.usatoday.com/news/politics/election2008/cmg-original.htm.

unique visitors to its online "Candidate Match Game" in just over eight months, launching an updated version after Barack Obama secured the Democratic Party nomination. The game aims to help readers get an idea of which presidential candidates come closest to their own views.

The Institute for Interactive Journalism (www.jlab.org) helps news organizations use innovative computer technologies to develop new ways for people to engage in critical public policy issues. The J-Lab supports interactive news ideas and teams newsrooms with computer scientists to build software and dynamic news experiences. It also is a great site to read up on ways newspapers are leveraging the Internet.

One example of this leveraging is the type of initiatives launched by New York City's Gotham Gazette (www.gothamgazette.com), a city news site published by the New York Citizens Union Foundation. In late 2003, the Gazette had three major interactive exercises:

The Ground Zero Planner (http://www.gothamgazette.com/rebuilding_nyc/ groundzeroplanner/) went online in May 2002 to provide a clickable map of the World Trade Center site. The exercise provided a simplified simulation of what professional architects and planners were doing in crafting their plans for the WTC site. The Gotham Gazette timed the exercise so that input from ordinary people would occur at the same time that city planners were considering proposals from professionals.

The City Budget Game (http://www.gothamgazette.com/budgetgame/budget game.html) went up a year later and was one of the first efforts to apply the basic format of the state budget game to a city budget. This interactive exercise summarized a dull, ongoing story in an interesting and engaging way.

So You Want to Be a Judge (http://www.gothamgazette.com/judgesgame/) is an ethics quiz that highlights alleged corruption in the Brooklyn Supreme Court. The game took a team of eight Gazette employees roughly a month to complete.

Another example of how media outlets are embracing interactivity is MSNBC's Big Picture, which won a 2003 Batten Award for innovation in interactivity. This series integrates video, audio, text, interactive polls and games and solidified MSNBC's status as a leader in interactive, multimedia storytelling. The sophisticated series provides in-depth guided tours on Iraq, the elections and the Oscars. The Iraq module is on the Web at http://stacks.msnbc.com/ modules/bigpicture/iraq/.

Going Mobile

Another trend to carefully watch in journalism is the rush to the mobile Web, a trend fueled by developments such as the iPhone, the proliferation of handhelds, and Google's and Microsoft's commitment to cloud-based software, or software housed on Google or Microsoft servers and used remotely by individual users. *The New York Times*, another traditional news organization not historically known for avant-garde products or services, announced in January 2008 its text messaging service to deliver, according to the *Times*, "the latest news, features and columns from the newspaper as well as features from The Times Magazine to cell phones and mobile devices."

Again, media companies are recognizing and responding to long-term trends in Internet and phone use. The Pew Internet & American Life Project found in March 2008 that 62 percent of American adults have either accessed the Internet wirelessly or used non-voice data applications, such as texting,

AIM Pages	Asianavenue	Bebo	BlackPlanet	Bolt	Cyworld
Facebook	Flixster	Friendster	HiS	Imeem	LinkedIn
LiveSpaces	MiGente	Multiply	Myspace	MyYearbook	NetLog
Orkut	Piczo	Stickam	Tagged	TagWorld	Tribe
Virb	Yahoo.360	AOLPictures	Break	DesktopNexus	DIVIX Stage6
Flickr	Fotki	Metacafe	Photobucket	Slide	UncutVideo
Veoh	Vimeo	WebShots	YouTube	blogmarks.net	Delicious
Furl	Ma.gnolia	Simpy	Spurl.net	StumbleUpon	Blogger
LiveJournal	Tabulas	Technorati	Typepad	Vox	WordPress
Xanga	FineTune	iLike	lastfm	MOG	Pandora
SoundClick	Uber	Meet Up	Upcoming	yelp	DIGG
Gamespot	IGN	Xuga	DeviantArt	Ebay	Plentyoffish
Twitter					

The "social network grid" at mashable.com, demonstrating the proliferation of social networks and sites devoted to users sharing content with one another (see http://my.mashable.com/links/network).

emailing, taking a picture, or recording video with a handheld. A majority, then, uses a mobile phone for more than calling and talking. On the average day, 42 percent of those with cell phones or other wireless-enabled handhelds use the devices for at least one non-voice data application, according to the study.

Pew identified a demographic it calls the "Mobile Centrics," a group more oriented to the cell phone than to desktop Internet access. This demographic also is diverse in its racial and ethnic make-up. When it comes to digital content, Mobile Centrics are not much into blogging or using the Internet as a destination to pass the time, but increasingly turn to their phones for a multiplicity of uses, including getting their news. In 2007, 51 percent of respondents said, "it would be very hard to give up their cell phone," a marked increase over 2002's 38 percent. The Internet was second in 2007, at 45 percent.

Mobile centrism will only grow. As of mid-2009, the iPhone boasted more than 30,000 applications, with roughly 5,000 apps added each month. For a taste of what these apps can do, including everything from help with a search for a kennel or organic grocery to playing flute-like music with an app called Ocarina, visit Apple's App Store. The Store recorded more than 800 million apps downloaded in its first month. For the Web writer, the iPhone's 3.5-inch (diagonally) screen presents severe spatial constraints. On the plus side, hyperlocal gains new meaning when any app can know precisely where a user is located because of global positioning technology in use by most cell phone service providers.

Closely related to mobile phone and handheld use is growth in what is called "cloud computing," which moves applications and data storage away from the desktop or laptop to remote servers managed by high-speed networks. Computing applications and users' data archives will increasingly be accessible by different devices anytime, anywhere over fast and widely available wireless and wired networks. As evidence of this, in May 2008 Google began giving users instant electronic access to their health histories using cloudware. Called Google Health, the service allows users to link to information from a handful of pharmacies and care providers, joining Microsoft's HealthVault and Revolution Health in health information cloudware.

Apple's App Store is organized by department or general use heading. This is the section for apps that can be used around the house, such as the iPhone-as-TV-remote app.

A YouTuber demonstrates Ocarina (http://www.youtube.com/watch?v=
u3WO6sonxl4).

Twittering the News

Related to the trend toward mobile Web use and news consumption is a micro-blogging software called twitter, a social networked hybrid of texting and blogging that is being leveraged by news organizations such as *The New York Times, Newsweek* and CNN. Limiting blog posts to 140 characters, twitter rewards a tight writing style and a sense of immediacy, both of which are qualities of good online journalism. The application by news organizations, then, would seem to make sense. *The Wichita Eagle* in April and May 2008 employed twitter to give readers moment-by-moment updates on a high-profile murder trial, providing a stream of coverage not unlike Kelly Sipe's of the sniper trial for *The Virginian-Pilot*.

Note that the Wichita newspaper gives readers some background on twitter, provides an alternative or traditional story format for trial coverage, links to all of the past trial coverage, and offers a slideshow. Readers could also sign up for an RSS feed specific to the trial coverage.

Here's how twitter works, according to twitter's own instructions:

> When you send twitter a mobile text (SMS), it gets sent out to your group of friends and also saves to your twitter page. Your friends might not have phone alerts turned on so they might check your web page instead. Likewise, you receive your friends' mobile updates on your phone.

Twitterers (or tweeters) can also post updates through the twitter Web site at www.twitter.com.

Because twitter is mobile and its messages are concise, most tweeters are accessing or using the software through their mobile phones, making it another important distribution channel for news organizations. Services that deliver "tweets" to users' phones include iTweet.net, PocketTweets.com and Hahlo.com. Sports scores, traffic alerts and travel advisories, event promotions,

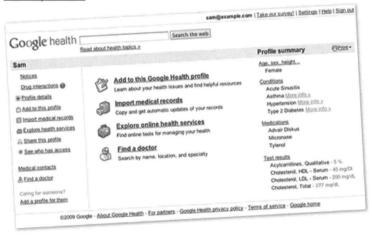

and breaking news are natural information categories for twitter. The *Orlando Sentinel*, for example, used twitter to send out updates on the Atlantis and Endeavour space shuttle launches during summer 2007. Some examples of *Sentinel* posts:

- Countdown has resumed. 9 minutes and counting to 6:36 p.m. shuttle launch . . . 06:28 PM August 08, 2007 from web.
- After three attempts, NASA gets shuttle hatch closed, so we're a go at moment for 6:36 p.m. launch. 05:23 PM August 08, 2007 from web.
- Accident closes State Road 46 near Seminole-Brevard line; use another route if you are on way to shuttle launch. 03:44 PM August 08, 2007 from web.
- Fueling is done, looking good for 6:36 p.m. shuttle launch.

THE STATE V. BURNETT

- **The trial:** Ted Burnett, 51, is charged with aggravated kidnapping and capital murder. He could face the death penalty if convicted.
- **The crime:** Chelsea Brooks, 14 and nine months pregnant, had just completed eighth grade at Allison Middle School when she disappeared from Skate South, 1900 E. MacArthur, on June 9, 2006. Her body turned up six days later in a shallow grave in a wheat field on Mulberry Road in Butler County.
- **Also charged:** Everett Gentry, then 17, pleaded guilty July 14, 2006, to murder as a juvenile and avoided the death penalty. Now 19, he is the prosecution's key witness. Elgin Robinson, 22, is scheduled for trial in September.
- **Prosecutors:** Deputy District Attorney Kevin O'Connor and Chief District Attorney Marc Bennett represent the state of Kansas.
- **For the defense:** Gary Owens and Mark Manna represent Burnett.

TWITTER UPDATES

Eagle staff writer Ron Sylvester is sending ultra-brief updates on the Burnett trial via Twitter. They're also fed here:

- Burgess: "With that, ladies and gentlemen, we'll be in recess until 9 o'clock tomorrow morning." about an hour ago
- Burgess: Jurors will receive their instructions Thursday morning, followed by closing arguments from the lawyers. about an hour ago
- Judge Burgess is releasing the jury for the rest of the day. Lawyers and the judge will spend the afternoon finalizing jury instructions. about an hour ago
- Manna: "Your honor, at this time the defense elects to present no evidence, and we rest." about an hour ago
- Judge Burgess asked the jury to return to the courtroom. about an hour ago

What is Twitter? It allows you to keep track of your friends, and they keep track of you, using frequent, very short messages (140 characters or less). Visit Ron's Twitter page to get started. We also send out Kansas.com's top headlines via Twitter all day. More updates

Murder trial coverage at *The Wichita Eagle* (www.kansas.com/chelseabrooks).

Hyperlocal News

Many of the same fundamentals that have fueled social networking online have also placed priority for many news organizations on hyperlocal news, or a very local, community-by-community approach to news online. Community news is not new, of course. News 400 years ago was shared in coffee houses and public houses, and it was all very, very local, or as Adam Holovaty of Everyblock.com refers to it, "address-specific news." But using online to reach and tailor news for even individual neighborhoods is quite new and represents an opportunity for traditional news organizations migrating to digital. Global positioning satellite technology, mobile phones, twitter, RSS and other client-specific, geocoding or locating technologies have helped make hyperlocal news approaches attractive.

Independent hyperlocal news sites like WestportNow.com in Connecticut, iBrattleboro.com in Vermont and VillageSoup.com in Maine are thriving, according to the *American Journalism Review*, at least in terms of reader interest. As a business model, however, hyperlocal news remains "financially marginal." There are few success stories, and fewer still that actually pay its founders full-time salaries. One of the biggest, for example, Baristanet.com, is run by two part-timers not ready to give up their day jobs.

In Rome, Georgia, the hyperlocal HometownHeadlines.com does quite well, at least in terms of attracting traffic and in providing news and "nearly news" that the local print newspaper misses for various reasons. Hometown Headlines delivers news people want, such as when and where Starbucks is

A map at Everyblock.com showing the stories from or about the Chelsea neighborhood in New York City.

Rome, Georgia's hyperlocal HometownHeadlines.com.

coming to town, when a cell of storms and high winds is headed Rome's way, and the latest scuttlebutt regarding real estate development in town. Washingtonpost.Newsweek Interactive's Jonathan Krim calls this reaching an audience at "a granular level."

The *Chi-town Daily News* (http://www.chitowndailynews.org/), founded in March 2007 thanks to a Knight Foundation Challenge grant, uses a network of 40 or so citizen journalists throughout Chicago and software that helps identify where this network lives and the subjects and topics its members like to cover. When a building collapsed in Wicker Park, the *Daily News* had a citizen journalist there in minutes. To accomplish hyperlocal, the site aims to put at least one citizen journalist in all of the city's nearly 80 neighborhoods, recruiting and training each one. To find these volunteers, the site has reached out using Craigslist, Facebook and MySpace and by communicating with Chicago bloggers.

In January 2008, the *Las Vegas Sun* (http://www.lasvegassun.com/) provided a clinic on how to do hyperlocal journalism. A fire at the Monte Carlo hotel and casino gave the newspaper and Web site a chance to show off its new site

CONTINUOUS NEWS UPDATES

💬 24 COMMENTS   🖨 PRINT   📧 E-MAIL   🔗 SHARE

Unclear when fire-damaged Monte Carlo can be reopened

By Mark Whittington · January 25, 2008 · 7:44 PM

Monte Carlo Fire

It's unclear when the Monte Carlo will reopen after a fire burned for an hour today atop the casino on the Las Vegas Strip.

"I can tell you that it won't be tomorrow," said Ron Lynn, the chief building inspector for Clark County.

The first alarm came at 11 a.m. as smoke rolled off the top of the building and flames licked the Monte Carlo sign. Smoke and fire poured from windows four floors from the top of the 32-story building.

SAM MORRIS / LAS VEGAS SUN

AUTOPLAY   CAPTION   ⊡

Burning foam and a stiff breeze blowing smoke back into the building made it difficult to fight the fast-moving fire, said Capt. Warren Whitney of the Clark County Fire Department. Some firefighters had to hang out of windows to pour water on the fire above them.

It's an unusual way to fight a fire," Whitney said.

One of the "continuous news updates" on the Monte Carlo hotel fire, from the *Las Vegas Sun*.

design and hyperlocal approach. The paper responded with, among other steps, a live blog updated by several members of the newsroom staff, an overview of the hotel's history, and a flurry of videos on the fire, all while the hotel was still burning. The site also accommodated user-contributed coverage, such as photos (via Flickr) and videos (via YouTube).

The story was very local; the paper made it the top priority. Adequate resources were deployed, coverage was continuously updated, readers were included in the coverage, and the Web was leveraged for multimedia, in particular for video. In short, the paper kept drilling down, as if for oil.

A pioneering father of the hyperlocal approach online is Rob Curley, who helped WashingtonPost.com build a mesh of microsites, beginning with LoudounExtra.com in July 2007, to cover the newspaper's markets one by one. Curley also developed video-centric hyperlocal models at the *Lawrence Journal-World* (http://www2.ljworld.com), including its KUSports.com site

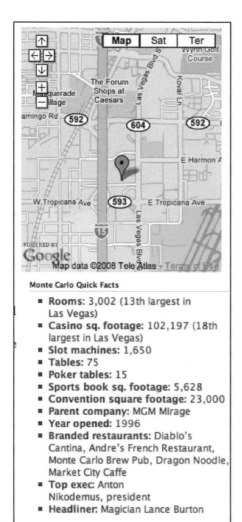

Monte Carlo Quick Facts

- **Rooms:** 3,002 (13th largest in Las Vegas)
- **Casino sq. footage:** 102,197 (18th largest in Las Vegas)
- **Slot machines:** 1,650
- **Tables:** 75
- **Poker tables:** 15
- **Sports book sq. footage:** 5,628
- **Convention square footage:** 23,000
- **Parent company:** MGM Mirage
- **Year opened:** 1996
- **Branded restaurants:** Diablo's Cantina, Andre's French Restaurant, Monte Carlo Brew Pub, Dragon Noodle, Market City Caffe
- **Top exec:** Anton Nikodemus, president
- **Headliner:** Magician Lance Burton

Map of the Monte Carlo, with baseball card-like stats on the hotel.

Las Vegas fire history

By Mary Manning
Fri, Jan 25, 2008 (12:32 p.m.)

Las Vegas residents and visitors have witnessed previous fires in various hotels. They include:

2005 – A three-alarm fire at the Aztec Inn, just north of Sahara Avenue on the Strip, forced the evacuation of the casino and caused an estimated $200,000 in damages but no injuries. At the time, it was the third fire that the hotel suffered in several weeks, but fire investigators did not connect the trio of blazes.

Feb. 18, 2003 – A pre-dawn smoky fire at the Aladdin hotel and casino, sparked by a lit cigarette in a laundry chute, caused the evacuation of the 21st and 22nd floors and resulted in six people being treated at the scene for smoke inhalation.

2003 – The historic Moulin Rouge hotel and casino on West Bonanza Road burned to the ground in May. It was the first hotel in Las Vegas where African American entertainers who performed on the Strip could stay. Fred Ball, 45, and John Antwan Caver, 29, were arrested on arson charges.

July 1998 – Fire investigators believed that lightning sparked a fire that erupted at the Palace Station, after flames blasted through the 21st floor during a torrential thunderstorm.

1998 – The Las Vegas Hilton Hotel reported $1 million in damages from a fire that forced the evacuation of six floors during a two-alarm fire, but no one was injured.

Hotel fires through history

AUTOPLAY   CAPTION

Fires on the Strip

- Palace Station damaged by rain, fire (06-20-1998)
- Flames Engulf Under-Construction Observation Tower (08-29-1993)
- Killer fire sweeps LV Hilton (02-11-1981)
- MGM BURNS (11-22-1980)
- Million Dollar Fire Belts Hotel Sahara (11-26-1964)
- Nearly Finished Resort Hotel Damaged By Fire (04-07-1955)

History of hotel fires in Las Vegas, posted at LasVegasSun.com.

More about the Monte Carlo

By Mary Manning
Fri, Jan 25, 2008 (1:22 p.m.)

Here are some facts and historical information about The Monte Carlo Resort and Casino, which was damaged in a three-alarm fire on Friday, Jan. 25, 2008.

- The casino brought the magic of Lance Burton, who performs in his own theater at the Strip hotel. Burton, who had formerly performed at the Hacienda since 1991, has signed a 13-year contract with the Monte Carlo.
- The MGM Mirage currently owns and operates the resort.
- The 32-story hotel offers 3,002 guest rooms, including 259 luxury suites.
- Modeled after the opulent Place du Casino in Monte Carlo, the hotel currently has an AAA rating of four diamonds.
- Guest room features include Italian marble, cherry furniture, cable/pay TV, 24-hour room service and data ports.

Information box posted on the hotel.

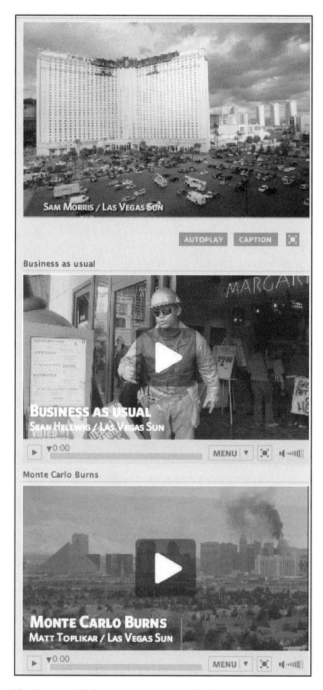

The *Sun* provided a constant stream of video coverage from the scene of the hotel fire.

dedicated to University of Kansas sports, and at the *Naples News* (http://www.naplesnews.com/studio55/) in Florida. Curley left the *Post* in May 2008 for the *Las Vegas Sun*, taking his hyperlocal Internet development team with him.

The premise of most hyperlocal sites is that the metro daily newspapers cannot compete with online news sites in delivering breaking news, but that they can own or dominate what happens in their backyards. This is the approach taken by *The Washington Post*, *The Atlanta Journal-Constitution* and the *Las Vegas Sun*. When that backyard is small and defined, with a discernible set of common interests, like Bluffton, S.C., then tailoring a site to that community is relatively straightforward. When the backyard is defined by geography and little else, as are many of the *Post*'s "backyards" (Arlington, Va., and Loudoun County, Va., for example), defining "hyperlocal" is problematic.

Hyperlocal site models range from the database-rich, amenity-driven, like LoudounExtra.com, which has databases on every church, school and restaurant in the county, to the more open models dependent on reader contributions in the form of blogs, contributed photography, video and commentary, like the New West Network (www.newwest.net). Other hyperlocal examples on the Curley model include Gridiron Central in Rome, Georgia (http://www1.romenews-tribune.com/multimedia); Chicagocrime.org in Chicago, which also is from Adam Holovaty, focusing on crime statistics; Holovaty's EveryBlock (http://www.everyblock.com/) for block-by-block coverage in Chicago; Ski Space.com (http://www.skispace.com/) for skiers; and BlufftonToday in South Carolina (http://www.blufftontoday.com/).

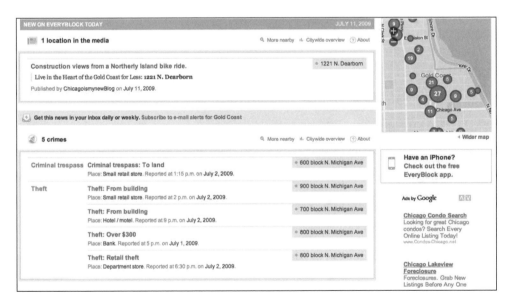

Neighborhood-specific crime information from Chicagocrime.org.

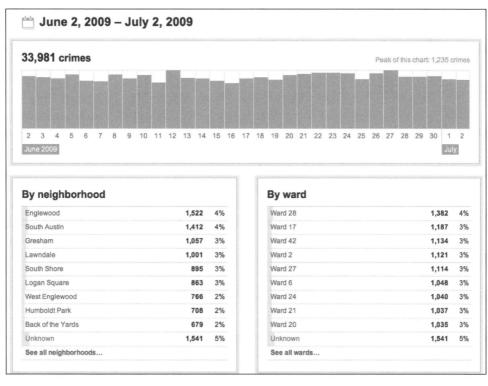

June 2, 2009 – July 2, 2009

33,981 crimes   Peak of this chart: 1,235 crimes

2 3 4 5 6 7 8 9 10 11 12 13 14 15 16 17 18 19 20 21 22 23 24 25 26 27 28 29 30 1 2

June 2009   July

By neighborhood

Englewood	1,522	4%
South Austin	1,412	4%
Gresham	1,057	3%
Lawndale	1,001	3%
South Shore	895	3%
Logan Square	863	3%
West Englewood	766	2%
Humboldt Park	708	2%
Back of the Yards	679	2%
Unknown	1,541	5%

See all neighborhoods…

By ward

Ward 28	1,382	4%
Ward 17	1,187	3%
Ward 42	1,134	3%
Ward 2	1,121	3%
Ward 27	1,114	3%
Ward 6	1,048	3%
Ward 24	1,040	3%
Ward 21	1,037	3%
Ward 20	1,035	3%
Unknown	1,541	5%

See all wards…

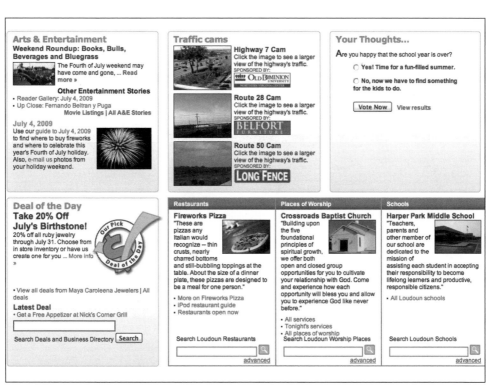

Arts & Entertainment
Weekend Roundup: Books, Bulls, Beverages and Bluegrass

The Fourth of July weekend may have come and gone, … Read more »

Other Entertainment Stories
- Reader Gallery: July 4, 2009
- Up Close: Fernando Beltran y Puga

Movie Listings | All A&E Stories

July 4, 2009
Use our guide to July 4, 2009 to find where to buy fireworks and where to celebrate this year's Fourth of July holiday. Also, e-mail us photos from your holiday weekend.

Traffic cams
Highway 7 Cam
Click the image to see a larger view of the highway's traffic.
SPONSORED BY:
OLD DOMINION UNIVERSITY

Route 28 Cam
Click the image to see a larger view of the highway's traffic.
SPONSORED BY:
BELFORT FURNITURE

Route 50 Cam
Click the image to see a larger view of the highway's traffic.
SPONSORED BY:
LONG FENCE

Your Thoughts…
Are you happy that the school year is over?

○ Yes! Time for a fun-filled summer.

○ No, now we have to find something for the kids to do.

Vote Now   View results

Deal of the Day
Take 20% Off July's Birthstone!
20% off all ruby jewelry through July 31. Choose from in store inventory or have us create one for you … More info »

Our Pick — Deal of the Day

- View all deals from Maya Caroleena Jewelers | All deals

Latest Deal
- Get a Free Appetizer at Nick's Corner Grill

Search Deals and Business Directory [Search]

Restaurants
Fireworks Pizza
"These are pizzas any Italian would recognize -- thin crusts, nearly charred bottoms and still-bubbling toppings at the table. About the size of a dinner plate, these pizzas are designed to be a meal for one person."

- More on Fireworks Pizza
- iPod restaurant guide
- Restaurants open now

Search Loudoun Restaurants
[   ] advanced

Places of Worship
Crossroads Baptist Church
"Building upon the five foundational principles of spiritual growth, we offer both open and closed group opportunities for you to cultivate your relationship with God. Come and experience how each opportunity will bless you and allow you to experience God like never before."

- All services
- Tonight's services
- All places of worship

Search Loudoun Worship Places
[   ] advanced

Schools
Harper Park Middle School
"Teachers, parents and other member of our school are dedicated to the mission of assisting each student in accepting their responsibility to become lifelong learners and productive, responsible citizens."

- All Loudoun schools

Search Loudoun Schools
[   ] advanced

The Washington Post's LoudounExtra.com, which in 2008 was struggling to build a critical mass of readership.

Geomapping

Geomapping is a common feature found on hyperlocal news sites, which makes perfect sense given the geographical focus of hyperlocal news. Geomapping software (readily available as freeware) allows you to create customized maps related to news coverage. The news aggregator site YourStreet.com, for example, takes third-party news coverage and aggregates it based on locality, using software to place "push pins" on top of a Google Map to show where news stories take place geographically. A YourStreet.com user can scan the map to quickly find local stories. The push pins are placed by an algorithm that extracts geographical information from stories, such as street names, neighborhoods, and cities, then geo-codes the articles against a longitude and latitude database so that it can place them on a map. Of course, presenting the news is only half the story. The site is also selling its ability to sell ads on very "pinpointed" local level, even a street-by-street basis.

Widgets

A byproduct of the social networking phenomenon is the widget, which online refers to, as Wordpress defines it, as a "self-contained piece of code that you can move into, out of and anywhere inside your [blog's] sidebar. You can use it to personalize your blog and deliver information you want."

YourStreet's marriage of news coverage and Google Map geomapping technology.

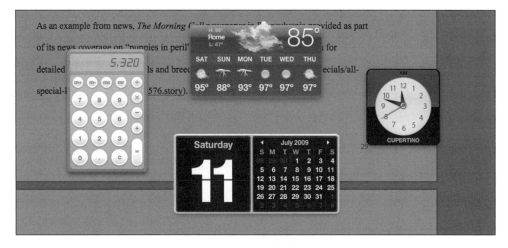

Apple's standard Mac widget with calendar, calculator, clock and real-time weather information.

Widgets also are used by Web sites in general and news sites, specifically. One of the most common types of widget provides real-time weather information. Apple also has embraced widgets by allowing and providing them as part of the Mac and iBook series. As an example from news, *The Morning Call* newspaper in Pennsylvania provided as part of its news coverage on "puppies in peril" a widget that allows users to search for detailed information on kennels and breeders (http://www.mcall.com/news/specials/all-special-kennel-031107,0,5454576.story).

Most widgets are portable or replicable, so any reader could add the widget to his or her blog, allowing that blog's readers similarly to search for specific kennels by accessing *The Morning Call*'s extensive database. Facebook opened

A Pennsylvania newspaper's widget for finding kennels.

The Abazab.com widget allows MySpacers to post
video using their mobile devices.

its platform to widgets in 2007, producing a flood of widgets any Facebooker can add to his or her page. As of June 2008, outside developers had created more than 24,000 programs and widgets, from allowing users to send virtual hugs to sharing movie and music recommendations. The top 1 percent of these applications accounted for approximately two-thirds of all application activity. One widget allows geographically disparate users to play the same game of Scrabble (called Scrabulous), for example, a widget used by Facebook founder Mark Zuckerberg and his grandmother. According to O'Reilly Media, the

Widgetbox's directory of widgets.

most popular Facebook applications in 2008 were those used to "enhance communication." Second most popular were those that allow users to compare themselves with other users. Playing social games ranked third.

After Facebook opened up to outside code developers in May 2007, the site saw its number of unique monthly U.S. visitors increase 81 percent. Not surprisingly, then, MySpace began allowing software developers to build new services for its members in February 2008, enabling new uses for the platform such as sharing travel plans, exchanging fashion advice and competing in multiplayer games.

Of course, there are blogs and sites devoted to making, finding and reviewing widgets, including SexyWidget (http://www.sexywidget.com/), WidgetBox (http://www.widgetbox.com/) and RockYou (http://www.rockyou.com/).

Evolving Online Writing and Editing Roles

As the explosions of applications for the Web and for mobile media suggest, writers' and editors' roles are evolving. Increasingly, these professionals will serve as researchers and guides, as traffic generators and as community managers.

Researcher and guide

The sheer amount of Web-based information is a double-edged sword. All this great stuff is wonderful in theory, but wading through page after page of search results can be quite tiresome. Most people need help. Web journalists can help by sorting through articles, blog posts and RSS feeds in the constant hunt for something interesting or useful. Journalism students should be introduced to research and organization techniques, how to use a feed reader, how to stay on top of a specific trend via email alerts and search feeds, and how to develop source relationships with blogs, instant messaging and email.

Academia should not overestimate students' Web skills or mistake technological prowess or knowledge with research expertise. There is little transferable skill between a well-managed MySpace profile and effective online research. Students should gain experience with the Web tools in use in industry.

Traffic Generator

Writers online are learning that it helps to think about the bottom line, even though such thoughts are antithetical for older generations of journalists. Good content attracts readers, and it is the reader who creates the page views. The page views attract advertisers, who generate the revenue. It's this revenue that provides us with a paycheck. As generators of the content that nourishes the rest of the food chain, perhaps the discussion is more about roles than it is about making money. An example: Advertising metrics reward page views. It might be a tactically wise move, then, to decide against the fancy Flash application in favor of an HTML-based slideshow, knowing as you do that slideshows are page-view bonanzas.

Online Community Manager

Online chat, discussion and community aren't always messy, but online community is no place for wimps. This third core online skill, which is largely absent from journalism pedagogy, has to do with how to lead and moderate communities. A successful forum or blog relies upon a robust user community. However, these communities do not magically or easily form. They require an enormous amount of time, effort and leadership. If you are lucky enough to develop a community, the work only gets harder maintaining and growing that community. A forum or blog moderator is equal parts discussion leader, party host and diplomat.

What does this have to do with journalism? Online, writers and editors are expected to interact with the audience. Audience interaction can yield better stories and more interesting content, but it also opens the door to arguments, mindless debates and comments so inane, so egregious, that you might want to pull the plug on the whole enterprise. Moderators have to swallow that first impulse, step back and remind themselves of the benefits. They need to see opportunity amidst the arguments and the story ideas amidst the flame wars. They need to lead the discussion and prod it when it falters. These community moderating skills can only be developed through experience, and that experience should begin as early as possible.

The Future of Journalism

No one can give definitive answers on what the future of journalism will be, but based on the trends we can discern some key traits or hallmarks of the profession going forward. Journalism in the future likely will be, for better *and* for worse:

- delivered via devices that are mobile, portable and always on;
- socially networked, and therefore contextualized, shared and commented upon almost immediately;
- hyperlocal, though "local" should not be defined in purely physical or geographic terms (The Politico.com, for example, is "hyperlocal" to those interested in inside-the-Beltway politics, regardless of where they physically reside);
- rich in media, particularly the visual;
- transparent, and therefore increasingly accountable (they are "fact-checking your ass," as one prominent blogger put it);
- hyperlinked, cross-linked and meshed (for an elaboration, watch EPIC's Google Grid video at http://idorosen.com/mirrors/robinsloan.com/epic/);

- only one part of a greater media environment or landscape rather than a destination location. A proliferation of distribution channels guarantees this;
- participative and collaborative (the producer–consumer, sender–receiver dichotomies are gone);
- open-ended, in process and always in play rather than being about finding or producing or reporting the "minted" truth;
- entertaining, though not always necessarily overtly so;
- datamapped, customized and, again, highly contextualized and atomized;
- unbundled (think of *The Long Tail* and its niches and sub-niches; the old news containers will no longer be relevant);
- a profession in which reputation, independence, integrity and trust will still matter, and they will matter a lot; how these values will be demonstrated and measured, however, will change and is changing;
- a business sector where breaking news is merely a commodity, and one that will reward perspective, analysis, sensemaking and meaning, as well as new, more interpersonal elements like community and collaboration;
- de-massified, related to the unbundling of journalism; for lots of small audiences (the tail) rather than one mass audience;
- a conversation rather than a lecture, or more like improv, with audience participation, and less, therefore, like opera buffa.

Chapter Assignments

1 Generate a map using any Web-based mapmaking software, such as Google Maps (http://maps.google.com/) or MapBuilder (http://www.mapbuilder. net) to show site visitors where in the city there are WiFi hotspots for wireless Internet access. (See p. 202, top.)

Place markers on your map indicating where in town there are WiFi hubs or access points. Finally, publish your map to a blog or Web page. (See p. 202, foot.)

2 Amend or edit a Wikipedia entry. Choose a subject for which you have expertise, but don't worry. It's easy. You will probably want to create an account first so that your ISP is not made public. (See p. 203, top.)

3 Sign up with twitter (twitter.com) and "tweet" a news event, concert, meeting or conference—something. You will want to experiment with twitter before you're on assignment, before you *need* to know how to use it.

The goal here is merely to become familiar with the service, with the 140-character format and with the dynamic of frequently, briefly posting to a network of readers who you know might immediately receive the information. Of course, there are often cases where richer prose is effective, even essential.

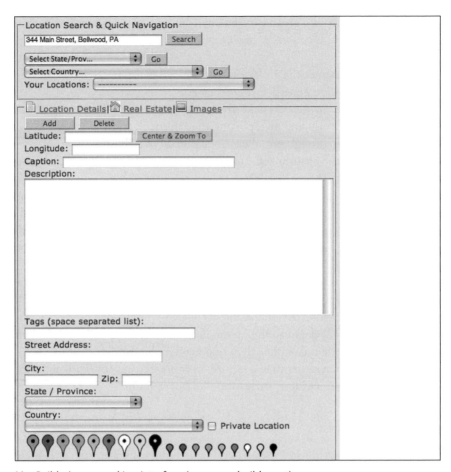

MapBuilder's map-making interface (www.mapbuilder.net).

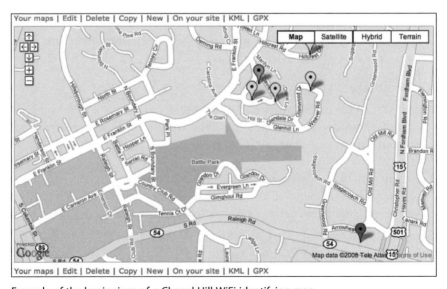

Example of the beginnings of a Chapel Hill WiFi identifying map.

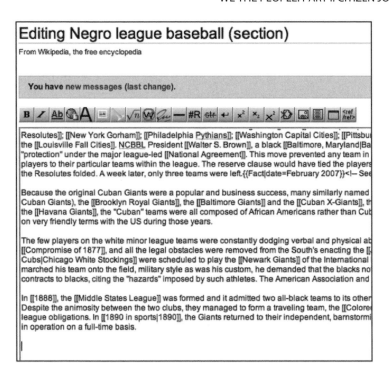

Editing Negro league baseball (section)

From Wikipedia, the free encyclopedia

You have new messages (last change).

Resolutes]]; [[New York Gorham]]; [[Philadelphia Pythians]]; [[Washington Capital Cities]]; [[Pittsbu
the [[Louisville Fall Cities]]. NCBBL President [[Walter S. Brown]], a black [[Baltimore, Maryland|Ba
"protection" under the major league-led [[National Agreement]]. This move prevented any team in
players to their particular teams within the league. The reserve clause would have tied the players
the Resolutes folded. A week later, only three teams were left.{{Fact|date=February 2007}}<!-- See

Because the original Cuban Giants were a popular and business success, many similarly named
Cuban Giants), the [[Brooklyn Royal Giants]], the [[Baltimore Giants]] and the [[Cuban X-Giants]], th
the [[Havana Giants]], the "Cuban" teams were all composed of African Americans rather than Cub
on very friendly terms with the US during those years.

The few players on the white minor league teams were constantly dodging verbal and physical ab
[[Compromise of 1877]], and all the legal obstacles were removed from the South's enacting the [[
Cubs|Chicago White Stockings]] were scheduled to play the [[Newark Giants]] of the International
marched his team onto the field, military style as was his custom, he demanded that the blacks no
contracts to blacks, citing the "hazards" imposed by such athletes. The American Association and

In [[1888]], the [[Middle States League]] was formed and it admitted two all-black teams to its other
Despite the animosity between the two clubs, they managed to form a traveling team, the [[Colore
league obligations. In [[1890 in sports|1890]], the Giants returned to their independent, barnstormi
in operation on a full-time basis.

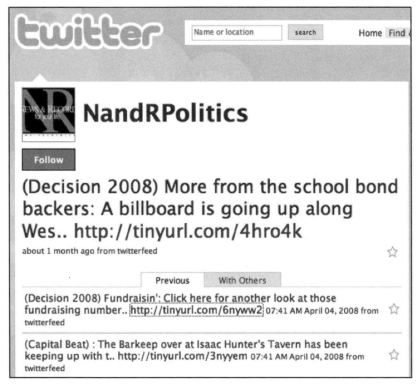

Greensboro, NC, *News & Record*'s twitter feed of political coverage, or, more accurately, of pointers to its political coverage, at https://twitter.com/NandRPolitics.

For an example of how twitter can help you, see "How Twitter Finally Taught Me to Be an Editor," by Craig Stoltz, from May 2008, available: http://2ohreally.wordpress.com/2008/05/27/twitter-taught-me-to-be-an-editor/. Stoltz's blog entry on his experience with twitter is written in 140-word (or fewer) tweets, or twitter posts.

You can also find local twitter-ers by searching TwitterLocal (http://www.twitterlocal.net/) and even subscribe to the RSS feed for the result of that search. Another resource is TweetScan (http://tweetscan.com/), which you can use to check up on breaking news or events.

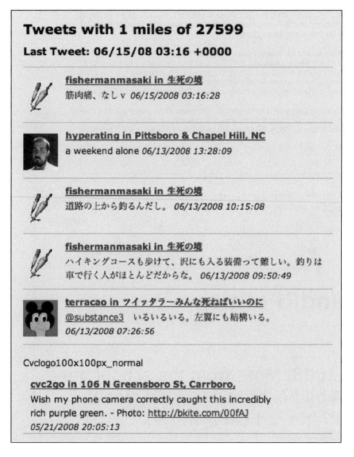

Results of a TweetLocal search in Chapel Hill, N.C.

Online Resources

Barista of Bloomfield Avenue
   http://www.baristanet.com/
   Hyperlocal blogger Debbie Galant of New Jersey.

BrooWaha

http://losangeles.broowaha.com/

Online collection of news, reviews and opinion pieces covering LA.

Chi-Town Daily News

http://www.chitowndailynews.org/

Hyperlocal news by Northwestern's Medill School of Journalism students.

Gannett's Information Center

http://gannett.gci/infocenter

The "Newsroom of the Future," a hyperlocal, crowdsourced multimedia platform.

NewAssignment.Net

http://newassignment.net

Traditional journalism, but assignments made by citizens.

Northwest Voice, Bakersfield, CA

http://www.northwestvoice.com/

Citizen journalism site.

NowPublic

http://www.nowpublic.com/

This site describes itself as "fresh, crowd-powered media."

Syracuse Goldring Arts Journalism program

http://artsjournalism.syr.edu

Backpack journalism master's program covering the arts and architecture.

WikiNews

http://en.wikinews.org/wiki/Main_Page

"The free news source you can write."

You Witness News

http://news.yahoo.com/you-witness-news

Reuters' and Yahoo News' effort to create an international multimedia news agency.

Sources

Chris Anderson, *The Long Tail* (New York: Hyperion Books, 2006).

Hal Berghel, "E-mail—the Good, the Bad, and the Ugly," *Communications of the ACM*, 40, no. 4 (April 1997): 11–16.

Mark Briggs, *Journalism 2.0* (Knight Citizen News Center, 2007), available: http://www.kcnn.org/resources/journalism_20/.

"Creative Destruction: An Exploratory Look at News on the Internet," Joan Shorenstein Center on the Press, Politics and Public Policy (August 2007), available: http://www.hks.harvard.edu/presspol/research/carnegie-knight/creative_destruction_2007.pdf.

Cecilia Friend and Jane B. Singer, *Online Journalism Ethics: Traditions and Transitions* (Boston: M.E. Sharpe, 2007).

Cecilia Friend, Don Challenger, and Katherine C. McAdams, *Contemporary Editing*, 2nd ed. (New York: McGraw Hill, 2005).

Jolene Galegher, Lee Sproull, and Sara Kiesler, "Legitimacy, Authority, and Community in Electronic Support Groups," *Written Communication*, 15, no. 4 (October 1998): 493.

Lee Gomes, "Why We're Powerless to Resist Grazing on Endless Web Data," *Wall Street Journal*, March 12, 2008: B1.

Rich Gordon, Beth Lawton, and Sally Clarke, *The Online Community Cookbook* (Arlington, VA: Newspaper Association of America, 2008).

Frederick Hertz, "Don't Let Your Case Get Lost in an E-Mail: Be Careful What You Say in an E-Mail, Because You Never Know For Sure How Far the Forwarding Process Might Take It," *New Jersey Law Journal* (September 2, 2002): 30.

Eric Hoffer, *The Ordeal of Change* (London: Hopewell Publications, 2006).

John B. Horrigan, "Seeding the Cloud: What Mobile Access Means for Usage Patterns and Online Content," Pew Internet & American Life Project (March 2008), available: http://www.pewinternet.org/Reports/2008/Seeding-The-Cloud-What-Mobile-Access-Means-for-Usage-Patterns-and-Online-Content.aspx.

Jeff Jarvis, "Argue with Me," *BuzzMachine* (November 2004), available: http://www.buzzmachine.com/archives/2004_11_11.html#008464.

Bill Kovach and Tom Rosenstiel, *The Elements of Journalism: What Newspeople Should Know and the Public Should Expect* (New York: Three Rivers Press, 2007).

"The Latest News Headlines—Your Vote Counts," Journalism.org (September 12, 2007), available: http://journalism.org/node/7493.

Charlene Li, *Social Technographics: Mapping Participation in Activities Forms the Foundation of a Social Strategy* (Cambridge, MA: Forrester Research, 2007).

Jenny Preece, *Online Communities: Designing Usability, Supporting Sociability* (New York: John Wiley, 2000).

Jay Rosen, "The People Formerly Known as the Audience," PressThink.org (June 27, 2006), available: http://journalism.nyu.edu/pubzone/weblogs/pressthink/2006/06/27/ppl_frmr.html.

9 WE THE PEOPLE
Part II: News as Conversation

I will provide the people of this city with a daily newspaper that will tell all the news honestly. I will also provide them with a fighting and tireless champion of their rights as citizens and human beings.
Charles Foster Kane II in the movie *Citizen Kane*

In any format, through any medium—isn't an understanding of the events of the day still a salable commodity?
David Simon, writer and executive producer
of HBO television series *The Wire*

Whether explaining or complaining, joking or serious, the human voice is unmistakably genuine. It can't be faked.
Doc Searls, *The Cluetrain Manifesto*

Chapter Objectives

After studying this chapter, you will be able to:

* analyze case studies to understand how news sites are engaging readers and seeking to include them in online communities;
* understand how online community is enabled and maintained;
* explain how the architecture of the Internet and Web sites affects the nature of community, communication and the sharing of content;
* discuss the potential of social networking for news.

Introduction

In addition to the participatory journalism model discussed in the last chapter, professional newsrooms are exploring many other ways to increase interactivity on their Web sites. This chapter will explore a wide range of these approaches that seek to move beyond merely presenting news to readers and toward engaging readers in a conversation. Some of these approaches to increasing interaction between news outlets and news users include allowing users to customize the site; opening up to users databases such as those for public spending or of restaurant and hotel reviews; providing extended coverage not possible or available in print or on air; and administrating bulletin boards and chat. *The Spokesman-Review* in Spokane, WA, for example, built a database for its BizFinderNW.com site, which offers any area business a listing with address, store hours, a map and a photo, all for free. Businesses wishing to add more or to determine placement can pay.

Methods like BizFinderNW.com are part of the transition from the one-way, journalist-centered monologues (or lectures) traditionally presented in newspapers to a more audience-centered conversation between news outlets and their readers, and among the readers themselves. This new conversational model of journalism seeks to serve by going beyond just presenting the news to engaging readers and building relationships with the communities they serve.

Pulling Back the Curtain

One example of this attempt to foster conversation and inclusiveness is a blog started up by the *Dallas Morning News*'s editorial writers. Called Edblog (http://www.dallasnews.com/sharedcontent/dws/blogs/opinion/), it aims to "allow [editorial] board members to share their evolving thoughts on a variety of issues, and to allow readers a window into our opinion-development process," according to the blog's introduction. In short, the newspaper is inviting the public into editorial meetings in an effort to make the paper's decision-making process more transparent.

An experiment that did not pan out was Michael Kinsley's "wikitorial" at the *Los Angeles Times*. The open, reader-written editorial allowed anyone with a computer to participate in online discussions with the newspaper and even "re-write" the *Times*'s editorials. The experiment lasted three days, after which the newspaper suspended the feature. Users flooded the site with foul language and pornographic photos, a perpetual problem for anonymous online forums.

Let's look briefly at two newspapers taking an aggressive approach to incorporating some of the social capacities of the Internet, the *News & Record* in Greensboro, North Carolina, and the *Lawrence Journal-World* in Lawrence, Kansas. The two newspapers' experiments testify to the range of possibilities for news organizations seeking to tap into the community-building taking place online.

Case Study 1: The *News & Record*

One of the more ambitious attempts to foster community and facilitate inter-activity with readership has been ongoing at the *News & Record*. One of the newspaper's editors, Lex Alexander, wrote that the newspaper hopes to better understand "how we can work on and with the Internet (i.e., with users of that medium) to expand the quantity and quality of the local news, information and dialogue we provide" (see http://journalism.nyu.edu/pubzone/weblogs/pressthink/2005/01/04/lex_report_p.html).

OPINION

EARN REWARDS FOR EXPRESSING YOURSELF

We want to hear from you.

How can we make the News & Record better? Listen to our readers, of course! We'd like to know what you think about our newspaper. Join our Internet-based reader's panel and share your valued opinions. It's fast and easy and you'll earn points toward rewards!

The *News & Record* solicits reader contributions in a number of ways, including this entry to its "reader's panel" program, which awards gift certificates for participation.

Out of that effort to promote dialogue, the paper launched several initiatives:

- More blog-style journalism done by its staff, which the paper has enabled though not financially incented.
- More participatory or open source journalism where readers or "affiliated" bloggers from the community become the knowledge engine and the agenda setters.
- A new and strikingly different Web philosophy for www.news-record.com, stressing open standards, transparency, interaction, dialogue and linking.

Among the proposals the newspaper has considered:

- Assigning local bloggers to cover in-depth topics the paper does not, like individual high school sports teams.
- Recruiting one blogger per neighborhood, like the Chi-Town effort described earlier.
- Enabling comments on all local news content.
- Re-launching "Letters to the Editor" as a blog, with each letter having its own permalink and comments.
- Doing obituaries as a searchable blog, ordered by page, with comments ("guest book") capability for each.
- Digitizing archives and making them available online, free.
- Linking to everyone—other local blog aggregators, other local media, even competitors.

- In news content, reversing policy from "don't link out" to "must link out" to resources anywhere on the Web that help users or make sense.
- Posting a permanent biography page for each full-time reporter and editor, with photo, contact information, background, political and religious affiliation.
- Opening up planning and editorial meetings to local bloggers who may blog about them.
- Posting, and inviting comment upon, the *News & Record* mission, vision and coverage priorities for the year.
- Starting "moblogs"—blogs to which people can submit text and/or images via email or wireless (mobile) phone.
- Creating an ad network to begin compensating bloggers who participate with the *News and Record* online.

Case Study 2: The *Lawrence Journal-World*

The *Lawrence Journal-World* in Kansas is another newspaper worth watching. Serving a city of 85,000, the newspaper is experimenting with personalized newspapers, allowing subscribers to tailor their own edition of the paper by choosing from a series of options. Providing hyperlocal coverage seems to be the common denominator in the newspaper's many ventures. Live chat, blogs, user-written restaurant reviews, chat rooms devoted to ongoing legal proceedings and access to reporters are some of the many ways users can connect. *Journal-World* blogs include "the Gay Kansan in China" and "the Born-Again Christian Blogger." One initiative even calls for every Little League player in town to be able to create his or her own personalized electronic trading card, complete with biography, photo, statistics and introductory audio clip.

Other steps the Lawrence paper has taken include routinely filing and posting Freedom of Information Act requests and public records; installing WiFi

The *Journal-World*'s mobile version.

spots throughout Lawrence; sending content to mobile phones; and publishing podcasts of local news.

Saving the Whale

The *News & Record* and the *Journal-World* are news organizations attempting to evolve, seeing themselves less as newspapers and more as information providers and community-builders and facilitators. As organizations adapting to a fast-changing media ecosystem, they suggest a metaphor. The newspaper industry is in some ways like a giant whale threatened with extinction. This whale historically has supported an entire ecosystem of plankton, smaller fish, and barnacles that depend on the beast for sustenance. Now the ecosystem is changing, and forcing the great whale to evolve, to change, to adapt. Whales don't do this very easily, willingly or quickly. Yet an entire ecosystem depends on this evolution's success. What should the whale become next? What new appearance or behaviors should it take on? No one knows for sure, but if it does not change, it will surely die.

Newspaper readership, circulation and market penetration numbers have been in decline since the 1960s (market penetration peaked in the 1920s). June 2008's announcement that McClatchy Newspapers, once the nation's most consistently profitable, would be cutting 1,400 jobs at its newspapers across the USA is just one in a string of such announcements. McClatchy-owned newspapers include *The Miami Herald*, *The Sacramento Bee*, the *Fort Worth Star-Telegram*, *The Kansas City Star*, *The Charlotte Observer*, and *The News & Observer* in Raleigh, NC. In the same month, the Tribune Co., owners of nine newspapers including the *Los Angeles Times* and the *Minneapolis Star-Tribune*, announced it would cut 500 newspaper pages per week across its holdings in response to falling advertising revenues.

The decline in newspaper readership is part of general shift away from push media (newspapers and broadcast) to online pull media (i.e. digg.com, RSS, twitter), according to a study from the Shorenstein Center on the Press,

CNN provides site visitors with a range of methods to share the news.

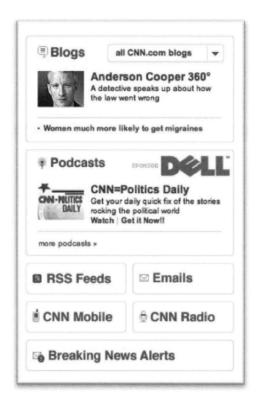

Politics & Public Policy (http://www.ksg.harvard.edu/presspol/carnegie_knight/creative_destruction_web.pdf). "Our evidence suggests that the Internet is redistributing the news audience in a way that is pressuring some traditional news organizations," according to the report. "Product substitution through the Web is particularly threatening to the print media, whose initial advantage as a 'first mover' has disappeared." Interestingly, the study also found that while traffic to many of the national "brand-name" newspapers is growing, the same is not true for the sites of local newspapers.

Part of the problem for traditional print newspapers transitioning to online publishing models is perhaps related to self-perception. What business are newspapers in, exactly? The newspaper business? Or, considering how dependent they are on their delivery trucks, the transportation business? In 1960, Theodore Levitt analyzed the railroads' then current economic problems in a *Harvard Business Review* entitled "Marketing Myopia." (Wikipedia has a robust entry on the article and its legacy, http://en.wikipedia.org/wiki/Marketing_myopia.) Levitt wrote that the railroads thought of themselves as being in the railroad business rather than the transportation business. The railroads thought they had a monopoly, but failed to see new competing forms of transportation collectively eating away at their core business, just as newspaper companies have seen, suffering a death of a thousand cuts.

Similarly, newspapers have faced new competition on every front. In classified advertising, sites such as Craigslist and Monster.com have eaten into revenue. Sites such as Google News and MyYahoo! have commoditized news to some extent, especially international news. Thousands of sites specializing in sports, weather and entertainment diminish the need for a printed newspaper each morning.

Phil Meyer explained in his book *The Vanishing Newspaper* (Columbia: University of Missouri Press, 2004) that newspaper publishers have essentially four choices for survival:

1 Think of another use for their product. Baking soda manufacturers, for example, faced extinction by marketing their product as an air or refrigerator freshener. Their product's main purpose—cleaning teeth— was usurped by toothpaste.

2 Write and edit for those who are still buying and reading the printed product, the elderly. (This obviously is not a good long-term strategy.) Jim Roberts, digital editor at *The New York Times*, told the blog Portfolio.com in May 2008 that the newspaper "is not going to be obsolete in print for a long time. So whatever it takes to keep breathing life into it, we're going to do. We are blessed, in a sense, because in Manhattan there are people who will not give up their papers. It's like the Charlton Heston quote—we'll have to pry it from their cold, dead fingers."

3 Enter the substitute (or encroaching) industry, which for newspapers is online news and digital information.

4 Or, as many corporate media companies are doing, harvest the business for whatever can be salvaged before the enterprise goes under. Raise prices. Reduce quality by laying off editorial staff. Take the money and run.

Evidence of the popularity of the fourth option is the 2,400 jobs lost by the newspaper industry through the first six months of 2008. The whale is dying, begging the question of whether it can evolve fast enough to survive. The stakes are incredibly high. As Bill Kovach and Tom Rosenstiel argued in their book *The Elements of Journalism* (2007), journalism is for democracy, for citizenship, for building community, for providing citizens with the information they need to be free and self-governing. If this whale dies, will the news media ecosystem be able to support itself or achieve these same goals?

Talking Back

The Internet has given the subjects of news coverage a voice, a fact that must inform news organizations' survival strategies. The people formerly known as the audience use their own blogs and Web sites to "correct" the record, add to coverage, deconstruct articles and coverage about them, and expose what they believe are biases. As journalism professor Jay Rosen noted, citizen journalism has moved the interview to the midpoint between source and media. "You produce things from it, and we do, too," he said. No longer are sources merely sources. "It has forced greater transparency on the part of mainstream media in how they do what they do" (quoted in Seelye 2006: C3).

To illustrate this new element of the news media landscape, consider an ABC News Nightline package that aired during summer 2005 on the Discovery Institute, a conservative organization that advocates a theory of the world's origins as a product of intelligent design. In response to the coverage, which focused on the marketing of intelligent design, the Institute published the next day the entire transcript of the hour-long interview, only excerpts of which had appeared on Nightline (ABC News has since posted the entire transcript, as well).

Here is what is interesting: The Institute did not accuse ABC News of error. It asked readers to examine the transcript and Nightline's questions, believing that they revealed a "predictable tone" of skepticism and critique. "Here's your chance to go behind the scenes with the gatekeepers of national media to see how they screen out viewpoints and information that don't fit their stereotypes," wrote an Institute spokesman on the site.

In May 2008, the White House balked at how NBC News edited an interview with President George W. Bush, demanding that the network broadcast Bush's answers to some of the questions "in full." White House counsel Ed Gillespie called NBC's editing "deceitful . . . misleading and irresponsible," according to the *Wall Street Journal* (quoted in UPI 2008). In what has become routine practice for news media, the full interview was posted after the television broadcast, but before Gillespie's criticisms, which elicited this response from NBC News's president, Steve Capus: "Editing is a part of journalism. We take the collective body of information surrounding a story, distill it and produce a report. We strive in all cases to be fair and accurate. In some instances, where appropriate, we offer interviews in their entirety— in live broadcasts, or posted on our website" (quoted in Stelter 2008).

The increasingly networked media ecosystem is proving resistant to editing and filtering, seeing in that process an incompleteness and bias. News media have responded by providing the raw materials for their reporting on their Web sites, a practice modeled first by bloggers. Craig Crawford, a columnist for *Congressional Quarterly*, told *The New York Times*, "We've pretended to be priests turning water into wine, like it's a secret process. Those days are gone" (quoted in Seelye 2006: C3).

"Print is Dead"

To quote Harold Ramis's character in the film *Ghostbusters*, "Print is dead." In *BusinessWeek* magazine in July 2007, media critic Jon Fine asked the related question, "When do you stop the presses?" When should a print newspaper, facing the worst fiscal years for the industry since the depression, consider moving all of its operations online? The logical candidate for Fine: the *San Francisco Chronicle*, a newspaper with a strong Web presence already, a Web-savvy readership and private ownership. The question for the *Chronicle*, as for all newspapers, is how to replace enough of the revenue streams that have long supported print fast enough to continue to fund news and editorial operations, and do it while facing new competition on every front. Fine put the *Chronicle*'s subscription revenue conservatively at $24 million, which would be difficult to walk away from, not to mention the suddenly useless assets such as a truck fleet and printing press.

In April 2008, *The Capital Times*, Madison, Wisconsin's 90-year-old daily newspaper, stopped printing to devote itself to publishing a daily report on the Web. Though the company still produces two print products, a free weekly entertainment guide inserted in Madison's remaining daily newspaper, the *Wisconsin State Journal*, and a news weekly that is distributed with the daily, the company is staking its future on online. In recent years, the newspaper's circulation dropped to about 18,000 from a high in the 1960s of more than 40,000, according to *The New York Times*.

"We felt our audience was shrinking so that we were not relevant," Clayton Frink, the Madison paper's publisher told the newspaper. "We are going a little farther, a little faster, but the general trend is happening everywhere" (quoted in *The Cleveland Leader*, April 2008).

Newspapers could perhaps learn from the world's largest publisher of technology newspapers and magazines, International Data Group. Publisher of 300 or so periodicals, including *Computerworld*, *PC World* and *Macworld*, the company began generating most of its revenue from online beginning in 2008 after several years of trial and error, experimentation and migration from print to digital. This print-to-online migration has been profitable for IDG

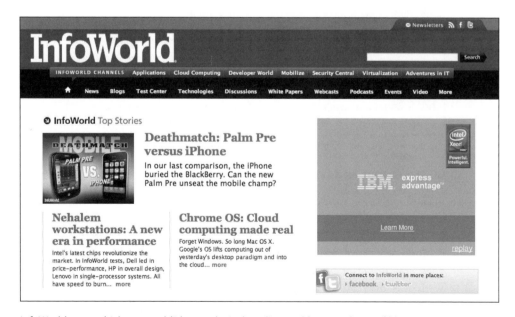

InfoWorld.com, which now publishes exclusively online and boasts a bevy of bloggers.

and precious few others, at least so far. Compare the 52–48 percent ratio, online to print, in advertising revenues for IDG in 2008 to the 86–14 percent ratio the other way just six years prior, in 2002.

IDG was brave enough, prescient enough, to move its flagship publication, *InfoWorld*, completely online in April 2007, a switch that generated an operating profit margin in its first year of 37 percent, according to the company. The year prior to the switch, the magazine was losing 3 percent per month, according to *The New York Times*. InfoWorld.com is the biggest of 450 IDG Web sites, one that emphasizes much shorter articles than its print predecessor; a multiplicity of media, including video and animation, podcasts and webcasts, blogs and even online petitions; and a great deal of packaging of information into "digestible chunks," its editor, Eric Knorr, told the *Times* (Lohr 2008).

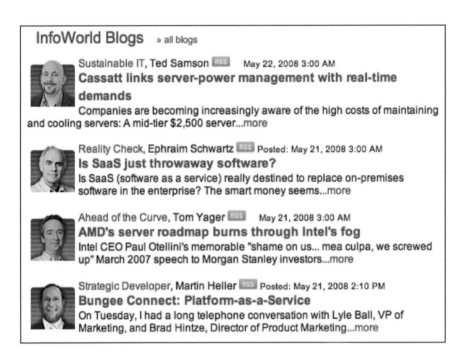

Collaboration and Cooperation

Because news is turning into more of a collaboration, much more of an interactive process, the reader has more of a say in determining or at least selecting the big issues of the day. Such a collaborative, distributive ecosystem is inherently more democratic, but that does not necessarily make the more open system better for democracy or for a democratic form of government. With less powerful watchdogs, with poorer watchdogs less able to fund investigative journalism, which is expensive (talk shows, by contrast, are very, very inexpensive), government is increasingly able to creep yet more into the shadows, offering but one example of the new dangers implicit in a more commercial, more recreational news media ecosystem.

Clearly this changing ecosystem is increasingly enabling and rewarding participation by individuals. Through the creation and exchange of social capital through social networking and crowd-sourced journalism, blogs and other forms of personal publishing are encouraging and rewarding participation. (Briefly, "social capital" is the value created in and through social networks as people seek to achieve mutual goals, and it is a theory about the reciprocal relationships we create in social networks.) These venues are collectively showing that the ethos of this new ecosystem is one based on values such as inclusiveness and community, participation and deliberation, and free and unfiltered expression. Because it is communal and not hierarchical, this ecosystem is pitted in philosophical and strategic opposition to many traditional news media, which historically have had and are fighting to protect control. There is room in traditional news media's tent for the ethos communicated and valued by these emergent media, and many news organizations, like IDG, have figured this out.

Case Study 3: The BBC

Perhaps no news organization in the world has been more aggressive in exploring and exploiting digital media than the BBC (the British Broadcasting Corporation, or the "Beeb"), a government-subsidized company. For example, the BBC has had a presence on the mobile Internet since 1999, adding color and images to its mobile content in 2003. As new devices have emerged and audiences have grown, the BBC has switched from a lowest-common-denominator approach to one that aims to provide the richest possible experience based on the capabilities that handheld and phone users have.

The BBC in 2008 began allowing visitors to customize the BBC home page, re-orienting placements and excluding categories of information supplied by BBC television, radio and online. This is a signal of the BBC's awareness of changes in the ecosystem, moving away from the silos of radio, broadcast TV and print and toward purposeful digital delivery of all forms of content. With growth in British households of broadband, the site has in fact emphasized audio-visual content and developed proprietary video player software to make it easier to access video content.

Taking a cue from YouTube, in 2006 the BBC transferred 300,000 hours of archives, or 25 percent of its inventory, online. And like U.S. networks, the Beeb has begun making full programs available online just after airing on television. To enable this, the BBC offers its visitors the iPlayer, which is used to watch television or listen to radio programming from the past seven days, and has partnered with YouTube to distribute video content.

The partnership with YouTube is just part of a strategy to make the BBC more of an online community. Users can use the BBC, for example to set up blogs, to contribute to databases and reporting projects, and to share files,

The BBC's citizen journalism portal for the 2008 Olympics.

The BBC's home page in 2008, which gave users more control over how the page renders and where news is placed.

Video site Hulu.com launched in March 2007.

including home videos. This blended distribution strategy of using various platforms to deliver content is at the heart of the BBC's approach to digital. As another example, the BBC joined with ITV and Channel 4 to develop an online, on-demand service called Kangaroo, much like Hulu.com, which is a joint venture of NBC Universal and News Corp designed to compete with YouTube.

Socially Networking the News

The popularity of Facebook has spurred many news organizations to develop social networking strategies and ways of leveraging social networking behavior to deliver the news (and the advertising that funds its production). In 2008, social networks became must-have partners for news organizations eager to maximize or grow the distribution of their content online. For many of these organizations, including ABC News, *The New York Times*, *USA Today* and the BBC, it has meant moving away from simply using their own branded portals to adopting a broader approach to content distribution.

ABC News began collaborating with Facebook in late 2007 to reach the millions of mostly college-age social networkers on the online platform. Facebook members can use the site to follow ABC reporters, view video and participate in polls and debates. Facebookers can also send private messages to reporters or post them on the reporters' public Facebook pages. For ABC News,

Facebook created a "U.S. Politics" category and co-sponsored with ABC News a round of presidential debates in New Hampshire to bring attention to the collaborative effort.

ABC's move likely is harbinger of many marriages as the need for content meets an equally compelling need for distribution of content. *The New York Times* and *The Washington Post* have produced pages on Facebook, and some newspapers, magazines and television stations have invited users to join special pages that are set up to follow reporters' political coverage.

Some big social networking sites are looking to produce their own content, as well. In 2008, News Corp's MySpace began co-producing "webisodes," or entertainment specifically for online viewing. Another social networking hub, Bebo, unveiled in 2007 its Open Media initiative, which offers content owners distribution and ad revenues generated around the content in exchange for hosting on Bebo. More than 60 organizations, including the BBC and MTV, signed up to participate, each hoping to reach the social networking site's 40 million 15- to 23-year-olds, an attractive demographic for advertisers.

Not long ago, traditional media believed they could co-opt digital with traditional command and control tactics. The new time-shifted, on-demand,

Yahoo's Buzz, which asks readers to rank the news and order the page, much like digg.

CNN iReport's Second Life blog.

Web 2.0 media world punishes attempts to control, however, rewarding instead the ceding of control and a liberal approach to content distribution. Thomson Reuters has recognized this. In addition to putting a reporter full time into the online virtual environment Second Life, the company welcomes crowd-sourced reporting, video, photography and blogs.

There does seem to be an awakening on the part of newspapers that their status as destination Web sites is diminishing and that the news they produce has to be mobile, fed, shared and sent in myriad ways as people customize

Thomson Reuters's Second Life "News Center."

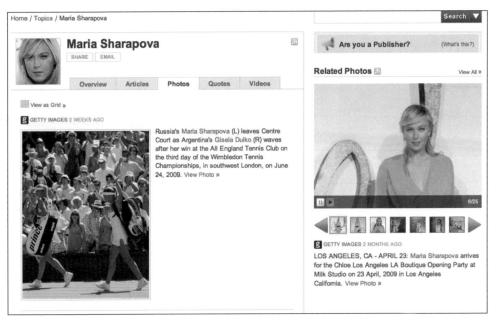

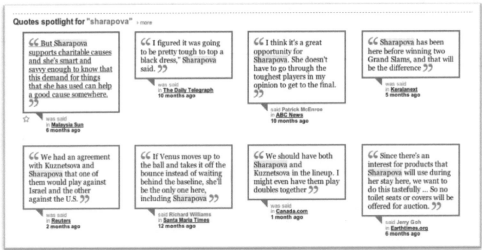

A search on Daylife for coverage of tennis player Maria Sharapova turned up a bank of news coverage, images from her loss at Wimbledon and quotes from news coverage.

their Web experiences and cherry-pick what they want to see and read. The Web's news economy, in other words, is becoming increasingly driven by the link.

An example of the link-driven economy is a relatively new news aggregation model called Daylife. Competing against Newser and Inform, among others, Daylife provides subject-specific news feeds to clients' sites that enable those sites to present content-rich home pages and always-refreshing rosters of news, photos and blog posts. Daylife charges between $10,000 and

$18,000 per month to clients such as *The Huffington Post*, *USA Today* and the *Daily Telegraph* in London to power news to those sites. The Daylife platform gathers news from thousands of news sites, wire and image services, and blogs worldwide, then classifies and indexes the content, which is organized around hubs or subject areas.

Case Study 4: Gannett

The publisher of *USA Today* and 90 other U.S. newspapers, Gannett began crowd-sourcing many of its newsgathering functions in late 2006 and has expanded those efforts since. In 2006 the company re-named its newsrooms "information centers" in an organizational structure oriented around digital delivery. This digital-centric model replaced a structure organized by section (metro, state, sports departments) and emphasized user-generated content and crowd-sourced methods of investigative or watchdog journalism. Also important is the new model's acceptance of a 24/7 news cycle rather than the increasingly anachronistic daily news cycle to which many newspapers still cling.

One of Gannett's earliest crowd-sourcing successes came in Fort Myers, Fla., where the *News-Press* partnered with readers to look into the suspiciously high prices charged to connect new homes to water and sewerage lines. Readers partnered with a team of reporters and editors to blow the whistle on government, to examine complaints and to put together the data that informed the reporting. The reader response overwhelmed the newspaper. According to *Wired* magazine, "retired engineers analyzed blueprints, accountants pored over balance sheets, and an inside whistle-blower leaked documents showing evidence of bid-rigging" (Howe 2006).

A useful metaphor here, perhaps, is ant behavior. Put some sugar on the kitchen counter, then watch ants find and share it by networking. A big part of crowd-sourcing is finding ways to put the sugar on the counter. Research conducted at the University of Southern California has found that new and richly interpretable information triggers a chemical reaction that makes people feel good, a feeling that in turn causes people to seek out more. The corollary or inverse of this finding: People are averse to boredom.

The collaboration at the *News-Press* boosted traffic to the newspaper's Web site and ultimately resulted in the city reducing utility fees by more than 30 percent. Gannett is rolling out a similar crowd-sourcing approach in many of its newsrooms, including those at newspapers in Indianapolis, Cincinnati and Burlington, Vermont.

Case Study 5: *The Atlanta Journal-Constitution (AJC)*

Another newspaper reorganization at the *AJC* in early 2007 cost 80 employees their jobs and pulled the newspaper out of circulation in parts of South Carolina, Alabama and Florida. An interesting quote from the internal memo distributed to employees read,

Online, we will show that we know Atlanta best, providing superlative news and information and becoming the preferred medium for connecting local communities. In print, we will really listen to our core readers and create a newspaper that offers distinct and valuable content.

The concentration on "core" means a return or reinforcement of a commitment to local and hyperlocal news coverage. The strategy of using online to reach everyone and print to reach the geographically local makes sense. Beyond Atlanta, much of the print newspaper is not relevant or useful, but online, the *AJC* site still would have much to offer. Online visitors can pick and choose.

The reorganization created four main divisions, including two content areas—news and information, and enterprise—and aligned with two distribution channels—digital and print. The *AJC* created a stand-alone division for digital on equal footing with everything else, a division charged to seek to grow "interactivity and social networking." This new structure centers on digital delivery, as Gannett's does, and moves away from the print model while retaining allegiance to original reporting and enterprise journalism. One of the *AJC*'s first social networking ventures is a platform for mothers in the Atlanta area, a model based on the success of IndyMoms.com (http://www. indymoms.com/), a site in Indianapolis that has been a huge financial success story for its owner, the Indianapolis Star Media Group. More than 180,000 women connect using IndyMoms.

IndyMoms.com is both an information resource and a "place" where "moms can connect, ask questions, share advice and discuss the topics that are relevant to their lives as moms and as women," according to the Web site's FAQ list. The network combines an energetic design, intuitive navigation, stringent privacy settings and a multiplicity of ways to connect and share content, and the *Indianapolis Star* also publishes a monthly print edition of *IndyMoms* focused on mom-to-mom communication.

Web 2.0

Media companies are picking up on the fact that the Internet connects more than computers; it connects the people who are using those computers (and all sorts of other networked devices from mobile phones to video game consoles). Web 2.0—the term for this increasingly social form of the Internet—is more than just a communication technology phenomenon, it is a thoroughly human activity. We are social beings, perpetually trying to connect. The Internet might be the best connector yet. The earlier references to corporations turning to social networking signal the rush to capitalize on the ways people are connecting online.

Big business is taking notice, as well. Serena Software of San Mateo, Calif., introduced to its 800 employees in November 2007 "Facebook Fridays," or one day a week on which employees are encouraged "to find fun and personal connections in the workplace." Each Friday, Serena Software employees are granted one hour of personal time to spend on their Facebook profiles and connect with co-workers, customers, family and friends. Serena President and Chief Executive Jeremy Burton describes himself as an avid user of Facebook, turning to it to keep in touch with employees, friends and business partners. He said he wanted "to bring the benefits he gains from using Facebook to his company, and allow employees to have more fun combining their personal and professional lives." This corporate embrace of Facebook had the effect of turning the social network into a sort of de facto corporate intranet.

Fostering Online Community

Because people have different desires in terms of levels of interactivity, the more options there are for participation, the better chance the site has to create and sustain community-building. These options include, on the low end, allowing readers to email and interact with reporters, an option that requires buy-in among reporters; rating and recommending; voting in polls and surveys; and, on the high end, blogging or contributing to a wiki.

Offering a multiplicity of options for interactivity will only become more important. A 2008 report from Forrester Research, indicates that 52 percent of online adults are "inactives," meaning that they do not interact with news sites. However, "inactives" make up only 17 percent of the 18–21 age range, as compared to 70 percent of those 62 and older. The young are the most likely

Bring together your photos and video.
Create muvees with your friends and family.

Share privately
All albums are by invitation only. Share privately with your friends and family without having to worry about where your photos and video end up.

Simple to use
Invited guests don't need to sign up to view your albums. Contributing to the album is as easy as replying to the invite with their photos or video attached.

Make a muvee
Create fun home movies that we call muvees! You choose the content, pick a style, your choice of music, and with the click of a button, shwup will make you a muvee!

The Shwup photo-sharing site, a competitor to Flickr.

to interact, in other words, and Facebook demonstrates this perhaps better than any other digital artifact.

The time being spent with Facebook is of tremendous significance. The average reader of a print newspaper spends more than seven hours per month with the paper, according to Northwestern University's Readership Institute, while the average user of a newspaper Web site spends only 43 minutes per month on the site. Sites and networks like Facebook are capitalizing on interpersonal conversation, which appears to drive usage and cultivate loyalty much better than having good things to read. Interactivity and social connectivity are proving more important than passively receiving content, in other words.

Types of Internet-enabled Interpersonal Communication

The communication methods enabled by the Internet are defined as much by their technical infrastructure as they are by their purpose. They each depend on supporting software developed specifically for the application or type of communication. A listserv, for example, delivers email messages to subscribers, but it requires specific software to facilitate this. Bulletin boards, however, ask users to have threaded discussions. Email is one-to-one, typically, whereas listserv-delivered mail is one-to-many.

Email

Email offers several technical advantages, such as fast transmission, asynchronous communication and automated archiving. It has weaknesses, too, such as a susceptibility to abuse, most notably spam and computer viruses. Email also is not considered very nuanced, a limitation acknowledged by the widespread use of emoticons to compensate for the lack of body language and facial expression.

The desktop metaphor for email is the United States Postal Service, or snail mail. Think of the AOL "You've Got Mail" campaign. Email's ingredients, symbolically, include a message (letter) delivered to an address in an envelope via a carrier that figures out how to get it from here to there. We lack a vocabulary to discuss and describe new technologies, so we use analogies of ordered and familiar relationships. In this case the metaphor belies radical, comprehensive differences in the nature of email communication and postal mail. For example, email messages—and any of their attachments—are broken down into small chunks of data called *packets*, which travel independently, weaving their way along with innumerable other packets traveling to different server destinations. It is as if each page of a letter was mailed separately. On the way, the packets are passed from one server to the next until they reach their final destination. Any given message's packets and attached file(s) may travel by several different routes, so the components often arrive out of order and at different times. Once all the packets have arrived, they are recombined into their original form.

Packet-switching makes sending the message faster because it does not require transmitting one large, bandwidth-hogging piece of data. But an entire message can be held up if one piece is missing. Usually, the entire process takes only seconds to complete, so email's advantages include (usually) fast transmission.

As a networked medium, email eliminates transmission delays imposed by geographical distance. In addition, because email is asynchronous, it does not require scheduled "meetings." The sender and receiver can interact with a message autonomously. Because email is transmitted in a digital medium, it can be manipulated by computer-based tools and applications available on the "desktop," including file management tools. Email is paperless and automatically archived. If not free, it typically is inexpensive relative to other one-to-one or one-to-many communication methods.

Email has definite social implications, as well, though there is no agreement on what they are. In the absence of interpersonal communication cues such as gestures, intonation and eye movement, email communication is more easily misinterpreted than might have been predicted in the 1970s when it emerged. This phenomenon added a new term to our vocabulary—**flaming**, which refers to email that either is or is perceived to be insulting.

Email can remove social distance as well as geographical distance. Email can support and sustain communities of interest, and it can be a tool in organizational politics. There also is evidence that email communication can both contribute to and ameliorate users' feelings of isolation. Email can lead to communication slavery, however. And one normally can't ignore email as one ignores the telephone.

The convenience of email encourages abuse at the interpersonal level. It can easily circumvent established organizational information routes, and there is no cost to the sender associated with transmission. Multiply this by a factor of 1,000 and the result is **spam**. Alias and distribution lists make email bombing and spamming inevitable. Like telephony, the advantages of email are most evident as point-to-point communication; and like hard-copy junk mail, the disadvantages of email are most evident when it is broadcast.

The consequences of sending the wrong email or attaching the wrong document can be devastating. Using the wrong address, accidentally replying to all senders or forwarding an email to the wrong person are other examples of the bad things that can happen. Most of us have participated in one or more of these scenarios, either as a receiver or as a sender.

UseNet News and Newsgroups

UseNet was pioneered at the University of North Carolina and at Duke University in the late 1970s and early 1980s to facilitate the formation of hundreds of thousands of newsgroups. Someone with an overwhelming passion for rose gardening could use UseNet to find other rose gardeners with whom to swap tips, to use one example. These connections predicted in some ways the social networking trends more than two decades away.

A **newsgroup** is a publicly posted discussion forum, a kind of electronic clubhouse for people with shared interests. The messages are organized in lists, or *threads*, that show the original message, the responses to the message and the responses to the responses so that a person can follow an entire conversation or just the parts in which he or she is interested.

A browser alone will not let a person get to newsgroups, but reading and posting messages can be done using either stand-alone news reader software, such as Forté's Free Agent, or a news reader that is a separate part of a Web browser package.

A news reader allows a subscriber to check newsgroups the way a browser enables surfing among Web sites. UseNet is the world's largest collection of public newsgroups, which go by a complex set of abbreviated names. The first set of letters of a newsgroup's name indicates its primary subject, such as *rec* (recreation), *soc* (society) or *comp* (computers). Additional abbreviations are separated by periods and tacked on to indicate subtopics. It is not uncommon for an individual newsgroup to have five or more elements in its name. For example, microsoft.public.inetexplorer.ie.setup is a newsgroup devoted to people who, presumably, use or work on Internet Explorer.

After acquiring UseNet, Google integrated the past 20 years of UseNet archives into its own Google Groups, which offer access to more than 700 million messages dating back to 1981. This is by far the most complete collection of UseNet articles assembled, and it is a fascinating, first-hand historical account of the growth of the Internet. The messages in newsgroups are stored on news servers owned by Internet Service Providers, universities, companies and other large entities all over the world. Most news servers keep only the more recent posts or they would soon run out of storage space.

Bulletin Boards

Another metaphor—the bulletin board, or the **electronic message board**. The messages on most of these boards are available for everyone to see. Unlike on listservs, users have to go to a bulletin board to get messages. They are not mailed or transmitted to individuals. Many are embedded within Web sites, giving them context and defining their purpose. Many also are moderated, which helps to facilitate discussion and to maintain civility. Most bulletin boards present messages in chronological order of receipt. Some have threading capabilities, meaning replies are positioned or threaded with the message to which they relate. Because bulletin boards are asynchronous, participants have time to think as they compose their messages.

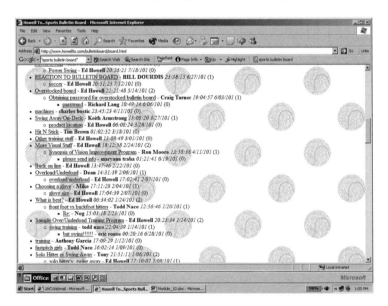

A bulletin board for baseball aficionados focuses on how-to information. The threaded discussions begin with a top line posting, then threaded replies are indented in a stair-step fashion. Also included are usernames, post dates and post times. The messages on this board are presented in chronological order, which is typical of most bulletin boards.

Chat

Online chat is similar to **telephone conversation**—another analogy—except it uses text. Users type messages that appear letter by letter, word by word on the screen in real time. There are millions of chat groups and instant message conversations, and they are searched using Web browsers and search engines. Many require "chatters" to register. The Internet Relay Chat network is one of the oldest. Some chat "rooms" are hosted like call-in telephone discussions, with experts available to answer questions. Some are scheduled while others, more like a conversation in a café, are ongoing and loosely organized. Different chat rooms are devoted to different discussions or conversations. As with email, *emoticons* are used to connote different emotions, like happiness :-> or sadness :-(. Expressing emotions in emoticons helps mitigate the problem of not being able to see body language. AOL's popular Instant Messenger service operates in similar fashion.

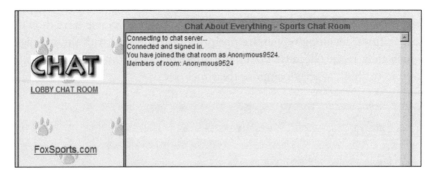

A typical chat environment uses a main screen that displays the identification names of those participating. In this case, the "chat-er" is all alone, waiting for someone with whom to chat.

Chat rooms or chat groups can be very large, with membership in the thousands or tens of thousands. Participants can be anywhere as long as they have access to a computer linked to the Internet, and they can communicate with other group members whenever they wish. Their communication occurs asynchronously, across time and place among people who are unlikely to have met one another face to face. Group discussion in electronic support groups is visible to any computer user who cares to read the posted messages. Readers, or lurkers, can participate without revealing anything about themselves, sometimes including their presence.

For writers, or posters, these chat rooms offer a venue for presenting ideas, thoughts and feelings apart from their physical selves. By using nicknames and anonymous re-mailers, they can participate without making their true identities known. The large size and non-local geography of electronic support groups, as well as the invisibility of readers and comparative anonymity of writers in these groups, imply several important features. Electronic groups offer the possibility of encountering people of any age or social category, learning about many different perspectives on a given problem and finding people with similar problems.

Moderating Community Forums

One of the nagging questions facing newspaper sites that offer discussion and other forms of online community is how to invite and enable the very highest levels of participation but at the same time limit the pollution, personal attacks and unhelpful comment. How can moderators enforce "civility," in other words, while keeping discussants on topic *and* avoiding censorship? As a rule, the easier it is to participate, the more monitoring that will be required. Topix.com, for example, allows anyone to post without registering, allowing anonymous posts, therefore. The result, not surprisingly, is a relatively high number of posts that include objectionable content.

AOL's Instant Messenger service sign-in.

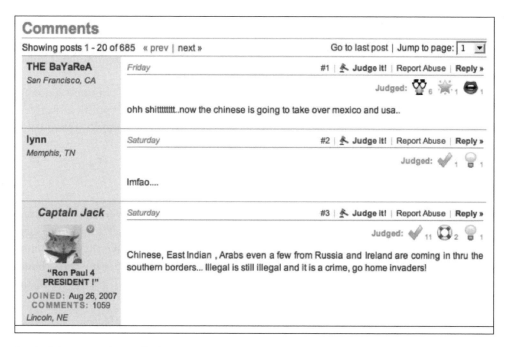

A colorful conversation at Topix.com.

In addition to prominently publishing and enforcing use policies and inviting users to help police the rhetoric, there are several things community moderators can do to build the community and counter attempts to undermine it. These steps include:

- Welcoming new users and helping to orient them.
- Enabling user profiles so that people can be identified and get to know one another.
- Being transparent. When a moderator edits or removes something, all users should be notified.
- Stepping in when there is trouble. Being scared to stop a thread out of fear of being called a "censor" will likely hurt more than it can help. Online spats and inappropriate threads can quickly escalate. If a moderator sees trouble brewing, he or she should warn the users and closely monitor the thread.
- Doing more. Moderators should not simply moderate. If community members know the moderator only as an editor or censor, they will naturally become antagonistic. Participate in discussions simply to interact with users. A moderator should always identify him- or herself, of course, but by participating the moderator is demonstrating that he or she is not there to simply be the "bad guy." Similarly, the moderator can highlight, reinforce and reward the desired kind and level of participation. Celebrate good contributions.
- Including email address and phone number with all communications to invite and encourage feedback and to communicate accessibility.
- Demonstrating a thick skin. People will criticize, complain and provoke. If the moderator is a good sport, the attitude can prevent ill will and running feuds. People can be emotional when posting online. Humor can often diffuse the situation.
- Anticipating problems. Realize that some topics will routinely generate hostility, topics such as sports, social issues and politics. Actively patrolling these threads or discussion areas can help moderators quickly respond to objectionable content.

Summary

In *The Beautiful Cigar Girl*, author Daniel Stashower delivers a non-fictional account of a murder in New York City in 1841 popularized a few years later by Edgar Allan Poe. The murder of a beautiful cigar girl gave the city's penny presses a carnival of twists and turns, suspects, clues and police mistakes. James Gordon Bennett, editor of the *New York Herald* and called the father of the penny press, claimed his newspaper would

> outstrip everything in the conception of man . . . What is to prevent a daily newspaper from being made the greatest organ of social life? Books have

had their day. The theaters have had their day. The temple of religion has had its day. A newspaper can be made to take the lead of all of these in the great movement of human thought.

(Stashower 2006: 111)

Books, theater, religion and newspapers all have at least one thing in common: A lack of interaction/feedback, at least on a grand scale, by and from their readers, who are largely passive. They read, watch, listen and believe. The Internet, citizen journalism and blogging each have the potential to fill these participatory voids, allowing for more active participation. This means very new and evolving roles for newspapers, which have been explored in this chapter. Publishers will have to tailor increasingly specific content for self-defining specific audiences, producing a narrowcasting model (as opposed to broadcasting). Newspaper presses and the massive rolls of newsprint that feed them are fast becoming as quaint as steam engines and whale oil.

One online writing student likened the new role for old news media as overseers of a power grid.

> I see news-gathering becoming less centralized, as in so many facets of our society. Electric utilities now talk about a 'distributed' generation, which means solar modules on individual rooftops, all feeding the grid. The gazillion bloggers already out there and the growing use of personal electronics that turn everybody into a reporter, which we witnessed again in [terrorist attacks on hotels in] Mumbai [in November 2008], shows a parallel trend in journalism.

The student's power grid analogy recognizes that technology has enabled anyone to commit random acts of journalism. But filters will still be needed. Someone will have to organize and oversee the grid. Professionals likely will continue to serve as this journalistic grid's caretakers and overseers, providing a conduit through which news flows from a universe of sources. Hopefully, readers will continue to demand good prose, thorough reporting and vetting that only trained and experienced writers and editors provide.

Chapter Assignment

1 Report, source, write, edit and post one news story on any topic. The article must have or rely upon at least three human sources. The more timely, the better, and the story should demonstrate impact or consequence. Keep it simple, and very short stories are fine. Beware, however, of **conflicts of interest**. This means avoiding friends, family members and business associates as sources, and stories that could materially affect those companies and entities with which you are affiliated.

Post with the story the **questions you asked** your sources, a list of the **facts you checked** and verified, and a list of the **sources you attempted to contact** (not merely those you were able to include in your story). Also identify your intended audience(s).

As you are completing this assignment, think about **what might be added** to your main story for publication online, including multimedia and interactive features. Because online you would have all the space you would need, consider the range of added features that could be developed, including fact boxes, an FAQ list, a podcast or video extra, interview notes and transcripts, maps, charts, a glossary, slideshow, animated graphic, poll, related stories and opinion, and perhaps an area where readers can contribute reactions, story ideas, photos and comments. No need to do any of these things, but consider what might make a strong story package online.

For non-journalists, if you need guidance getting started, Poynter offers a good source through its "NewsU." Look for "Hot Courses" on left panel, http://www.newsu.org.

The five basic journalism questions:

> WHO is involved in what you're covering?
> WHAT are they doing—and accomplishing?
> WHERE are they doing it?
> WHY are they doing it in the first place?
> HOW do they make it happen?

Warning: Do not wait to get started. Procrastination results in sloppy, harried work, and you might have difficulty reaching your sources. Build in time for callbacks, for failure to reach people. Sources are best reached early in the morning and just after 5 p.m., or after most people are gone and the phones are relatively quiet.

Online Resources

"Best Practices for Newspaper Journalists"
http://www.freedomforum.org/publications/diversity/bestpractices/
bestpractices.pdf
Written by Bob Haiman and published by the Freedom Forum, this .pdf download was developed to help journalists achieve fairness in their reporting.

"Poynter Guide to Accuracy"
http://www.poynter.org/content/content_view.asp?id=36518
A collection of articles by Poynter writers to help journalists in the area of accuracy, including helps in fact-checking, grammar and punctuation, and quotations and attribution.

"Principles of Citizen Journalism"
http://www.kcnn.org/principles/
Published by the Knight Citizen News Network, this guide provides the basic principles and covers the fundamental values of good journalism.

Sources

Hal Berghel, "E-mail—the Good, the Bad, and the Ugly," *Communications of the ACM*, 40, no. 4 (April 1997): 11–16.

"Creative Destruction: An Exploratory Look at News on the Internet," Joan Shorenstein Center on the Press, Politics and Public Policy (August 2007), available: http://www.hks.harvard.edu/presspol/research/carnegie-knight/creative_destruction_2007.pdf.

"Daily Newspaper Shuts Down Print Operations," *The Cleveland Leader*, April 2008, available: http://www.clevelandleader.com/node/5423.

Jolene Galegher, Lee Sproull, and Sara Kiesler, "Legitimacy, Authority, and Community in Electronic Support Groups," *Written Communication*, 15, no. 4 (October 1998): 493.

Rich Gordon, Beth Lawton, and Sally Clarke, *The Online Community Cookbook* (Arlington, VA: Newspaper Association of America, 2008).

Frederick Hertz , "Don't Let Your Case Get Lost in an E-Mail: Be Careful What You Say in an E-Mail, Because You Never Know For Sure How Far the Forwarding Process Might Take It," *New Jersey Law Journal* (September 2, 2002): 30.

Jeff Howe, "Gannett to Crowdsource the News," *Wired*, November 3, 2006, available: http://www.wired.com/software/webservices/news/2006/11/72067.

Bill Kovach and Tom Rosenstiel, *The Elements of Journalism: What Newspeople Should Know and the Public Should Expect* (New York: Three Rivers Press, 2007).

Charlene Li, *Social Technographics: Mapping Participation in Activities Forms the Foundation of a Social Strategy* (Cambridge, MA: Forrester Research, 2007).

Steve Lohr, "Publisher Tested the Waters, Then Dove In," *New York Times*, May 5, 2008, available: http://www.nytimes.com/2008/05/05/business/media/05idg.html.

Jenny Preece, *Online Communities: Designing Usability, Supporting Sociability* (New York: John Wiley, 2000).

Katherine Q. Seelye, "Take That, Mr. Newsman! Answering Back to the News Media," *New York Times*, January 2, 2006: C3.

Daniel Stashower, *The Beautiful Cigar Girl: Mary Rogers, Edgar Allan Poe and The Invention of Murder* (New York: Penguin Books, 2006).

Brian Stelter, "The Caucus: White House v. NBC," *New York Times*, May 20, 2008, available: http://query.nytimes.com/gst/fullpage.html?res=9800E4DF123BF933A15756C0A96E9C8B63.

United Press International, "White House: NBC News 'deceitful,'" May 19, 2008, available: http://www.upi.com/Top_News/2008/05/19/White-House-NBC-News-deceitful/UPI-72651211242712/.

10 GETTING DOWN TO BUSINESS

Intranets, Extranets, Portals

For a company with 10,000 employees, the cost [in lost productivity] of a single poorly written headline on an intranet home page is almost $5,000.

Jakob Nielsen, Web design expert

When the Web came along, lots of companies just took their existing applications, spent a few million dollars to create a Web user interface, and— presto!—they had an intranet.

Oliver Muoto, portal developer

Chapter Objectives

After studying this chapter, you will be able to:

- determine the appropriate writing styles for online business communication;
- identify trends in intra-organization communication via the Internet;
- understand how intranets, extranets and portals function, and how they are different.

Introduction

Intranets, extranets and portals are among the most important online information spaces in business today, particularly for U.S. companies. Each has its strengths and weaknesses, and together all three are part of an evolution in online business communication that began quite innocently with email. The goal of this chapter is to help students understand these unique business communication arenas. While many of the general online writing skills discussed in this book will apply to these spaces as well, this chapter will also introduce some of the special writing requirements that intranets, extranets and portals demand.

Intranets

An intranet is a private or internal, Internet-enabled network. Intranets are typically used by companies, government and other large organizations to share files, post internal information and policies, communicate with employees and facilitate collaboration between them. In contrast to the "world wide" Web, intranets are private networks, or singular internal Webs, though most port into or otherwise utilize the open Web as well.

Intranets are usually built around a company or organization Web site, and they provide everyone in the organization with access to email and sometimes chat, IM, blogs, wikis and even Facebook-like social networking, along with other communication tools.

The term "intranet" was coined in 1994, about the same time the World Wide Web was becoming a popular way for people to use the Internet. By 2000, there were more than 4.7 million intranet Web servers in the United States, according to Data Analysis Group. One company—3M—operates 180 intranet sites running on 40 servers to reach its employees worldwide. At Hewlett Packard in 2002, more than 100,000 computers and 600 sites in 120 countries connected employees via intranets, chat rooms and other intranet applications.

In an ideal world, intranets save time, money and paper. They facilitate the sharing of knowledge, empowering and informing employees across departmental and divisional barriers. They can also foster a sense of community, bringing isolated employees or separate offices into the whole of the organization. Commonly accessed information including personnel policies and procedures, a company directory, news and downloadable forms are often posted on intranets, making the information easy to access by all staff and reducing staff time required to find and provide that information. Bulletin boards, payroll information and calendars are other common sections or features of most intranets.

Because intranets are private, they require a unique set of writing and editing skills. Intranet writers go by many names: intranet editor, Web editor,

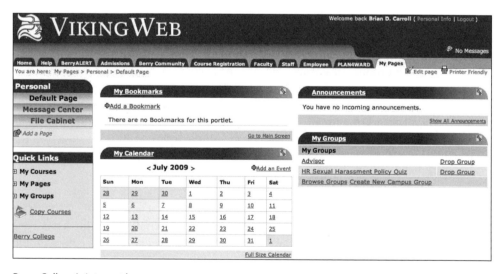

Berry College's intranet home page.

online editor, electronic writer, new media writer, content writer, technical writer, content manager, content editor, even Webmaster, and that is when a company has had the foresight and wherewithal to hire specialists dedicated to online communication. At many businesses, intranet content providers and editors wear other hats as well.

Special Requirements of the Intranet Writer

Writers for the intranet should have about the same level of understanding of the technology that powers intranets as, say, the company's or organization's middle managers and executives. In other words, intranet writers should understand the basic principles and implications of intranet technology to effectively communicate within and throughout the company.

Some companies require their intranet writers to know coding languages such as XHTML, CSS, XML or SQML at a basic level. Expertise in one or more of these languages is rarely required, but it is a tremendous asset for a writer to understand the limitations and capabilities of the medium for which he or she writes.

Given the narrower audience, writing content for an intranet can be an easier task than writing for a Web site. The intranet writer typically possesses:

- comprehensive and specific knowledge of the audience;
- knowledge of the corporate jargon, and therefore of important key words that can be used to tag and organize content;
- knowledge of the search engines used by employees and how these engines process queries;
- some knowledge of the computers, browsers and Internet connections being used;
- access to more than ample bandwidth, which enables large file sizes, rich media and downloads.

And there are other advantages of intranet writing. First, there usually is no need to sell a product or attract new visitors. Second, new users can be directed to a special section of the intranet to orient them. Third, feedback is guaranteed, especially when something goes wrong. Fourth, users reward simplicity; most employees are not looking for award-winning Flash movies and other whiz-bang effects, but rather the quickest way to the information they need at the moment. Finally, intranets are much more secure than any Web site because they are closed systems.

Much of an intranet writer's work is related to adapting basic business documents for access and use on the company site. These documents must be adapted with care. Sick-leave policies, training materials, procedures manuals, presentations, job descriptions, directories, and calendars and schedules should be edited and re-formatted for online publication, not merely dumped into the site or attached as a .doc or .pdf file. These .doc or .pdf versions are

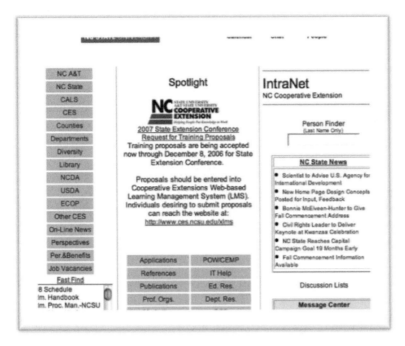

NC State's Cooperative Extension intranet.

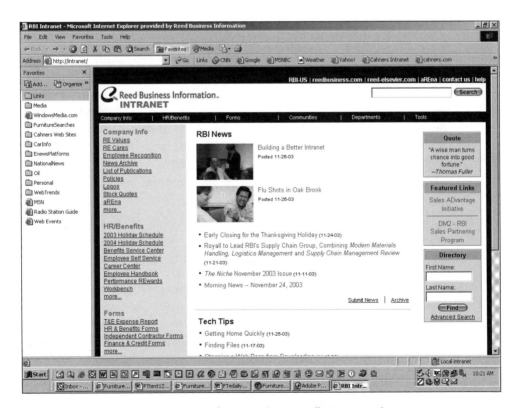

Intranet home page for Reed Business Information (www.reedbusiness.com).

attractive portable options for downloading and printing, however, so they should be offered in these formats too, as additional viewing options. When .doc and .pdf files are offered, they should be clearly labeled as downloads, warning users what will happen when they are clicked.

Business documents will need additional care in the form of creating key word search terms in their XHTML meta tags, which help the intranet search engines readily find the right document. Other common responsibilities of the intranet writer include:

- re-writing and reformatting paper manuals for online use;
- writing titles and meta tags for intranet pages;
- writing summaries to precede posted reports and business documents;
- adding headings, subheads and other sign posts for scanning;
- commissioning, writing and editing articles and news items;
- testing new site features;
- working with management to ensure that messages are accurate, clear and consistent;
- training members of the organization to publish and update content relevant to their department, division or specific job or role.

The Need for Style Guides

Style guides and Web page templates speed the preparation of online documents. Online style guides for intranets should explicitly outline how formal the writing should be, what structure information should take (including headlines, headings, subheads, etc.), what tone the information should have and which documents are most important and therefore should be most frequently updated. A great deal of information and content developed for intranets will age quickly. There often is little urgency or impetus to take outdated information down on an intranet, and some degree of perpetual obsolescence is perhaps inevitable. A conscientious intranet editor will regularly schedule some time for housecleaning, however.

There also are some challenges unique to the format. Every corporation has its own culture. If the intranet writer is part of the organization's regular communications staff, that writer is a part of this culture and can probably work and navigate within it. Freelance intranet writers, however, will need to learn an organization's culture, including its sensitivities, taboos, priorities and blind spots.

Success is also related to the degree to which a communications staff is connected and included in the organization's decision-making processes. The more included and connected, the better able that staff will be to build and maintain a relevant, useful, empowering intranet. Many companies give merely lip service to internal communications, however, and no one intranet editor is powerful or resourceful enough to alter a company's culture alone.

Size Matters

Because intranets are private networks, it is difficult to get access to the many different varieties and therefore to be able to discern best practices, which is a shame, because the sheer size of most intranets makes the challenge of creating and maintaining one all the more difficult. Jakob Nielsen (2000) estimates that intranets are 10–100 times the size of the same companies' external Web sites. Sun Microsystems, for example, had 2 million pages in its intranet in 2000 while at the same time offering 20,000 pages on its public Web site.

Because they are so large, it is common for an intranet to be split across multiple sites, each managed by a different department but connected by a hub or central information gateway. The Reed Business intranet site is an example of this multi-dimensional, multi-site intranet joined by or through a type of online "lobby" or entryway, directing constituents to the right sub-site. External or public sites usually project a unified image and feel and behave like a single, holistic site.

All intranet home pages should have at least three elements:

- A directory hierarchy that structures all content
- A search field connected to a robust search engine
- News and updated information, which often replaces email and newsletter updates.

Corporate departmentalization has implications for writers for intranets since the writing might have to be highly compartmentalized or segmented, as well. Because the intranet makes it possible to get information from other organizations or departments unobtrusively, people are more likely to follow up on hunches and see whether information from other departments might be useful. This, too, should be considered when generating content for a specific department or constituency. Specialized writing might include content for specific projects, content for an organizational unit or department and content for individuals, like top executives. It is easy to see how intranets grow so large so fast, and why the good ones offer robust search engines.

Another of the benefits of writing for an intranet is the high degree of equipment and software **standardization**. A company's employees are probably using roughly equivalent hardware and software, browsers and monitors, in sharp contrast to those accessing the open Web. Web designers and writers for intranets can predict with a high degree of accuracy how their pages and content will be seen, downloaded and otherwise consumed, so certain assumptions can be made in design, writing and programming that could not be made for general-use, external Web sites.

Extranets

Extranets typically flow from or are extensions of an intranet, providing a distinct constituency with connectivity to the corporation separate from that

An extranet page at Castle Worldwide, demonstrating the modular format of most extranets.

used by those who are employed directly by the corporation. Extranets are designed to serve and connect privileged third-party or external users, in other words, and these third parties are granted special access permissions. Typically they see and interact with only designated sections and pages of the corporate intranet, or they access company information in a site created especially to be an extranet. In the latter case, information often comes from the same databases driving the corporate intranet. Suppliers, contractors and consultants are typical users of extranets because they need access to information within a company in a secure environment. Suppliers might need to check on an invoice or a demand forecast; customers might need to access updated delivery information; and consultants need project-sensitive information often from the company's core information systems. Extranets make all of this possible without opening up the company's information systems to the general public.

As with the Internet, extranet designers and content providers have to assume variety in computer systems, download speeds and software in use among extranet users because not all users are company employees. They are coming from all over. Also, because extranets rely on the Internet and not an internal system, and because many extranet users likely are on the move, the design and the content should assume slower Internet connections between the company's servers and remote extranet users. Finally, unlike the intranet for its users, the extranet is not the center of the online environment for its users. It is one of many sites the user frequents.

There are important similarities between intranets and extranets, however. Both are accessed by people who have a relationship with the company.

The extranet is used for specific reasons and tasks, like the corporate intranet. Finally, both should be designed to save time, to be easily navigated and to reward use. There is a significant productivity impact implicit in both intranets and extranets.

Intra-business Communication: An Evolution

Email fundamentally changed the nature of organizational life in most companies. With more people in the loop on decisions, people who had relevant information or ideas were given a better way to influence the outcome of those decisions. But like most everything else, a little was good but a lot became problematic. After email came intranets, which have replaced for most companies the broadcast emails and mailing lists. Before intranets the various business units that make up any company, from R&D to marketing to human resources, were largely invisible to most people working at the companies. Intranets have made companies more transparent. People who had never gone on a sales call could see for themselves how the company was presenting itself to customers; people whose work was affected by a particular team could look directly at what that team was doing. Unlike email, intranets index and archive information, which can be searched and accessed when needed.

Portals are the next logical progression in business communication. The term merely means "gateway," but on the Web it has come to mean entry pages that are customized and personalized. Portals are different from intranets in their comprehensiveness, aiming to customize Web use and interaction by putting pre-determined databases, information, applications and software proximous to the employee. Portals also are designed to facilitate collaboration by interconnecting employees by task or work group.

Portals are therefore intended to be the desktop destination for anyone in an organization and the primary vehicle by which people do their work. In a portal environment, each person's start page reflects his or her view of the enterprise. KrispyKreme is an example. The Winston-Salem, N.C.-based doughnut maker embraced portals several years ago and continues to refine them for use throughout the company, including its many franchises.

Store managers have one type of portal start page; suppliers have another; and administration personnel still another. Each employee can customize his or her start page to give certain information automatically, like KrispyKreme's stock price, local weather and futures prices on flour and sugar, for instance. The user is in charge.

Fast Company magazine unveiled its FastCompany.com portal in mid-2008, an approach to accessing the Web that uses the magazine site as the engine for customizing Internet use. After registering as a member of the magazine's social network, any one user's home page will continuously refresh with messages, new contacts and updates on who is viewing his or her profile. The home page also puts the activities of blog post writing, accessing recommended articles and sending messages one click away. Incorporating social networking, the portal includes running updates on what "friends" or "contacts" are talking and blogging about, recommending and commenting. In addition, a news and content aggregator searches and collects stories and features to recommend, searching 300 *Fast Company* editor-recommended sites and blogs.

An intranet is a collection of links to various resources that may be useful to people in a company—most of them internal, some of them external. Most intranets capture what leaders in the company think is important: They reflect

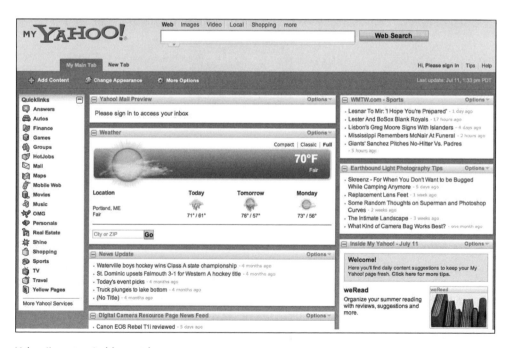

Yahoo!'s customizable portal page.

a top-down view of what's happening in the organization. A portal is a **centralized** starting point for everyone in an organization. It allows users to personalize in ways that make sense to them, bringing some information closer and distancing other, less important information. In a company of 500 people, there might be 500 different start pages, each one based on what that individual needs to do his or her work and what that individual needs in order to track developments in the outside world.

On a portal's start page, there might be modules such as "My Company," "My Department" and "My Favorites," or their equivalents. The content of each module, such as information updates and links to key sites, is based on choices the employee has made about what is needed to do the job. The company may support hundreds of R&D projects, but the individual employee may be involved in only a handful of them. Instead of navigating a generic intranet site, the employee can create links and sign up for updates that relate only to the relevant projects. An employee might be in sales and need to track three big competitors and what they are doing. The employee could select an information service and a stock-price service for just those competing companies.

KrispyKreme recognizes that its employees also are parents, sports fans and community activists, so the portal enables them to choose modules that feature news headlines, sports scores, stock updates and weather reports, among other things. This helps to persuade people to spend time using the portal. Service that is useful, relevant and compelling is service employees will want to use. Portals reflect a new view of the relationship between an organization and its people, one that is more democratic.

For a look at how portals are developed, visit Materna, one of the growing number of portal providers, at http://www.materna.de/Internet/englisch/ Products/Information/e-Business/e-Portals/e-Portals.jsp; this is not to endorse Materna but merely to show one example of how a company is pitching the concept of portals and to provide a sample of some of the services these portal developers are offering.

Newsletters

A related form of business communication is the newsletter. To save postage, copying and distribution costs, newsletters are increasingly moving away from print and instead to an email distribution model or to Web site presentation or both. Newsletter editors historically have been constrained by small production budgets. Digital publishing removes many of these constraints and, as a result, employee newsletters, association newsletters, house organs and niche publications are proliferating on the Web.

The writing required for these vehicles is very similar to that recommended for intranets and extranets. And the same print-to-Web transition and adjustments should be made with content when moving a newsletter online from the print model.

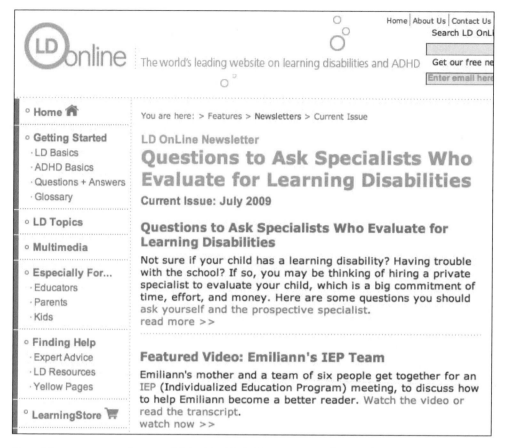

One of the many e-newsletters published by LD OnLine, one specializing in learning disabilities. Note also the navigational aid above the story signaling exactly where in the site the reader has landed.

Wikis and Cloud Computing

Wikis have been embraced by business because they are inexpensive, easy to deploy and easy to use. Wikis are online writing surfaces or documents that any number of Web users can write on, edit and otherwise change (i.e. adding pages, sections, headings, etc.). Wikis are used to enable people within an enterprise, even people in disparate geographic locations, to collaborate. They require no special knowledge of coding, either to write or to publish, and they are conducive to hyperlinking and interlinking, or linking within or beyond the wiki. Wikipedia is the best known of this category, and most wikis behave or operate much like Wikipedia.

For some of the same reasons that wikis are popular, cloud computing is gaining momentum in business. This form of networking puts the software and the data and information onto third-party servers connected via the Internet. Individual users, therefore, do not need to have specific software, nor do they really have to have anything other than a Web browser on their own computers.

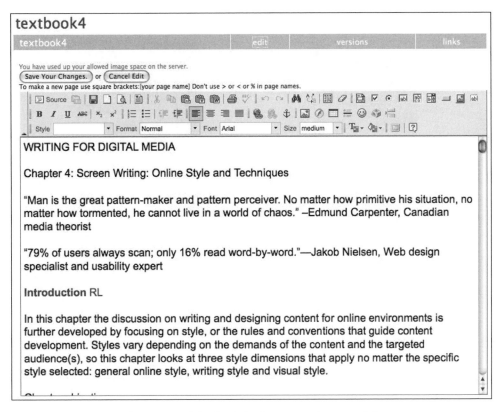

The wiki used to edit early versions of this book. "RL" was one of many collaborators.

The "brains" of the operation reside on servers "up there," or in the clouds. Like wikis, cloud computing can reduce costs by eliminating the need for individuals to own software and software licenses. Also reducing costs are the diminishing needs for memory on individual work computers.

Virtual Networks

Companies such as Vera Wang, Cisco, Sony, Intel, Audi and Nissan are using virtual worlds online to test and prototype products, ad slogans and branding techniques, all at a fraction of the cost of product development and consumer research in the physical world. Other companies, like advertising agency Leo Burnett, use Second Life to encourage collaboration among staffers around the world, without requiring them to travel. Leo Burnett's 2,400 employees tele-conference using Second Life married with Skype voice over Internet (VoIP). The virtual world provides a meeting room and visual tools that can simulate a real-world board meeting or conference. These computer-generated environments can offer tools for employees and business partners to collaborate.

IBM is developing its own virtual world/social networking platform for similar purposes, spurred in part by skyrocketing fuel and travel costs.

IBM used Second Life to debut its SmartBank system, displayed on its own
Second Life island.

The company uses Second Life for meetings, training and recruitment, but runs
Second Life software on its own servers for security purposes.

Starwood Hotels, which owns Westin and Sheraton, prototyped and
marketed a mid-priced, loft-style hotel chain exclusively on Second Life.
Starwood also set up a blog to engage potential customers and get them in on
the planning of the new division, www.virtualaloft.com/. The virtual hotel
launch gave Starwood input on, among other things, what types of interiors and
furniture people gravitate towards and which ones are ignored. In one mini-
market test, several different fabrics were draped over ottomans in the hotel's
bar area to see which ones Second Life "residents" liked or responded to.

The lobby of Starwood's Virtual Loft hotel in Second Life.

In addition to Linden Labs's Second Life, computer-generated environments are offered by Makena Technologies (There.com) and MindArk (Entropia Universe), among others. Software vendors such as Activeworlds, which is working with IBM, and Forterra Systems, Qwaq and Sun Microsystems offer software to enable companies to develop in-house virtual worlds.

As of May 2008 there were more than 13.4 million residents of Second Life, though only 340,623 had logged on in the previous seven days. Those users were spread out over 65,000 virtual acres, many of them making real U.S. currency creating and selling that real estate.

Conclusion

Whether for intranets or on a virtual whiteboard inside Second Life, good writing in business contexts is rare. Produce some and you will likely stand out from the crowd. According to a survey of 120 American corporations by the National Commission on Writing, one-third of employees in the nation's blue-chip companies wrote "poorly." The study also found that businesses were spending as much as $3.1 billion annually on remedial training (Dillon 2004).

Fortunately, many if not most of the writing skills, techniques and sensitivities discussed throughout this book are transferable to online business environments and publications. In short, writing well will make you money, and doing it on deadline could make you invaluable to the enterprise.

Chapter Assignment

Create an interactive FAQ help page for some entity (publication, company or organization), preferably one with which you have some formal connection. Suggested is the entity you selected for the assignments for Chapter 5. This frequently asked question section should anticipate common problems and questions users might have about that publication, organization or company.

The objective is to think for our audience(s) and anticipate their questions and needs. It is, therefore, the process that is most important, not the product. This means that you do not have to worry too much about design or layout or aesthetics.

The page should have:

- Clear, comprehensible instructions
- Clear organization
- Thorough consideration/anticipation of user questions
- Informative, helpful answers to FAQs
- Design that promotes, rather than impedes, page usability.

Online Resources

The Intranet Journal
http://www.intranetjournal.com
Online journal devoted to news and practices about and for intranets.

Intranet Reference Site
http://www.intrack.com/intranet
For those researching, planning, designing and/or implementing an intranet or intranet project.

Professional Writing Handouts and Resources
http://owl.english.purdue.edu/handouts/pw/
From Purdue University, this site points to online resources for "workplace writers," including how-to information and best practices.

Sources

Dan Baum, "Battle Lessons: What the Generals Don't Know," *New Yorker* magazine, January 17, 2005; available: http://www.newyorker.com/archive/2005/01/17/050117fa_fact.

Dan Bricklin, "How to Write for the Intranet," especially the "Techniques" section; available: http://www.gooddocuments.com/homepage/homepage.htm.

Jim Candler and Eric Brown, *The Elements of Intranet Style* (San Francisco: Cyberpress, 1999).

Sam Dillon, "What Corporate America Can't Build: A Sentence", *New York Times*, December 7, 2004, available: http://209.157.64.200/focus/f-news/1295982/posts.

Jean Folkerts and Stephen Lacy, *The Media in Your Life: An Introduction to Mass Communication* (Boston: Allyn & Bacon, 2003).

Rachel King, "The Global Virtual Office," *BusinessWeek* magazine, May 2, 2008, available: http://www.businessweek.com/technology/content/may2008/tc2008052_842516.htm.

Steve Lohr, "Computer Age Gains Respect of Economists," in *Living in the Information Age*, Erik P. Bucy, ed. (Belmont, CA: Wadsworth Publishing, 2005): 177–80.

Rachel McAlpine, *Web Word Wizardry* (Berkeley, CA: Ten Speed Press, 2001).

John Nichols, "Newspapers . . . and After?," *The Nation* magazine, January 2007.

Jakob Nielsen, *Designing Web Usability* (Indianapolis, IN: New Riders, 2000).

11 LEARNING THE LEGAL LANDSCAPE

Libel and Privacy in a Digital Age

He who receives an idea from me, receives instruction himself without lessening mine; as he who lights his taper at mine, receives light without darkening me.
Thomas Jefferson, in a letter to Isaac McPherson, August 8, 1813

Monsieur l'abbé, I detest what you write, but I would give my life to make it possible for you to continue to write.
Voltaire, in a letter to M. le Riche, February 6, 1770

The future we're rushing towards isn't one where our every move is watched and recorded by some all-knowing "Big Brother." It is instead a future of a hundred kid brothers that constantly watch and interrupt our daily lives.
Simson Garfinkel, journalist and privacy scholar

Chapter Objectives

After studying this chapter, you will be able to:

- understand the legal contexts in which Web writers gather information and in which they publish, including the limits on and freedoms for both activities;
- discuss how privacy law has changed in and for a digital age;
- know the basics of libel law as it applies to publishing in general and, more specifically, to publishing via or to the Web;
- explain the basics of intellectual property law as it relates to digital content;
- analyze the tensions in the law as competing interests vie for priority;
- appreciate the implications of international law for publishing on a global medium.

Introduction

Internet communication and publishing has introduced new tensions in the law. Decisions and policies are being made within the content, electronics and computer industries about how to protect copyrighted material in digital media and how to protect the information privacy of citizens more vulnerable to privacy invasion, fraud and identity theft. The Internet as a global publishing tool created the potential jurisdiction of 190 countries, which complicated the already confusing area of libel law.

This chapter focuses, therefore, on media law as it relates to writing for digital media, but it in no way is meant to offer a comprehensive survey of all law related to press and to media. After exploring the rights of access to information, the chapter looks at two of the more intractable problems in American society generally and for publishers of digital media specifically—privacy and libel. Finally, the chapter addresses new intellectual property questions raised of the law by digital content, or content that is easily copied, stolen, shared and distributed.

Gathering Information

> *Congress shall make no law respecting an establishment of religion or prohibiting the free exercise thereof; or abridging the freedom of speech, or the press; or the right of the people peaceably to assemble, and to petition the Government for a redress of grievances.*
>
> (First Amendment to the U.S. Constitution)

The First Amendment guarantees the right to publish information about government and about public issues, but it doesn't help much with access to that information. After the attacks of September 11, 2001 and, later, the onset of the Iraq war, access to U.S. government information and records became even more problematic for news media. For bloggers and other online media writers, the absence of clear definitions determining just who is a journalist and who is not makes getting information from government all the more difficult.

Constitutional law scholar Thomas Emerson said, "a democracy without an informed public is a contradiction," and democracy implies a significant level of transparency in government. When print periodicals first emerged in Europe in the 17th century, they saw their role as investigatory. During the English Civil War, when press freedom in England began to emerge, these periodicals promised that they would investigate what was going on and tell their readers. *The Parliament Scout*, a publication that began in 1643, stated it would "search out and discover the news." The next year, in 1644, a publication calling itself *The Spie* promised readers that it "planned on discovering the usuall cheats in the great game of the Kingdome. For that we would have to go undercover."

Thomas Jefferson famously said that he would rather live in a nation with newspapers and no government than in a country with government but no newspapers. But there are tensions, or competitions of interests and priorities when the Fourth Estate seeks to watchdog government. Like most bureaucracies and institutions, government seeks to do its business behind closed doors and out of the public eye. Sometimes the secrecy is warranted. National security often demands secrecy, to name one instance. Individuals want their health, personnel or employment information kept secure and private. With a raft of federal laws promising information privacy, we arguably have more privacy than any generation before us. We also have more surveillance than any generation before us, both by governments and corporations ("Big Brother") and by each other ("Little Brother").

Two landmark Supreme Court cases that established a constitutional right to access to information for all citizens, including but not especially journalists, are *Richmond Newspapers v. Virginia* and *Branzburg v. Hayes*. The case of *Richmond Newspapers v. Virginia* (1980) gave U.S. citizens "a right to know" how their government administrates justice. The U.S. Supreme Court ruled that the First Amendment in fact does establish the right to attend criminal trials. This constitutional right is for everyone, not just or especially news media. This decision could have been extended to cover legislatures, council meetings and review boards, but it wasn't. For access at those levels, in most cases we must turn instead to statutory law, the product of legislatures, rather than constitutional law. Statutes that provide some guarantees of access include the Freedom of Information Act, state open meetings and state-level open government laws.

Whether reporters should be allowed to protect confidential sources is a recurring question for the law, a question addressed in *Branzburg v. Hayes* (1972). Paul Branzburg, a reporter for the *Louisville Courier-Journal* newspaper, had cultivated sources within a drug ring; a grand jury not surprisingly wanted access to those sources. To protect the identities of those sources, and to fulfill his promise of confidentiality, Branzburg argued that the First Amendment's protections of a free press should shield him from government requests for his privileged information.

In a very close, contentious 5–4 decision, the Court ruled that

> it has generally been held that the First Amendment does not guarantee the press a constitutional right of special access to information not available to the general public . . . Newsmen have no constitutional access to the scenes of crime or disaster when the general public is excluded.

Complicating *Branzburg*, however, was the majority opinion by Justice Byron White that stated that "without some protection for seeking out news, freedom of the press could be eviscerated." Despite the logic of White's dissent, journalists historically have had no more right or access to information than the general public, as the *Richmond Newspapers* case demonstrated, and therefore no special right to gather information from within government or about government.

In other words, the information buffet is open, so grab a plate and help yourself, media, but do not expect the government to come to you to wait on your table. Can you get exactly what you want? No, the buffet is what it is— meat loaf and baked potatoes. There is a public prison tour at 8 a.m. There are slideshow photos in the gift shop. These are available to anyone, including media, but no one will be coming to your table, saying, "Hello, my name is Eric Holder. I'll be your Attorney General today. I'd like to tell you about a few specials on the information menu." As mentioned earlier, since 9/11 the buffet has been shrinking. More and more information entrées, especially information on national infrastructure, transportation and law enforcement records, are being taken off the table.

A few other Supreme Court cases should illustrate or elaborate the buffet metaphor. In *Zemel v. Rusk* (1964), the Court ruled that the constitutional right to speak and publish does not carry with it the unrestrained right to gather information. Ten years later, in *Saxbe v. The Washington Post*, the Court stated that even though the First and Fourteenth Amendments prevent government from interfering with the press, the Constitution does not require the government to provide to the press information that is not available to the average citizen. The Court argued that the lack of this requirement in fact does not represent an abridgement of First Amendment rights of the press.

The *Zemel* and *Saxbe* cases set up *Houchins v. KQED* in 1978. Three years earlier, in 1975, an inmate committed suicide in a California prison. KQED San Francisco requested access to go inside the prison to document conditions. Sheriff Houchins said, paraphrasing, "The buffet is open. Take the prison tour." Of course, the prison tour didn't go into cells where conditions were reportedly poor or where the suicide took place, and no photography was allowed on the tour. KQED took the tour but failed to get much meaningful information, so the station sued the sheriff for violating the station's First Amendment right to a free press.

In another close and contentious decision, the Court ruled 4–3 in favor of the sheriff, stating that "neither the First nor the Fourteenth mandates a right of access to government information," which served to affirm *Saxbe v. The Washington Post*. In other words, the Court will defer to prison officials as long as rules are not content- or expression-specific. The rules have to apply to everyone all the time. A prison cannot provide access to *60 Minutes*, then deny access the next day to a blogger for a citizen journalism site. Without a constitutional imperative for government to open its doors, its files, prisons and courts, we have to litigate. We have to lobby. We have to plead for legislative relief.

One attempt at providing this relief is the Freedom of Information Act (FOIA), initially passed in 1966 and amended for the Internet in 1996. FOIA provides the disclosure of previously unreleased information and documents possessed by the federal government, but its effectiveness depends on cooperation from government. FOIA covers agency records and information collected, maintained, used, retained and disseminated by the federal government, and it is available to anyone, public or private, media and non-media. The 1996 amendment expanded FOIA to cover electronic information, including email correspondence. In addition, the Electronic Freedom of Information Act established priorities or rankings for agencies to use when petitioned for information:

- Top priority: where life or safety is at risk
- Middle: information requested by news media for the public's interest
- Low: everyone else.

Often, using FOIA becomes a cat-and-mouse game. A request is made. Government agencies drag their feet, claiming national security interests, Health Information Privacy Protection Act (HIPPA) or some other statute to block access to information. The Bush administration exercised what could be called reflexive secrecy. Then U.S. Attorney General John Ashcroft, for example, ordered a more intensive review of requests by agencies already reticent to fulfill requests.

In addition to a bureaucratic culture predisposed not to help media or private citizens obtain information, agency personnel called on to fulfill the requests typically have other job duties and roles, forcing a difficult choice: Either do their jobs or spend time fulfilling FOIA requests. Overburdened both by their own jobs and a large number of FOIA requests, many not surprisingly choose their jobs.

Good news came in December 2007, however, when President Bush signed into law the Openness Promotes Effectiveness in our National Government Act of 2007, also known as the OPEN Government Act, which amended FOIA by establishing a definition of "news media"; prohibited an agency from assessing certain fees if it fails to comply with FOIA deadlines; and established an Office of Government Information Services in the National Archives and Records Administration to review agency compliance with FOIA (read the law in full at http://www.opencongress.org/bill/110-s2488/show). The new definitions are liberal, meaning that most bloggers and Internet publishers are eligible for reduced processing and duplication fees available to "representatives of the news media." The law also broadens the scope of information that can be requested.

The OPEN Government Act was the first makeover of the FOIA in a decade, or since it was first amended to account for the Web. The Act also brings non-proprietary information held by government contractors under the law, which effectively reverses an order by former Attorney General John Ashcroft in the wake of 9/11 to resist releasing information when there was uncertainty about how doing so would affect national security.

The legislation also creates a system for the media and public to track the status of their FOIA requests, as well as a hotline service for all federal agencies to deal with problems and an ombudsman to provide an alternative to litigation in disclosure disputes. Whether the law can effect change and ensure greater compliance remains to be seen.

How do you use FOIA?

Follow these steps:

1 First, informally ask an agency public information officer for the information you want, a method that is quicker, cheaper, nicer and surprisingly effective.
2 If working with an information officer in person is either unsuccessful or not feasible, file a formal, written request under FOIA. Each agency must identify the person to whom to submit requests, as well as its FOIA procedures and electronic indices of those popular records it releases as a matter of course.
3 Once a request is made, the agency must release the documents or provide a reason for exemption. Exemptions must cover only the information it is applicable to, not the entire record.
4 FOIA gives agencies 20 days to determine whether to grant or deny a request, except for "unusual circumstances," such as sudden popular demand for a particular record.
5 If a compelling need is demonstrated, such as danger to human life, agencies are required to expedite requests.
6 Agencies can charge for information, including electronic information, to cover the actual costs of getting the information and duplicating it.
7 If 20 days expire, the person requesting the information can file a complaint in the federal district court.

Realize, however, that FOIA has several exceptions or exemptions:

1 National security, the broadest category, is the only one that allows the executive branch to determine the criteria for release of documents rather than Congress. This exemption covers military plans, weapons and operations, and intelligence activities; programs for safeguarding nuclear facilities; and U.S. foreign relations, among other categories.
2 Agency housekeeping practices or rules, which relate to internal personnel rules, parking policies and sick-leave policies. This exemption is meant to avoid swamping agencies with trivial requests.
3 Statutory exemptions, which include documents that Congress has declared in other statutes to be confidential. Examples are personal tax records, census bureau records, patent applications and Central Intelligence Agency records, including even names and titles. (The CIA does not have to turn down a request since the rejection might reveal that the agency has the document being requested.)
4 Confidential business information, including trade secrets, private commercial information, contracts or information related to seeking a contract.

5 Agency memoranda, including working papers, studies, opinions, policy drafts, staff proposals and reports used to make a final report, agency policy or agency decision of some kind. This exemption is similar in practice to the attorney–client privilege.

6 Personnel and medical files in which the release would warrant an invasion of someone's privacy.

7 Law enforcement investigations where the information released would interfere with law enforcement proceedings or investigations, invade personal privacy, disclose the identity of a confidential source, endanger someone's life, deprive a defendant of a fair trial, or reveal protected enforcement techniques.

8 Financial records and bank reports.

9 Geological data and maps concerning oil, gas and water.

In addition to the FOIA exemptions, other federal statutes can deny disclosure of information, and some of these laws are complementary to or redundant with FOIA exemptions. A few examples:

- The Homeland Security Act, section 214, states that government cannot disclose critical infrastructure information provided by agencies and private businesses, including information about the national electrical power grid, nuclear power plants or air transportation.
- The Privacy Act of 1974 states that government can only use "personally identifiable records" for the purpose for which they were created and for which the information was gathered.
- The Family Educational Rights and Privacy Act (FERPA).
- Student disciplinary records of nonviolent crime and violations of institutional rules.
- The Driver's Privacy Protection Act of 1994, which prohibits the release of driver's license information without a driver's consent.

Open Records and Open Meetings: Sunshine Laws

The Government in the Sunshine Act was passed into federal law in 1976, opening most federal government meetings to the public. In addition, all 50 states have their own "sunshine laws" on their books, laws aimed at increasing openness in government. These state laws offer different degrees of access along a wide spectrum of openness, making it difficult to generalize. The purpose of these laws is to hold government accountable. Georgia Supreme Court Chief Justice Charles Weltner wrote in a 1992 opinion, "Because public men and women are amenable 'at all times' to the people, they must conduct the public's business out in the open" (*Davis v. Macon*, 1992).

As was stated in a 1980 Georgia Supreme Court case, *Athens Observer v. Anderson* (1980), the purpose of open government and open meetings laws is three-fold. Government should provide access so that:

1 "The public can evaluate the expenditure of public funds."
2 The public can evaluate "the efficient and proper functioning of its institutions."
3 Accountability can "foster confidence in government."

Open records acts typically apply to documents, papers, letters, books, tapes, maps, photos and computer-generated information, and they cover every state department, agency, board, bureau, commission and authority; every county and municipal corporation, school district and political subdivision; and non-profits receiving funding from tax dollars. Similarly, open meetings acts generally cover meetings of any state, county and regional authority, municipality, school district and political subdivision, whether appointed or elected. The laws apply to non-profits receiving tax monies, but not to advisory groups and quasi-governmental bodies that collect information, make recommendations and advise government.

Voters have the right to know if the city budget is reasonable or whether the school board is making good decisions with the tax dollars allocated to the school system. But few like scrutiny, so an increasingly complex government seeks to do its business in the dark. Legal battles for freedom of information likely will be with us forever.

Privacy in the Information Age

One of the more controversial aspects of communication law is privacy, a term that does not even appear in the U.S. Constitution. This area of law is very active because of the vast amounts of private or personal information being kept in online-accessible databases, the actions of hyper-competitive news media in such celebrated cases as the paparazzi chase of Princess Diana, and the spread of technologies that make it ever easier to survey people without their knowledge.

Ask any group, "Are you concerned about your privacy online?" and you are likely to hear mostly affirmative answers. Ask that same group how many have read the user agreements or privacy policies for the Web sites they use most, including MySpace, Facebook, YouTube or even Google, and you will likely find that very few have taken even this nominal step toward safeguarding personal data privacy. Pair this general apathy or lack of concern with technological changes that make it easier to steal, survey, duplicate, buy and sell personal information, and the result is a general vulnerability of data privacy.

Since 9/11, the U.S. government has worked hard to make it easier to get wiretap permission and to share what is heard, and to survey and to collect information on individuals without their knowledge. According to a 2007 Wiretap report (http://www.uscourts.gov/wiretap07/contents.html), federal and state courts issued 2,208 orders for the interception of wire, oral or electronic communications in 2007, compared to 1,839 in 2006. Meanwhile, the Department of Defense is collecting the world's largest archive of human DNA for a robust database of digital dossiers and biometric data. The ability to invade what most citizens would define as a right to privacy or a right to be left alone clearly is outpacing the law's attempts to re-negotiate for a digital age just what privacy rights should look like.

Privacy is a notion or idea or ideal that is always being **negotiated,** rather than a static concept or right. City life brought privacy to the fore as an issue for the law in the 19th century. In the colonies, people had either no privacy in the fishbowl of village life or total privacy living on farms or estates, with the nearest neighbor perhaps miles away. In big cities, however, a person could have a high degree of privacy in a completely public place because in big cities it is possible to be anonymous. But where there is anonymity, there is little trust.

For most of this country's history, anonymity has been impossible for most citizens. Anonymity as a relatively recent phenomenon helps to explain in part why even a basic notion of privacy as a constitutional right came so late. Samuel Warren and Louis Brandeis interpreted into the Fourth Amendment a "right to be left alone," arguing this interpretation in an 1890 *Harvard Law Review* article, "The Right to Privacy" (http://swiss.csail.mit.edu/6805/articles/privacy/Privacy_brand_warr2.html). Warren and Brandeis published their article just as photographic technology began making it possible to take a snapshot, or in other words to "take" or "capture" someone's photo, with *or without* that person's permission. Technology raced ahead of the law, just as it does today. Brandeis further articulated the privacy right he and Warren had argued in a 1928 Supreme Court case, *Olmstead v. U.S.*: "The right to be left alone [is] the most comprehensive of rights, and the right most valued by a free people." (Brandeis was named to the Supreme Court in 1916.)

Privacy is a negotiated right because it constantly balances among or against many other interests and rights, at both the individual and the societal levels. Privacy is not, therefore, an absolute value, but one forced into accommodation with other important individual and societal values. It is not surprising, then, that privacy law varies from state to state.

Privacy law has **four general areas** or torts:

- Appropriation (of a person's name or likeness)
- Intrusion ("a man's home is his castle")
- Publication of private facts
- False light invasion of privacy.

For our purposes, for writing and publishing in and for digital contexts, we are most concerned with intrusion. Because intrusion has been made easier and therefore more prevalent by computers, especially networked computers, protecting privacy has become increasingly difficult and costly, which is why public interest in the regulation of spam, Internet cookies and information databases has grown. Privacy-invading technologies continue to improve, and legal restrictions are not likely to stop or slow them if history is any guide.

Here are a few episodes that demonstrate how vulnerable personal privacy is in a computer age:

- Identity theft victimized 10 million people in 2008, a 22 percent increase from 2007, making it one of the United States's fastest-growing crimes, according to the Federal Trade Commission.
- In May 2008, approximately 13,000 employees at Pfizer had their personal information compromised when a company laptop and flash drive were stolen. The same month a breach in an Oklahoma State University computer server exposed names, addresses and Social Security numbers of students, staff and faculty who had bought parking and transit services permits in the previous six years.
- Personal information on as many as 26.5 million military veterans, including their Social Security numbers and birth dates, was stolen in May 2006 from the home of a Department of Veterans Affairs employee who had taken the information without authorization.
- The personal financial records of more than 163,000 consumers in databases belonging to consumer data broker ChoicePoint were compromised, leading the Atlanta-based company in 2006 to pay $10 million in civil penalties and $5 million in consumer redress to settle Federal Trade Commission (FTC) charges. The FTC alleged that ChoicePoint's security and record-handling procedures violated consumers' privacy rights and federal laws.
- The FTC also charged that ChoicePoint violated the Fair Credit Reporting Act by furnishing consumer reports—credit histories—to subscribers who did not have a permissible purpose to obtain them, and by failing to maintain reasonable procedures to verify both their identities and how they intended to use the information. The agency charged that ChoicePoint violated the FTC Act by making false and misleading statements about its privacy policies.

ChoicePoint, Pfizer and OSU are not unique. These types of data thefts, breaches and lapses are becoming increasingly common, with repercussions for the privacy and identity protection of everyone (visit the Privacy Rights Clearinghouse for a chronology of these incidents to see how the rate is increasing: http://www.privacyrights.org/ar/ChronDataBreaches.htm).

Open Architecture and Privacy Breaches

The Internet's open architecture enables networking and file-sharing, which are primary reasons the Internet was developed. These characteristics also make it ripe for privacy breaches. A classic example is the Federal Bureau of Investigation's email wiretap system, popularly known as Carnivore. The system was designed to pick up email from targets of investigations and to give the FBI some of the eavesdropping capabilities the bureau has historically enjoyed to tap telephone communications. Carnivore has been widely criticized by civil liberties advocates and privacy advocates for its ability and perhaps tendency to breach private and personal privacy.

Carnivore's potential for abuse points to another player in the privacy drama—**Internet Service Providers** (ISPs), or those services and companies that provide Internet connectivity to businesses and individuals. Carnivore's lapses, according to some in the Bureau, were the result of "outdated settings" for the targets' computers, settings that are provided by ISPs. With the cooperation of ISPs, Carnivore can tap the communications stream of the ISP to obtain email messages to and from an investigation target, putting ISPs at the center of several tugs-of-war between legislative and judicial bodies attempting to regulate Internet activities.

The New Jersey Supreme Court, for example, found that ISPs must protect user information and that a valid subpoena is needed before the providers can disclose private data about subscribers, ruling,

> We now hold that citizens have a reasonable expectation of privacy, protected by Article I, Paragraph 7, of the New Jersey Constitution, in the subscriber information they provide to Internet service providers—just as New Jersey citizens have a privacy interest in their bank records stored by banks and telephone billing records kept by phone companies.

Though the Privacy Act of 1974 establishes "fair information practices" and restricts government collection and use of personal information, the U.S. government has been active in surveillance and data collection. Launched as a response to 9/11, the Total Information Awareness (TIA) plan announced by the Pentagon in October 2003 was designed to analyze vast amounts of computer data about citizens and visitors to the United States in order to search for patterns of terrorist activity.

TIA did not go forward, in part because of its ominous name and logo (pictured). What many people do not realize is that although TIA was defeated, federal agencies and bodies still collect and search vast computer databases with information on individuals and are pooling that data and data analysis.

Backed by federal funding, many states are participating in the Multi-state Antiterrorism Regional Information Exchange System, or MATRIX, that links law enforcement records with other government and private databases to identify possible terrorists. MATRIX is owned and operated by a single, private, Florida-based company, Seisint. The system's "terrorist index" is compiled using factors such as age, gender, ethnicity, credit history, pilot and driver's licenses, and "investigational data."

The U.S. government is trying to catch terrorists and track suspected terrorists. U.S. citizens believe they have a right to privacy, however nebulous and changing that belief might be. This creates a tension between privacy and security. A danger is that while government collects increasing amounts of information on mostly innocent, law-abiding people, the government is able to do more in secret, citing security as its reason. A healthy democracy demands and depends on transparency in government and a respect for personal privacy.

Safeguarding Data

Carnivore and MATRIX are designed to uncover. **Steganography** and **cryptography** are designed to obscure, to hide and to secure data for privileged users and viewers. Data hiding is the practice of modifying data so that either its existence or its content is obfuscated. The hiding can be accomplished in a number of ways, including the use of mechanical methods and through social engineering. Encryption seeks to protect the integrity of data on a system.

Here are some definitions from the *Oxford English Dictionary Online*, accessible at http://www.oed.com:

- Steganography: the art of secret writing, or a form of cryptography, which is the enciphering and deciphering of messages in secret code or cipher.
- Watermark: a distinguishing mark or device impressed in the substance of a sheet of paper during manufacture, usually barely noticeable except when the sheet is held against strong light.

The use of these techniques can hide messages and confidential data, and they can protect intellectual property and copyright by marking a product with evidence of its provenance, or origin, and history of possession.

Digital watermarking came about as an outgrowth of steganography after the commercial market perceived it could apply the same data-hiding techniques to circumvent the theft of intellectual property and copyright-protected materials. Digital watermarking applications of stenographic techniques became prevalent with color copiers through concerns about realistic duplications of original data. Because of the apprehensions about counterfeiting, all color copier manufacturers agreed to put steganographically hidden data within their printed outputs that would allow law enforcement personnel to pinpoint which machine made any one copy.

With the appearance of computer-produced artwork and the modification and even wholesale alteration of digital photography, digital watermarking has become popular because it can mark, and therefore copyright, original work. One advantage to digital artifacts, be they photos or music or publications, is that they are all made out of 0s and 1s. This makes reproduction and distribution relatively easy and inexpensive. It also makes copies "look" and operate or behave exactly like the original, being in some ways indistinguishable from the original.

Here are some other technologies, terms and utilities for both safeguarding and threatening personal privacy in an online environment:

- **PGP encryption**: Pretty Good Privacy, or PGP, is a freeware program that runs on most platforms and enables encryption, or the secret encoding of computer files. The program, developed by computer expert Philip Zimmermann, encrypts (or scrambles) and decrypts (unscrambles) data. Zimmermann's address on the Web: http://web.mit.edu/prz/.

- **Cookie**: A short bit of text that a Web site stores on a user's machine in order to recognize return visitors and track their activities, including shopping, surfing and buying. The text file can be no more than 4,096 characters long, but it is often as short as 10 or 20 characters. Cookies cannot carry computer viruses, and most are configured to remain on a system for some specified period of time. Cookies also are used for convenience, to record personal preferences, usernames and passwords.

- **Bug**: In contrast to cookies, bugs allow a Web site to download cookies onto the user's system that were placed by other Web sites. It occurs in one out of every few thousand visitors (see Privacy.net, "Bugs"). These cookies can include the user's home address, email address and numerous user IDs from various Web sites.

- **Re-mailers**: A re-mailer takes an email, strips it of its personally identifiable information, then re-sends it anonymously to its intended destination. This is one of the technologies that drives most spam email and phishing, which is the attempt to acquire a person's sensitive information, such as bank account information, by sending an email that masquerades as coming from a trustworthy entity, like a bank or insurance company.

  From anonymous emails to chat rooms and instant messages, users can disguise their identities or simply lurk without disclosing their identities. Pseudonyms and anonymous speech allow users to maintain privacy and create diversity on the Internet and by sharing their thoughts, opinions and criticisms without inhibition.

- **Spam**: Another email-related issue is spam, or unsolicited and usually commercial (or junk) email sent to a large number of addresses. In May 2003, an AOL executive testified before the Federal Trade Commission that spam was customers' biggest complaint, with more than 2 billion unsolicited email messages arriving at AOL every day. Despite new laws, the amount of spam has only increased, as anyone with an email account well knows.

- **Opt-in/opt-out**: Related to spam is the issue of selling personal information to third parties, usually for marketing purposes. There are two primary approaches to protecting privacy in these cases, opt-in and opt-out. Opt-out is having personal information removed from databases and lists sold for marketing or other reasons. Personal information is collected on individuals in a variety of ways. Applying for a credit card or telephone service, entering contests and registering for a driver's license all are ways personal information is collected into databases, then sold to third parties for marketing. Companies often make 'opting-out' difficult or virtually impossible. Opt-in, which is far less common, is a policy that calls for permission from an individual before selling or sharing personal information.

- **Filters**: For First Amendment reasons, Internet filters are controversial. Filters screen Internet sites, pages and information for specific content. Library filters have been ruled unconstitutional in some cases because they have been determined to violate the First Amendment right of free speech. They are designed to screen the Internet for material harmful or offensive to minors, in particular pornography. Opponents argue that at worst filters programmed to flag or prevent showing pages with lists of words violate the First Amendment. At best they are inefficient. A list with the word "breast" on it, for example, would cause a filter to prevent a browser from navigating to sites commenting on breast cancer or boneless chicken breasts. Parents, citizens and the federal government, on the other hand, wish to protect children from the worst of the Internet, including pornography, and have turned to filters.

A fast-evolving online environment of technological innovation is one that is constantly bounding ahead of legislation and even Congressional and judicial understanding of the implications of the emerging technologies. Privacy is one of the issues that cuts across many if not most technologies regarding the Internet and information.

Trespass and Surveillance

The two most common forms of intrusion are trespass and surveillance. Trespass involves going onto private property without the consent of the owner(s). It does not matter what you find, or even whether you find anything, this type of intrusion can be against the law. Surveillance is a violation of a person's right to be left alone, which means that anything you can easily hear or see in a public place or in a private place generally open to the public is safe to photograph or record. Special devices, however, are not covered, such as telephoto lenses and high-powered mics. Journalistic codes of ethics, such as the one endorsed by the Society of Professional Journalists (see http://www.spj.org/ethicscode.asp), typically include a section on when and under what circumstances it is permissible to use hidden cameras and microphones, which is essentially when there is no other way to get the information.

Intrusion is the only realm of privacy law that has to do with how information is gathered, and it is the invasion of privacy we probably think of when we consider privacy law. Intrusion is the offensive, physical or mechanical invasion of another's solitude. As such, this tort can address the use of telephoto lenses, hidden cameras, computer cookies, clickstream data or going through someone's trash. The miniaturization of cameras and recording equipment has kept this a lively area of the law, as have the ability to retrieve even deleted email and the online publication of court documents, tax records and liens. Identity theft, computer hacking, infiltration and even spam can be governed by privacy law.

One principle that helps navigate this treacherous area of the law, and also the most important element in most invasion of privacy cases, is what the courts call "a reasonable expectation of privacy." Admittedly subjective, this principle determines when and where a journalist or information-gatherer is in legal jeopardy based on a person's expectation of privacy in the circumstances giving rise to the intrusion claim. What happens in public is generally not regarded as private, which makes sense. If what took place was visible and what was said was audible to others, it will be difficult to argue invasion of privacy.

Legislative Protections of Privacy

In an attempt to safeguard citizens' information privacy, Congress has passed legislation that limits, regulates and in some cases prohibits personal information-gathering and dissemination. Listed here are some of the most important pieces of privacy legislation to date:

1 **Electronic Communications Privacy Act (ECPA) 18 USC sections 2510, 2702:** The ECPA regulates the interception of private communications and access to and disclosure of stored electronic communications. The ECPA extends wiretap restrictions to digital media, and it specifically forbids the federal government from seeking information about online communications system users unless the government:

   (a) obtains a warrant issued under the Federal Rules of Criminal Procedure or state equivalent, or
   (b) gives prior notice to the online subscriber and then issues a subpoena or receives a court order authorizing disclosure of the information in question.

   The ECPA and a patchwork of privacy legislation do not provide the same privacy protection to sensitive personal data collected by private entities.

2 **Children's Online Privacy Protection Act of 1998 (COPPA):** COPPA specifically protects the privacy of children under the age of 13 by requesting parental consent for the collection or use of any personal

information of the users. After several constitutional challenges, the Act took effect in April 2000 as a response to a growing awareness of Internet marketing techniques that target children and collect their personal information from Web sites without parental notification.

COPPA applies to commercial Web sites and online services that are directed at children, requiring them to:

    (a) provide and abide by a detailed privacy policy describing the information collected from their users;

    (b) acquire verifiable parental consent prior to collection of personal information from a child under the age of 13;

    (c) disclose to parents any information collected on their children;

    (d) grant the right to revoke consent and have information deleted;

    (e) limit collection of personal information when a child participates in online games and contests;

    (f) protect the confidentiality, security and integrity of personal information collected online from children.

Since its ratification, COPPA has been successfully used by the FTC to prosecute companies for improper collection and use of information on and from children, usually as part of games or contests. The social networking/blog site Xanga.com, for example, paid a record $1 million to settle charges by the FTC that it violated COPPA. However, a study by the University of Pennsylvania found that only about 50 percent of children's Web sites that collect information were in fact following the rules.

3 **Privacy Act of 1974, 5 USC section 552:** Passed soon after the Watergate scandal, this Act broadly restricts the use of information by government agencies and regulates their information practices. The Privacy Act specifically requires that every federal agency maintain a system to permit the individual to control disclosure of the information in the record; retain records of information that have been disclosed; permit the individual to review and maintain a copy of the information in the agency's records; and allow the individual to request an amendment of information contained in an agency's records.

4 **Fair Credit Reporting Act of 1970, 15 USC section 1681:** The FCRA regulates the collection and use of personal information by consumer reporting agencies. It provides a list of permissible purposes for which personal information may be released without the consumer's consent, but only by credit-reporting companies.

5 **Federal Trade Commission Act, section 5 15 USC section 45:** The FTCA gives the FTC the authority to police unfair or deceptive acts or practices in commerce, including privacy policies and the information-gathering activities those policies cover.

Other laws covering personal privacy and information-gathering, or data-mining, include the Right to Financial Privacy Act and the Health Insurance Portability and Accountability Act. As their names suggest, these laws restrict government access to financial and health-related information.

Executive Efforts to Protect Privacy

Alongside legislative efforts, the executive branch is also active in Internet privacy issues, primarily through the Federal Trade Commission. The FTC's mission is to promote the efficient functioning of the marketplace by protecting consumers from unfair or deceptive acts or practices and to increase consumer choice by promoting vigorous competition. The Federal Trade Commission Act (FTCA) provides the Commission with broad law enforcement authority over entities engaged in commerce and with the authority to gather information about such entities. Commerce on the Internet falls within the scope of this statutory mandate.

For years, the FTC has monitored the data collection practices of popular Web sites and issued reports about the status of online privacy. Until May 2000, the agency favored industry self-regulation as opposed to legislation governing online privacy. Self-regulation is a system made up of voluntary compliance with industry guidelines, membership in privacy seal-of-approval programs and other practices that facilitate the protection of personal information. The FTC has consistently held that its proposed legislation, in conjunction with self-regulation, will ensure important protections for consumer privacy at a critical time in the development of e-commerce.

As the U.S. economy becomes increasingly dependent on the Internet and its related technologies, expectations of personal privacy no doubt will change. Law is only part of the solution. Something thought to have been an invasion of privacy in the past can become acceptable during a business transaction in order to get some benefit, such as online banking or buying via the Internet. The technologies promoting and protecting privacy, too, will continue to change, warring with those developed to better collect, aggregate, organize and disseminate personal information. "The campaign against liberty, identity, and autonomy in the 21st century is being carried out around the world, but nowhere are the attacks more evident than in the United States," wrote privacy expert Simson Garfinkel. "It's a campaign that is being pursued, hand in hand, by government, business, and ordinary citizens. We are all guilty. Privacy is suffering the death of a thousand cuts" (2000: 257).

Libel, Slander and Defamation

There are two forms of "malpractice" possible in the "practice" of journalism: invasion of privacy and libel, the latter being the most common way journalists get into legal trouble. Even the fear of libel litigation can silence journalists into self-censorship. While individual bloggers and Web writers generally aren't worth suing from a financial point of view, being poor is not a great legal defense when faced with a libel action. Even bloggers and freelance writers should be aware of the law and how to stay out of the courtroom.

Libel has three essential ingredients: the questionable material must be printed or published (written), erroneous or false, and defamatory. Spoken defamation is termed slander. Just like medical malpractice, libel is almost always a tort, or a civil wrong (from the French word for damage, *tort*), and not criminal, like seditious libel. About half of the 50 states still have criminal libel laws on the books, but criminal libel cases are extremely rare. There have been no cases in this area of the law in Georgia, to cite just one state as an example, since 1910. And libel is primarily state law, though the states' approaches are guided and shaped by U.S. Supreme Court precedent.

The premise in libel law is that a reputation has been damaged and that it can be repaired through the awarding of monetary damages. This reasoning is, of course, flawed, but it is the law's attempt at justice and, though not perfect, it is better than dueling.

Libel can appear in headlines ("Cops Think Kato Did It," for example), in a news story or editorial, in a press release or company newsletter, in a blog post, in advertising copy, in a letter to the editor, in a chat room, or in statements made orally at a public gathering. Even innuendo can be interpreted to be defamatory. Since 1997, the courts have viewed communication on and via the Web in much the same way as they have historically regarded or treated material in print, meaning that libel law as it has developed to deal with print also is relevant to online communication.

Allegations of libel are included in about three-fourths of all the lawsuits filed against mass media, but most libel suits are dismissed. When a suit does make it to trial, media are likely to lose. Juries are unpredictable. Ordinary citizens often think the media are unfair. Robert Lichter of the Center for Media and Public Affairs told the *American Journalism Review* that he thinks

> there's a feeling that journalists have overstepped their boundaries. People don't look on [journalists] the way journalists like to view themselves— as the public's tribune, speaking truth to power, standing up for the little guy. They don't look like the little guy anymore.
>
> (Farhi 2008)

In a national survey conducted by Sacred Heart University in January 2008, only 20 percent of respondents said they believed "all or most" reporting. An even larger portion, 24 percent, said they believed "little" or none of it.

Libel cases take an average four years to litigate, while lawyers typically take home 50 percent or more of the winnings. This litigation is no fun for anyone, in other words, except of course the lawyers. But people get mad at how they are reported in the news, and they want to sue. They can't win, typically, but they're hurt and angry. They should probably write a letter to the editor, or call the editor and talk to him or her about what happened, giving another side of the story, their side of the story.

So, **how do you protect yourself from a libel suit?** Know the law and do a good job, a professional job reporting and writing. Sometimes doing additional reporting or gathering more information or sources can prevent the problem. Good journalistic and communication practices are the best defense. Good, careful, accurate reporting generally prevents successful libel suits, so know the law, have a solid story and follow the records or documentation. Libel occurs only where or when what has been published is untrue. Stay away from things that are not true. Do enough reporting to discern the truth from what isn't true. Be fair and honest. If you are writing negatively about a person, give that person an opportunity to respond.

Michael Hiltzik, a Pulitzer Prize-winning investigative business reporter for the *Los Angeles Times*, said the single most important technique in his career has been "getting the documents." Get everything documented. The whole point of dealing with sources is to get them to point to things you can get in black and white, he said. Hiltzik and Chuck Phillips teamed to win a Pulitzer for a story exposing that the Grammy Awards, an event held supposedly for charity, generates huge income but scant little for charity. Grammy organizers threatened legal action, specifically a libel suit, but "couldn't lay a hand on us because everything was written down in documents," Hiltzik said (Committee of Concerned Journalists 2006).

Criminal libel cases occur when an individual is charged under criminal or statutory law. Some statutes, for example, make it criminal to disturb the peace by criticizing public officials. The person's speech is protected under the First Amendment, but the disturbance caused by the speech could land the person in jail for criminal libel. Often, when these arrests or charges are challenged, the law is found to be unconstitutional or overly broad or vague.

Who can sue for libel? Only the living can sue; the dead, obviously, cannot sue, and you cannot sue on behalf of a dead person. A person can sue, die and have the suit continued by survivors, however. Businesses can sue, as can non-profits, churches and charities. Companies (and the people who work for the companies) can sue for libeling of their products.

Who cannot sue? Besides the dead, government cannot sue, at least not successfully. Individual staff members, however, can sue. Whether they can win depends on a host of factors, including whether they are public officials (a governor or mayor) or private citizens (such as a secretary or administrator), a distinction that determines the level of fault on the part of the journalist or publisher that must be proven.

When someone sues, **the burden of proof is on the plaintiff**, who has to prove at least six things. There are therefore six elements of any successful libel suit, or six hurdles that a plaintiff must clear. And the plaintiff must clear all six, though some are relatively low and others higher. If a plaintiff trips or fails to clear any one, media win. The six hurdles:

- Defamation
- Identification
- Publication (and re-publication)
- Fault
- Falsity
- Injury.

Defamation

A plaintiff has to prove the published or printed material is in fact derogatory, or something that holds him or her up to hatred, ridicule or contempt. Accusing someone of a crime qualifies, as do accusations of serious moral failings or incompetence in business or professional life. Juries decide what is defamatory, which means that interpretations can vary with the times and even with geography.

A community would not think less of a doctor or businessperson who makes a single error, reasoning that gave birth to what is known as the **single mistake rule**. Stories that suggest a pattern of incompetence that goes beyond asserting a single error can be found to be defamatory, though not necessarily libelous. (Remember that libel has three ingredients, with defamation being only one of those three.)

There are three kinds of defamation: libel *per se*, libel by interpretation and libel *per quod*. **Libel *per se*** can occur with accusations that are obviously defamatory; the Latin means "libel on its face." A published statement such as "Smith killed the postal worker" is libel *per se* if in fact Smith did not kill the postal worker. It does not cover merely embarrassing information, like stating a person's age as ten years older than they really are or having them earn a PhD from the wrong school.

Libel by interpretation concerns something published that is or could be libelous depending on one of a number of competing interpretations. One of the competing interpretations is defamatory, whereas others are not. The plaintiff must prove, then, that the defamatory interpretation is the interpretation that was intended and that this interpretation was the one readers would be expected to hold.

Libel *per quod* concerns something that has been published that becomes defamatory when readers add something commonly known that does not appear in the story. Not surprisingly, this form of libel is very rare. The writer may or may not have knowledge of the added fact or element, and usually it is the plaintiff that provides this missing piece of information. Think of libel *per quod* as "instant libel: just add water!" The water is some other fact or piece of information that, when added to the published story, makes that story defamatory and therefore potentially libelous.

Identification

If you write that someone embezzled, you have defamed that person. He or she flies over the first hurdle. To prove identification, a plaintiff has to prove that at least one other person could read the story and identify the plaintiff as the person about whom the story is talking or describing. Publish the plaintiff's name and, of course, this hurdle has been cleared. Identification can also result from publication of a nickname, description, title or affiliation.

Publication

If the actionable material was published or broadcast, the plaintiff clears this hurdle, an easy requirement to meet. Did the accusation reach a third party? Sending a note to a second party doesn't count, but add just one intermediary and a plaintiff has met the minimum contacts requirement. Listservs, press releases, blog entries and even a broadcast email can all be found to have been "published." An interoffice memo, faxed or emailed press release, tombstone, post-it note on a cash register, or bounced check posted on a restaurant wall can all qualify as having been "published."

Under what is called **the republication rule,** a person reporting or writing the story is fully and legally responsible. That person's source can be sued for slander, but it is the reporter who is responsible for the published libel. "I just repeated what they said," is not a successful defense in a libel case. Repeating a rumor is not necessarily libelous, but publishing it could be because of minimum contacts; it takes a third party to qualify as libel. Keep in mind that anyone who participates in publication can be named in a suit: copyeditors, publishers, editors, press release writers, ownership. Plaintiffs not surprisingly go after the money, however, which typically puts ownership in the most jeopardy.

Fault

The most complicated area in or distinction for libel law is fault. Briefly, different types or classifications of plaintiffs have to prove different standards or levels of libel, specifically fault, a hurdle added in 1964 with the landmark U.S. Supreme Court case, *Times v. Sullivan*. Prior to this case, civil libel law had been governed by the doctrine of strict liability. In other words, reporters strictly and legally were responsible for what was published. "Did you write it? Then you are responsible."

Libel is much more complicated now. In *Times v. Sullivan*, the Court ruled that plaintiffs must prove what is known as fault or, specifically, that public or government officials must prove a standard of fault called "actual malice." By distinguishing public officials and assigning a higher level of fault, the Court ruled by implication that private citizens need prove only negligence as the fault level. All plaintiffs have to clear the hurdle, but different classifications of plaintiffs must clear varying fault levels. *Times v. Sullivan* put an end to strict liability.

Actual malice has a precise legal definition: a reckless disregard for the truth or knowledge of falsity. To clear this high level of fault, a plaintiff has to prove that the reporter knew the published material was false or that the reporter demonstrated a reckless disregard for truth. The term's definition underlines how good, honest, professional reporting can prevent successful libel claims. If you have three reliable sources, you cannot be guilty of actual malice-level libel. If you have no reliable sources, just the word of an unemployed former insurance salesman with a grudge (the source for a libelous *Saturday Evening Post* story on game-fixing in college football), you could be guilty of actual malice-level libel. Relying on only one discredited source can be interpreted as reckless reporting. A word picture might help: The reporter is driving down the highway of good journalism. Truth is just ahead, in the middle of this highway, with all lanes leading straight to it. The reporter swerves off the road, drives into the ditch, avoids the truth completely before swerving back up onto the highway to continue on his or her journalistic journey. This is a picture of a reckless disregard of the truth.

It is important to note from *Times v. Sullivan* that the majority opinion supported an aggressive, free press. Justice Brennan wrote that at issue was "a profound national commitment to the principle that debate on public issues should be uninhibited, robust, and wide-open, and that it may well include vehement, caustic and sometimes unpleasantly sharp attacks on government and public officials." Brennan's opinion established the actual malice defense. It is also important to note that in this case advertising, or commercial speech, was ruled protected by the First Amendment for the first time, though at a level lower than that for political speech. (Political speech in this context has nothing to do with politics; it refers to non-commercial speech, or the parts of the newspaper, for example, that are not advertisements. The term uses the Greek root *polis*, meaning "the people." Political speech, therefore, is the people's speech.)

In rulings after *Sullivan*, the Court made it clear that it wants more people to have to prove actual malice before successfully suing for libel. Public officials were joined by public figures, a category that includes celebrities and the well-known, as well as people with power and influence in society who therefore are worthy of media scrutiny. The Court had serious people in mind, but it is this strand of legal reasoning that ultimately evolved to include celebrities.

All plaintiffs must fall into one of the four plaintiff categories, a classification that determines the fault level that must be proven. The four:

- All-purpose public figures, such as Tom Cruise or Angelina Jolie
- Limited or vortex public figures, such as Richard Jewell, the security guard once suspected of being the Centennial Park bomber in the 1996 Olympics

- Public officials
- Private citizens.

Public figures make themselves public by seeking fame or notoriety (media attention), and public people have access to media to refute things said or written about them. They can call a press conference, for example, and media will show up. The same media that are allegedly libeling them can be used as a remedy to the libel.

The Court has sub-divided public figures into two categories:

- **All-purpose public figures**, or people with widespread fame or notoriety. These figures typically are household names, or people with special prominence in society. They are considered to have pervasive power and influence and are therefore continually newsworthy. Consider the relatively recent trend of celebrities selling their "exclusive" wedding or baby photos to periodicals for millions of dollars. Public figures have virtually no private aspects to their lives, at least in a legal sense. Their lives are wholly fair game, as the TV shows *Entertainment Tonight*, *TMZ* and *Access Hollywood* demonstrate. Once a person has been classified in this category, that public figure never falls out or lapses back to the lesser category, therefore becoming eligible for more libel protection.
- **Vortex or limited public figures** are people who were private at one time who have been pulled into the public sphere, like an object swirled into a vortex. The key court case for this category is *Firestone v. Time* (1972). The wife and heir to the Firestone tire fortune found herself listed in *Time* magazine as getting a divorce for cruelty and adultery. The magazine column was in error, however, so Firestone sued. The question for the Court was: Is Firestone a public figure who therefore must prove actual malice? The Court noted that she was a socialite, and that she had hired a publicity clipping service. Firestone was well-known, but for the purposes of the lawsuit she was classified as a private person. Her divorce was deemed by the Court a private matter. Had *Time* written about Firestone's role as head of a cotillion or charity, she likely would have been classified as a public figure.

Since the *Firestone* case, a test of sorts has emerged from case law to help courts determine a plaintiff's classification for the purposes of establishing a fault level:

1 Is the published material about *a public controversy or real dispute*, the outcome of which affects a substantial number of people? Firestone's divorce was a real dispute, but its outcome did not affect a substantial number of people, though the Court has not defined "substantial number of people."

2 Did the plaintiff *voluntarily participate* in the public controversy?
3 Did the plaintiff voluntarily participate to *affect the outcome* of the issue, question or controversy?

Case law suggests that a person cannot lose vortex public figure status once established, at least in connection with the issue or event that led to the status in the first place. This principle holds true for former public officials; they don't lose their public status once they retire or lose re-election.

In contrast to actual malice, **negligence** is simply failure to exercise ordinary or reasonable care. Private citizens need only prove this level of fault. Some courts rely on professional standards, calling in editors and academics to testify to standard practices. The Court is interested in the number and credibility of sources used, in red flags about the story's veracity, and in the newspaper's or Web site's policy and whether that policy was followed. Other courts follow what is known as the "reasonable person standard," which asks how a reasonable person might respond in similar circumstances. This so-called "reasonable person" is a fiction, of course, applied purely in the abstract.

The lack of thorough investigation, the lack of verification of information from official and reliable sources, and a lack of contact with the subject of the story have all been found to be negligent. What is deemed negligent, therefore, is not the same thing, necessarily, as what is considered good reporting practice or good journalism. The Court is looking for horrible reporting, for malpractice, not merely the absence of professionalism or good practices.

Falsity

Libel is by definition false, whereas defamation has nothing to do with truth or falsity. To win a libel claim, a plaintiff is going to have to prove that the published story is false, an element of libel law unique to the United States. Truth or falsity is not a factor in libel cases in, for example, Australia, New Zealand, Canada or England. The Court requires only substantial truth, at least for private citizens, and not that every word be true. Remember, public figures and public officials will have to prove actual malice; media therefore need only prove *the absence* of actual malice, not absolute truth. Careless errors are not enough to lose a libel suit. If a published report states that a person embezzled $75,000 and the actual amount was $70,000, the error likely will not qualify as substantially false. Report a felony where there was none? That will be a problem.

Injury

Another easy hurdle to clear is demonstration of injury. A plaintiff needs only one psychologist to testify to the need for medication, for example, for a plaintiff to clear this hurdle. In this category are types or classifications of damages.

1 **Compensatory (or actual) damages**—these compensate for harm done or harm proven and include damage to reputation and personal suffering. They are also called actual damages.

2 **Special damages**—these are the damages one might think are actual damages: loss of a job, and therefore income; the plaintiff had to move and sell his or her house; the plaintiff required three years of therapy.

3 **Punitive damages**—the jury takes care of these. No plaintiff fails to sue for punitive damages because it is this classification that promises the big money awards. Juries look at the financial status of the defendant and will seek to punish that individual or organization. The results typically are huge punitive damage awards, though almost all judgments are reduced on appeal. To win punitive damages, actual malice is the requisite fault level, even if the plaintiff is a private citizen.

A Few Additional Considerations for Libel Claims

Not all libel cases systematically proceed through the six hurdles. First, a judge can be motioned to dismiss a case, a ruling called summary judgment. If a defendant can persuade a judge that the plaintiff cannot possibly win, summary judgment is a possibility. Second, there is a **statute of limitations** for libel actions. In most states it is one year. If the actionable material was published or aired more than a year ago, the libel claim can be summarily dismissed. If the material was published online, typically the clock begins on upload, or when the site publishes it, as opposed to when someone downloads it.

In addition, jurisdiction can be very tricky. A reader in Canada claims libel against a publisher in Oklahoma. Which court has jurisdiction? Libel claims have proceeded against U.S. plaintiffs in British, Australian, Irish and Canadian courts, for example. For material published online, the question of jurisdiction often is the Court's first question.

Strategic Lawsuits Against Public Participation (or **SLAPP suits**) are those actions deemed by the Court to be intended to intimidate and/or chill the press and comment rather than to recover for injury due to defamation. At least 20 states explicitly bar or severely limit such lawsuits, and the high cost of defending a SLAPP suit is one the concerns spurring states to act.

In an example of an anti-SLAPP suit action, the Maine Supreme Judicial Court struck down in 2008 a defamation lawsuit filed against a former legislator who claimed that the plaintiff was using the court system to try to stifle free speech in a political debate. The defendant successfully sought dismissal of the lawsuit on the grounds that it violated Maine's anti-Strategic Lawsuit Against Public Participation statute, or Anti-SLAPP Law. Maine's law is intended to protect a citizen's right to directly or indirectly petition the government through public discourse, a right found in the First Amendment.

Absolute privilege is a libel defense that covers what is published in documents coming out of or as a part of senate deliberations, judicial proceedings and other official government business. No matter what is said or printed, this defense covers the speaker. The defense is not intended to shield media. Protecting media is the **qualified privilege (or fair report) defense**, which shields media against libel suits when they report on or with official government reports, lawsuits or government meetings, provided the reporting is fair, accurate and truthful. The courts recognize the importance of scrutiny of government proceedings, meetings and activities as part of news media's watchdog role. Courts have said news media can act as a sort of video camera and therefore are not necessarily responsible for truth, as long as the reporting is fair and accurate. A citizen at a city council meeting charges that an official took a bribe, for example. Accurate reporting of the accusation is protected. The qualified privilege defense is especially valuable in political campaign coverage, when it is particularly difficult to parse fact from fiction.

The First Amendment opinion defense covering rhetorical hyperbole, fair comment and criticism varies state to state and is based on common law. It covers opinions, arts and music criticism, parody and satire, among other things. The case *Ollman v. Evans* (1984) produced the **Ollman Test**, which is used by lower courts to guide use of the defense. The test asks:

1 Can the contested statement be proved true or false?
2 What is the common or ordinary meaning of the words?
3 What is the journalistic context of the remark?
4 What is the social context of the remark?

Generally, hyperbole, parody and exaggerated statements that no one would believe are protected. Political cartoons, parody and satire are strong vehicles for expressing public opinion, so they are generally protected even if they offend or inflict emotional injury. Statements incapable of being proved true or false also typically are protected.

In a 2003 case, *Batzel v. Smith*, the Ninth Circuit Court interpreted into libel law the same protections for bloggers that have been traditionally recognized for journalists. The Court ruled that bloggers, Web site operators and email list operators cannot be held responsible for libel in information they re-publish. The decision is based on Section 230 of the Communications Decency Act of 1996 (CDA), which states that "no provider or user of an interactive computer service shall be treated as the publisher or speaker of any information provided by another information content provider."

California attorney Ellen Batzel sued for defamation after someone in the Netherlands published an email on an international email list that accused Batzel of owning art stolen by the Nazis. The email author, Tom Smith, also accused her of being a descendant of famous Nazi Heinrich Himmler. The re-publisher of the email, Ton Cremers of the Netherlands, was ruled innocent of defamation under Section 230, which protected him from defamation liability. (Also of note, Cremers moved to dismiss Batzel's case under California's anti-SLAPP suit statute, but his motion was denied.)

Anonymous Speech and Section 230

Anonymous speech has become a staple of online communication as well as a growing problem for news sites and community platforms. There is a new nastiness emerging online, causing Web site operators and news sites concern and Congress to begin considering changing or removing the protections found in Section 230 of the CDA (full text of the section at http://www4.law.cornell.edu/uscode/47/230.html). Sites are concerned because of the sheer amount of problematic expression being posted behind the shield or cloak of anonymity.

As federal law, Section 230 pre-empts state laws, and the courts have rejected attempts to limit Section 230 to "traditional" Internet service providers. News sites and blogs, too, have been recognized by the courts as "interactive computer service providers." Practically, Section 230 protects Web sites when and where users are allowed to post or comment, even where those sites edit or delete entire posts. Sites run into legal jeopardy or liability when they contribute commentary or substantively change posts in editing, and the courts have yet to clarify what is and is not an acceptable amount or degree of editing. Sites such as Google, Facebook and WashingtonPost.com are not required to censor what users post. Additionally, these sites can restrict access to content they deem "objectionable," but they cannot be sued for choosing not to do so. Sites cannot be expected to review every single post, in the courts' view.

Copyright and Intellectual Property Issues

William Shakespeare wrote *As You Like It* between 1598 and 1600, basing his plot and his play's general outline on Thomas Lodge's 1590 play, *Rosalynde, Euphues Golden Legacie*. Lodge, in turn, had "borrowed" his play from Chaucer's *The Cokes Tale of Gamelyn*, a 14th-century poem. It is unlikely that under U.S. copyright law Shakespeare could write or, more accurately, publish *As You Like It*. It is also unlikely that Lodge could publish his work, either, without running afoul of U.S. copyright law.

In the United States, copyright law has changed almost completely since Thomas Jefferson first articulated it for U.S. law in 1790. Copyright law has, in fact, taken a 180-degree turn, which may help explain how Fox News could plausibly sue humorist Al Franken and his publisher for naming his book *Lies and the Lying Liars Who Tell Them: A Fair and Balanced Look at the Right* in 2003. Fox sued specifically for Franken's use of Fox's trademarked "Fair and Balanced." Fox's lawyers argued that use of the slogan would "blur and tarnish" the network's reputation. Franken was described in the lawsuit as being "unfunny," inspiring Franken to consider counter-suing for use of the word "funny," which Franken said he had trademarked. Fox lost its case, but that the question had to be answered in a court of law points to fundamental problems with intellectual property law as it is practiced in the United States.

For most works, there are two pieces of property: first, the physical or material content and the words (and/or visuals) in the physical document;

second, the organization of facts in that printed or published work. Consider this textbook. Whose is it? You own your physical copy of the book, which is why you can sell it to a second-hand bookstore or back to the student bookstore and keep the money. But the publisher and/or the author of the book own the copyright, protecting the expression of its ideas. The tricky part, then, is how to treat the two very different properties, or not to treat them as the same. Intellectual property is largely intangible, but it is treated under U.S. law more like tangible property, like a piece of land or a lawn mower.

Copyright, patents, trademarks and plagiarism are dealt with by different types of intellectual property law. Before we sink our teeth into copyright, let's take a look at its intangible cousins:

1 **Patents:** They protect and encourage technological development. If your invention were not protected, perhaps you would not share it. We could not benefit from nor improve upon it. The absence of patent law is precisely why Italy's great inventors, including Leonardo Da Vinci and Filippo Brunelleschi, wrote their notes in secret codes using cryptography. They were afraid of someone stealing their ideas and inventions. Patents cover inventions, secrets and discoveries, and they cover utility (machines or processes) and design (such as Michael Graves's teapot for Target).

The expansion of patent law in the last quarter-century has been tremendous. Demonstrating the extremes, a resident of California, John Moore, had his spleen removed to treat a rare form of leukemia. The University of California doctor who removed the spleen used the organ to develop and then patent a cell line, without Moore's knowledge or permission. The market value of this patent has been estimated at $3 billion. The doctor received $3 million in stocks from the Genetics Institute, which marketed and developed a drug based on the cell line. Moore sued for a share of the profits, because it was his spleen, after all. Moore lost and received absolutely nothing (McCleod 2005: 5–6).

2 **Trademarks:** These protect words, symbols, devices or combinations of these three. They are used to make a company or its goods or services recognizable and distinct. You can market a photocopier, but only Xerox can market a Xerox machine. You can develop a gelatin, but only Jell-O can market Jell-O brand gelatin dessert. Donald Trump trademarked "You're Fired." NBA coach Pat Riley trademarked "Three-peat" (even though none of his teams ever "three-peated"). The television network Fox trademarked "Fair and Balanced." After 9/11, someone tried to trademark "Let's roll," but the mark was not approved. These trademarks, if protected and enforced, can last forever. There are four functions of trademarks and service marks:

(a) To identify and distinguish a product, brand or company.
(b) To signify or verify that the product or service is made or provided by the company or entity signified by the mark.

(c) To signify or identify the relative quality of that brand or company, though not specifically "high quality," merely a certain level or degree of quality. For example, think of a Chevrolet as opposed to a Lexus, or a Walmart-brand shirt compared to a Brooks Brothers shirt. We associate with each certain quality attributes.

(d) To serve as instruments in advertising, marketing and selling.

Trademark law covers product names, like Kleenex, Rollerblade and Band-Aid; the shape of a bottle, like Coca-Cola soda and Absolut vodka; and buildings and sculptures, like the lions on the steps leading up to the New York Public Library. It can cover a slogan, like MasterCard's "Priceless," and 1-800 numbers. It can even protect the color of fiberglass insulation, like Corning's pink.

Trademark protection can also be lost. The owner has to use the mark, and he or she has to protect or enforce the mark. For this reason, trademark owners write and issue cease-and-desist letters with the threat to sue. Sometimes they do sue. Nylon, dry ice, escalator, raisin bran, linoleum, zipper and yo-yo are all examples of items or products for which the trademark was not enforced, and therefore lost. Brands have to sue, or at least threaten to sue, which helps to explain the watchfulness of companies like Nike, Disney and Coca-Cola.

3 **Plagiarism:** The act of taking ideas, thoughts or words from someone else and passing them off as your own is plagiarism, a word that comes from the Latin term for "kidnapping." Unfortunately plagiarism is very common, as this list of recent violators attests:

- 2001: Historians and best-selling authors Steven E. Ambrose and Doris Kearns Goodwin admit to accidentally incorporating the words and thoughts of others in their best-selling books.
- 2003: *New York Times* reporter Jayson Blair is caught basing his coverage on that of other news organizations, sometimes by watching television from a New York bar.
- 2004: The newspapers *Macon Telegraph*, *Vancouver Sun* and the Iowa State student newspaper each are found to have published plagiarized coverage; columnist Mike Barnicle of *The Boston Globe* confesses to having recycled the jokes of comic George Carlin, and *USA Today* star reporter Jack Kelley is discovered to have fictionalized accounts of conflict in the former Yugoslavia.
- 2005: Siddharth Srivastava, an India-based freelancer for the *International Herald Tribune* and *San Francisco Chronicle*, plagiarized material from an article in the *Guardian* newspaper. Ken Powers, a sportswriter from the *Telegram & Gazette* of Worcester, Massachusetts, was "sent home" from covering the Super Bowl after he plagiarized for his column using an article in *Sports Illustrated*. The *Los Angeles Times* ran a lengthy Editor's Note that outlined the inaccuracies,

"substandard" reporting methods, and unverifiable quotes in two stories by reporter Eric Slater. Two young reporters and the managing editor resigned from the *Reidsville Review* after it was revealed that the reporters fabricated quotes for a regular feature in the newspaper.

- 2006: Caught plagiarizing were a *Village Voice* reporter, a Harvard student newspaper editorial cartoonist and editorial writer, and Harvard sophomore Kaavya Viswanathan, the sophomore for stealing at least three portions of her book, *How Opal Mehta Got Kissed, Got Wild, and Got a Life*, from *Can You Keep a Secret?*, a chick-lit novel by Sophie Kinsella.

4 **Copyright:** "All works of authorship fixed in a tangible medium of expression" receive copyright protection, according to U.S. copyright law. This definition applies to writings, paintings, music, drama and recordings. It does not protect the ideas themselves, only their fixed expression, which is sometimes difficult to parse. How do you know the idea without its expression? You don't, so the two are in some ways indivisible.

Copyright as a concept was not necessary until the printing press, another example of how the law lags behind technological development and innovation. The Internet has put an unprecedented strain on copyright law as a result of the ease with which intellectual property can be copied, downloaded, uploaded, altered, mass-emailed and mass-duplicated. Further problematizing digital content is the fidelity of copies to the "original." The copies look or sound every bit as good as the original, which is unprecedented.

Copyright's Origins

Sixteenth-century British law protected printers only, not authors or painters, or those we would think of as the originators of the intellectual property. This changed in 1710 with "An Act for the Encouragement of Learning, by Vesting the Copies of Printed Books in the Authors or Purchasers of Such Copies, during the Time Therein Mentioned." This awkwardly named law gave a legal claim of intellectual property ownership to the creator, or to someone who bought the creative rights from the creator. It is this law that is the basis for U.S. copyright law.

In its beginnings, U.S. law gave the copyright owner the right to protect creation for up to 28 years, or for two 14-year terms. Registering provided the first 14 years; one renewal provided the next 14 years. In 1831, the timeline lengthened to cover the original 28 years plus an automatic 28-year renewal *and* an additional 14-year renewal—70 years in total. Musical compositions were added in 1831, while photography gained protection in 1865, largely because of the commercial value of photography of the Civil War. Translation rights were added in 1870.

Before 1978, copyright law was an opt-in system, granting protection only to those who registered and renewed their copyrights, and only if they marked their creative works with the © symbol. In 1978 Congress created an opt-out system, meaning that copyright protection no longer need be applied for. Protection is granted automatically to a created work once it is in fixed form, and this protection extends for nearly a century, whether the author or creator needs it or even knows he or she has it. In other words, the system once offered protection only to those who wanted it or needed it. Current copyright law universally grants it, regardless of need, even though according to the government's own study only about 2 percent of copyrighted works 55 to 75 years old have any commercial value.

Generally, the copyright owner is the author of the created work. Exceptions are works made for hire, such as newspaper, magazine or Web-published articles. Copyrights may also be sold or given away, such as in publication contracts that transfer copyright from an author to the publisher of the work. Reassigning copyright requires a written statement of transference. Acquiring a previously unpublished creation, such as a manuscript, does not mean that one has acquired its copyright.

In the last 40 years, Congress has extended copyright terms 11 times, each time favoring private incentive versus the enrichment of the public domain. When the Sonny Bono Copyright Term Extension Act (CTEA) added 20 years to existing and future copyrights in 1998, Eric Eldred and other commercial and non-commercial users of public domain works sued. On October 9, 2002, the U.S. Supreme Court heard oral arguments that the CTEA is unconstitutional. However, in January 2003, the Supreme Court ruled by a vote of 7–2 that the CTEA does *not* violate the constitutional commandment that copyrights be granted for a limited time.

The Bono extension, therefore, locks up or excludes a vast majority of creative works in order to protect the 2 percent with any commercial value. This means, as Kembrew McLeod put it, that we are "allowing much of our cultural history to be locked up and decay only to benefit the very few" (2005: 8). The song, "Happy Birthday to You," for example, will not enter the public domain because of the *Eldred* ruling until 2030. Copyrighted in 1935 by the Hill sisters, the song was sold in 1988 by Birch Tree Group to TimeWarner. That the song is protected explains why restaurants have their own versions of "Happy Birthday"; singing "Happy Birthday to You" in a public place would be regarded as a public performance of a copyrighted song.

Web sites typically include in their user agreements an articulation of copyright rights covering content produced for or published on those sites. MySpace's user agreement, for example, states that once you have logged on, you "grant MySpace.com the nonexclusive, fully paid, worldwide license to use, publicly perform and display such content on the Web site." This means that essentially all photos and blog entries, video and music clips are the property of News Corp, owner of MySpace.

Thomas Jefferson was not primarily concerned with protecting the commercial interests of the last known user of the property, but rather with fostering innovation, development, knowledge and progress. "He who receives an idea from me, receives instruction himself without lessening mine; as he who lights his taper at mine receives light without darkening me," Jefferson wrote. The founding ethos of the Internet is consistent with Jefferson's philosophy. Justice Sandra Day O'Connor wrote in her *Rural Telephone Service v. Feist Publications* decision in 1991 that "The primary objective of copyright law is not to reward the labor of authors, but to promote the process of science and the arts."

The danger, as McLeod wrote in his 2005 book, *Freedom of Expression®*, is in corporate interests wielding intellectual property laws like a weapon, and in overzealous owners eroding our freedoms. McLeod posits that we self-censor because we might get sued, even where there is no threat; we censor ourselves in backing down from a lawsuit even when that suit is frivolous, often because of the expense of even winning the case; and we are losing freedoms because everything from human genes and business methods to slogans, gestures and even scents are being privatized and commercialized. We should not be required to hire an expert to determine whether a symphonic orchestra can perform a work composed in 1945, or whether a library can display documentary photographs of the Japanese internment.

Having spelled out copyright's chronological protections, we should look at what it practically means to own a copyright. There are six permutations or specific rights:

1 reproductions
2 derivative works (or the right to someday create derivative works)
3 public distribution
4 public performance
5 public display
6 public digital performance of a sound recording.

The above list means that there are several works that are not covered, including:

- trivial materials
- ideas (remember, it protects only their **expression**)
- utilitarian goods (like a toilet or, more specifically, how the toilet works)
- book titles
- lists of ingredients
- standard calendars and rulers
- methods, systems, math principles, formulae, equations and the periodic chart of elements
- anything that does not offer its origin to the author (non-original works).

Copyright holders, then, have **five distinct rights** to a given creation: the holder can **copy, distribute, display, perform** and **create derivative works** from the original creation. These derivations include translations, abridgments and adaptations, such as making a movie from a novel. Another right, called a *moral right*, entails that one cannot change or mutilate a creation, such as removing an artist's name from a painting. Moral rights were originally recognized by European countries and are now recognized in the United States.

The *Rural Telephone v. Feist* case mentioned earlier has proved important for databases, CD-ROMs and digital anthologies. Feist Publications combined Rural's telephone directory with others to create a regional directory that it then sold for profit. Rural Telephone sued and lost. The Supreme Court allowed Feist's alphabetical listing of residents with a telephone, arguing that such public information cannot be copyrighted, that there is no "idea" there. The listing is not novel or unique, and copyright does not cover purely "sweat of the brow" labor, in Justice O'Connor's words. Since 1991, *Feist* as valid precedent has been expanded, even though it was a relatively narrow ruling when issued.

A related qualification is that facts cannot be copyrighted, only the way those facts are expressed. The naked truth cannot be copyrighted. URLs, for example, cannot be copyright protected, meaning a copyright holder cannot prevent or control their publication. Unique expressions of truth, including facts, however, often can be copyright protected.

The copyright protections we normally associate with print also govern the use of audio, video, images and text on the Internet and the Web. A safe assumption, then, is that materials found on the Web such as documents, images and video clips are copyrighted. We can also avoid infringement and legally use copyrighted materials if we understand and comply with fair use guidelines, or by obtaining permission for use from a copyright's owner.

Fair Use

Fair use is the most significant limitation on a copyright holder's exclusive rights, but determining whether the use of a work is fair or illegal is not a science. There are no set guidelines that are universally accepted. Owners' rights of copyright are exclusive and monopolistic except in four sets of circumstances. These are:

1 Where the work is not eligible for copyright protection; government information, for example, is not eligible, as it is the people's information.

2 Where the work is not an original; copyright does not cover copies, like a print of Van Gogh's *Sunflowers*, for example, but only the original.

3 Where the copyright has expired.

4 Where the work's copying is covered by fair use.

The doctrine of **fair use** is meant to provide "a rule . . . to balance the author's right to compensation for his work . . . against the public's interest in the widespread dissemination of ideas and information on the other," according to a district court opinion. Fair use generally covers:

- small amounts of copying, generally understood in print to be around 150 words or less;
- the advancement of ideas, education, information and knowledge, such as copies of a journal article distributed to students in a classroom;
- all intellectual property.

Since the U.S. Copyright Act was enacted in 1976, federal judges typically ask four questions in determining whether the use is in fact covered by "fair use." The individual who wants to use a copyrighted work must weigh four factors:

1 Is the use transformative? What is the purpose and character of the use?
2 What is the nature of the copyrighted work?
3 How much of the original work was changed? What amount and how much substantiality does that amount represent when viewed as a part of the whole?
4 What is the effect on the market or the potential market for the copyrighted work?

These questions are implicit in the U.S. Code, Title 17, Chapter 1, section 107, which reads in part,

> The fair use of a copyrighted work, including such use by reproduction in copies or phonorecords or by any other means specified by that section, for purposes such as criticism, comment, news reporting, teaching (including multiple copies for classroom use), scholarship, or research, is not an infringement of copyright.

To better understand this dense language, let's unpack these four factors.

1 What is the purpose and character of the copying? What is the copyrighted material being used for? Teaching? Comment and criticism? Scholarship and research? If so, it is probably covered. This factor permits a professor photocopying an article, even in full, and passing it out to students in a classroom. If the professor copies an article in full, then charges students $15 per copy? That will be a problem. Coursepacks, for example, are rare because of these restrictions. In general, educational copying must:

(a) be brief (usually less than 1,000 words);
(b) be spontaneous (where there is no time to get permissions from publishers);

(c) note with a copyright notice somewhere on the copied material(s), crediting or otherwise identifying the copyright owner;

(d) be equal to or less than the cost to the student of obtaining the original (if it cost the professor a buck, he/she can sell it for no more than a buck).

Finally, ask whether the new work offers something above and beyond the original. Does it transform the original work in some way? If the work is altered significantly, used for another purpose or appeals to a different audience, it is more likely to be considered fair use.

2 What is the nature of the copyrighted work?

(a) Is it a workbook made to be used only once? If that's the case, copying the workbook probably is an unprotected use.

(b) Is the work out of print? If it is, copying it is more likely to be considered fair use.

(c) Is it informational or creative? If it is a newspaper, your right to copy is probably protected because it is informational. A poem, however, is more likely to be protected. The more a work tends toward artistic expression, the less likely it will be considered fair use to copy it.

(d) Has the work been published? Copyright is meant to protect in order to encourage people to publish. If you are not the author and it has not been published, be very careful. The Court wants to protect the author's right of first publication. Generally, however, unpublished works are less likely to be considered fair use.

3 How much is used and, just as importantly, what does the use represent in terms of the essence or substantiality of the original work? Using only 150 words? The copying is probably a fair use, unless those 150 words are the heart and soul or essence of the piece. The more you use, the less likely it will be considered fair use. If the amount approaches 50 percent of the entire work, it is likely to be considered an unfair use of the copyrighted work. If the very small portion used is the essence of the work but it is used in a wholly different way, as in a parody or satire, it is likely permissible. To help us understand this last distinction, consider the Supreme Court case, *Campbell v. Acuff-Rose Music* (1994), which concerned 2 Live Crew's re-worked parody of Roy Orbison's "Pretty Woman." The 2 Live Crew version used the lyrics: "Big hairy woman, all that hair ain't legit; Big hairy woman, Cause you look like Cousin It," mimicking Orbison's, "Pretty woman, walking down the street; Pretty woman, the kind I'd like to meet."

The plaintiff's argument was based on two claims:

(a) The parody is a commercial use. 2 Live Crew is making money.

(b) 2 Live Crew is using the "heart of the original," or the essence of the song, so the amount appropriated should not be a factor.

The Court disagreed, recognizing that it is the "heart of the original" that makes the parody most likely to "conjure up the [original] song for parody." In other words, what was copied had to be recognizable to be recognized or heard as a parody. In ruling the Court also suggested that the four provisions or criteria for Fair Use are not binary. If you fail one or more, you still might not be infringing. Rather, the four exist on a sort of continuum, where an overall balance of fairness is struck between the old work and the new.

4 What is the effect on the market? This factor is often the most important, at least in the courts. This factor covers direct impact, such as lost sales, and indirect impact, like that on derivative rights. For example, *Castle Rock Entertainment v. Carol Publishing* in 1997 centered on a book titled, *The Seinfeld Aptitude Test*. Seinfeld's distributor, Castle Rock, won the case because of the effect on the market of the book in preventing Castle Rock from profiting from a similar work, a "Seinfeld"-based trivia test.

Generally, the more the new work differs from the original, the less likely it will be considered an infringement. If the audience for the new work is the same as that for the original, as was the case for *The Seinfeld Aptitude Test*, it will likely be considered an infringement. If a new work contains anything original, it is more likely the use of the copyrighted material will be seen as fair use.

The Internet and Copyright

As we have discussed, digital content—0s and 1s—is easy and inexpensive to copy and distribute, and digital copies have all the integrity of digital originals. Furthermore, the prevailing culture on the Internet is that content should be free and freely obtained, even where copyright-protected. We live in a cut-and-paste culture. Google, YouTube and MySpace are cut-and-paste, or record-and-stream, worlds. They bump up against U.S. law, specifically the Digital Millennium Copyright Act.

In the mid-1990s, the World Intellectual Property Organization framed digital copyright rules in negotiating two treaties. From those treaties came the **Digital Millennium Copyright Act of 1998 (DMCA)**. Among its provisions:

> You cannot circumvent copyright protection using devices or their technologies. You cannot, for instance, use a file-sharing software program like BitTorrent to circumvent copyright and copy and distribute music. You cannot alter the code in DVDs that prevents copying, or use a descrambler to pick up satellite broadcasts.

The DMCA has been at the center of a storm of litigation, including *MGM v. Grokster* in 2005, a case that echoed the famous Sony Betamax case (*Sony Corp. v. Universal City Studios,* 1984). In the Sony case, it was acknowledged that the VCR can be used to play home movies, and it can be used to illegally copy TV programming. Should VCRs, then, be illegal? The Supreme Court ruled that they should not. The manufacturer of the machine should not be held liable for the use to which it is put by the consumer. VCRs do not violate copyright, in other words, people do.

In *MGM v. Grokster* (and Streamcast), Grokster argued the Betamax defense: "Don't hold us responsible for miscreants." The Supreme Court ruled, in sending it back to the lower court for decision, that Grokster (and Streamcast) could be sued because there was evidence that the companies knew their software was being used primarily for illegal uses and did nothing about it. As a result of what basically was a loss at the Supreme Court level, Grokster shut down on November 7, 2005, agreeing to pay a $50 million fine. Grokster's Web site was changed to say that its existing file-sharing service was illegal and no longer available. "There are legal services for downloading music and movies," the message said. "This service is not one of them."

The *Grokster* decision significantly weakened lawsuit protections for companies that had blamed illegal behavior on their customers rather than the technology that made such behavior possible, which since 1984 had been an effective defense. This weakening has helped the recording and film industries in their campaigns against file-sharing, campaigns simultaneously being waged on several fronts.

> Hollywood could be brought to its knees by the digital anarchy perpetuated by 12-year-olds ... If the value of what [movie studios] labored over and brought forth to entertain the American public cannot be protected by copyright, then the victim is going to be the American public.

Jack Valenti, formerly chief executive officer of the Motion Picture Association of America, said this more than 20 years ago (McLeod 2005: 11). He was referring to the VCR.

In June 2009, a 32-year-old woman from Brainerd, Minn., lost her copyright infringement case over downloaded music and was assessed $1.92 million in damages, or $80,000 per song for the 24 songs she was accused of downloading. Of the more than 30,000 suits brought by the Recording Industry Association of America (RIAA) against alleged file-sharers, the Minnesota woman's was in summer 2009 the only one to go to a jury trial. The damage amount underlines the high stakes in downloading and sharing copyrighted digital content, and the lengths to which the RIAA is willing to go to protect its control regime.

Who, then, can best manage the commons, or the shared public resources, our culture, its icons and slogans and intellectual property? The people or private industry? Though it belongs to the people, as a matter of free speech, it is most often litigated as private, commercial property. Corporate interests are most often the winners; the commons or public good, then, is the loser.

The World's Biggest Publisher: The U.S. Government

An important exception to copyright, as described in U.S. Code 17, section 105, is that any work of the U.S. government is prohibited from being copyrighted. This includes works by governmental agencies and works commissioned by the government specifically for a governmental agency. This means that virtually everything published by the Government Printing Office, the world's largest publisher in terms of the sheer amount of information it disseminates, is fair game.

All Web pages, email messages and newsgroup messages are copyrighted, however, unless clearly stated otherwise. Copyright holders thus retain all rights to copy, distribute, display, perform and create derivative works from their Internet publications. For example, a user cannot distribute someone's email message without expressed permission; the private email correspondence is itself copyrighted and the user simply has one copy of its contents. Here is a form used by Internet book publisher O'Reilly to obtain permission to reprint quoted material, as an example:

Permission to Quote from Interview or Internet Posting

Permission is granted to O'Reilly & Associates, Inc. for non-exclusive world rights in all languages, for use of the material indicated below, in the book by _____ (author/s) titled _____ (title of book), and for any subsidiary use, promotional use, future revisions, and future editions of the same.

Copyright law generally allows hyperlinking without permission, and historically sites have welcomed links from others since this practice can boost traffic, advertising rates and revenues. In the high-profile *Ticketmaster v. Microsoft* case in 1997, Ticketmaster sued Microsoft for linking to its site without permission. Ticketmaster objected specifically to Microsoft's practice of **deep-linking**, or linking deep within Ticketmaster's site rather than to the event ticket seller's home page. Ticketmaster claimed, among other things, that Microsoft diverted advertising dollars by avoiding its home page. Though the complaint was based primarily on trademark law rather than copyright, in arguing deep-linking the case has copyright implications for Web writers and publishers. Linking, including deep-linking, generally is not considered a copyright or trademark infringement as long as there is no implication of an association with the linked site, though the issue still is somewhat unresolved. Ticketmaster and Microsoft settled out of court.

International Law and a Global Medium

Internet communication transcends geographic boundaries, and normally that is a good thing. For journalists who publish online, however, the transborder nature of the media format in particular and Internet communication in general could mean that local laws everywhere, from Australia to Zimbabwe, apply to them. Where an article is downloaded and read can be more important than where it is published, or uploaded, which makes online writers and publishers potentially subject to the laws of 190 countries. Not surprisingly, the result is dizzying jurisdictional complexity. With no international consensus to guide how or even where jurisdictional disputes should be resolved, online writers should beware.

The nature and popularity of Internet communication make international legal questions all the more important. Technological innovation means Internet communication exists in a permanent state of flux, with new ways of doing things perpetually posing legal questions without precedent. The sheer number of people online puts a premium on finding solutions to what is a growing number of transnational disputes and international jurisdictional questions.

Most journalists are proud of their editorial independence, and that is as it should be. In the United States, the First Amendment and a string of landmark Supreme Court cases affirm and protect that independence. But as English poet John Donne realized almost four centuries ago, "no man is an island entire of itself." The laws of many nations might apply. Any one journalist's loss in a foreign court is a loss for all journalists, including and perhaps especially those with blogs. In another echo of Donne, "Any man's death diminishes me because I am involved in mankind; and therefore never send to know for whom the bell tolls; it tolls for thee."

For journalists who write and publish online for large media organizations, awareness of potential legal challenges internationally could prevent legal actions that threaten to hale the employer organization into a foreign court. For lone, untethered writers who do not have the benefit (or bane) of large constituent legal departments, the lack of significant material assets abroad and relative anonymity likely provide ample protection against lawsuits.

Conclusion

Good, thorough, professional reporting and writing practices should keep you out of court. Corroborate a claim with three credible sources and you should be fine. Avoid intruding on a person's privacy by publishing what is protected by statute and you should be fine. Obtain copyright permission to re-publish digital content and you should be fine. But stay up on the news as it relates to digital content and the law. The fast pace of technological innovation and, in contrast, the slow pace of change in the law guarantees that lawyers will have plenty to do for a long, long time. Keeping up on news of these tensions can help you stay out of court.

Chapter Assignments

1 Read the posted privacy policy and/or user agreement of your favorite Web site, preferably one for which you supply information and/or content. Write a response to the policy that includes any objections to the ways in which the site reserves the right to use the information and content supplied to or published on it.

   Length: about 700 words.

Facebook's Privacy Policy

Facebook's Privacy Policy is designed to help you understand how we collect and use the personal information you decide to share, and help you make informed decisions when using Facebook, located at www.facebook.com and its directly associated domains (collectively, "Facebook" or "Website")

By using or accessing Facebook, you are accepting the practices described in this Privacy Policy.

Facebook is a licensee of the TRUSTe Privacy Program. TRUSTe is an independent, non-profit organization whose mission is to build user's trust and confidence in the Internet by promoting the use of fair information practices. This privacy statement covers the site www.facebook.com and its directly associated domains. Because this Web site wants to demonstrate its commitment to your privacy, it has agreed to disclose its information practices and have its privacy practices reviewed for compliance by TRUSTe.

If you have questions regarding this statement, please visit our privacy help page. If you do not receive acknowledgement of your inquiry or your inquiry has not been satisfactorily addressed, you should contact TRUSTe Watchdog at http://www.truste.org/consumers/ watchdog_complaint.php. TRUSTe will then serve as a liaison with us to resolve your concerns.

EU Safe Harbor Participation

We participate in the EU Safe Harbor Privacy Framework as set forth by the United States Department of Commerce. As part of our participation in the safe harbor, we have agreed to TRUSTe dispute resolution for disputes relating to our compliance with the Safe Harbor Privacy Framework. If you have any complaints regarding our compliance with the Safe Harbor you should visit our Help Center. If contacting us does not resolve your complaint, you may raise your complaint with TRUSTe at http://www.truste.org/users/users_watchdog_intro.html.

2 In this hypothetical, you are legal counsel to MyFacebookSpaceNews.com, which is facing a libel suit. Advise the news site as to how to avoid or win the libel action based on the following facts. On September 2, 2009, MyFacebookSpaceNews.com published a story with the following headline: "Six Killed in Pair of Wrecks." The published story:

> Six people were killed Saturday night in a horrifying pair of alcohol-related crashes near Yankee Stadium after a sold-out baseball game. Five of the six victims had stopped to help after the first accident.
>
> The accidents occurred about 11:45 p.m., roughly two hours after the Yankees' victory over the Red Sox on a congested street near the Stadium. The identities of the victims had not been released by early September 3. New York Police Sgt. Rocco T. Ruggiero said that a white Ford Explorer ran a stop sign and pulled onto East 161st Street. The Explorer was likely coming from the stadium and alcohol was a factor, Ruggiero said.
>
> The Explorer struck a silver Toyota Prius in the intersection. The driver of the Explorer that ran the stop sign was killed. Other motorists and one person riding a bicycle stopped to help.
>
> A green Chevy van heading east then slammed into the good Samaritans and into both the Explorer and the Prius. Ruggiero said that the third motorist was arrested on suspicion of drunken driving and faces "more very serious charges."
>
> The driver was not seriously injured, and he was taken to a local hospital to be treated. Ruggiero identified that motorist as David Simmons, a 19-year-old Brooklyn College student from Queens, N.Y., whose address is a campus dormitory. Brooklyn College officials confirmed that Simmons is enrolled there as a student. They said he is a soccer player and the vice president of the campus chapter of SADD, Students Against Drunk Driving.
>
> Five victims were pronounced dead at the scene; the sixth died en route to the hospital. Five of the six were males. Their ages were not released.
>
> As authorities blocked off streets in the area, bodies lay on 161st Street covered with sheets. Robin Hubier was leaving her apartment on a bicycle when she saw the green van pass her. "I heard a sound and saw something, but that's about all," she said. As she pedaled closer, she saw that the van had hit people. "It's a tragedy," Hubier said. "All I can say is that it's a damn tragedy. Whoever was driving the van was too much in a rush. I think people like that guy are just too stupid to know when it's unsafe to drive."

Simmons sues MyFacebookSpaceNews.com for libel *per se*, seeking $5 million in damages. Simmons said the story was libelous because it falsely reported that he was guilty of drunk driving and that it falsely portrayed him as stupid. Simmons said he was not drunk and that he's not stupid. He said he majors in inter-disciplinary studies at Brooklyn College.

In your advice to the site, provide counsel on the following concerns:

- What type of libel plaintiff is the court likely to name Simmons?
- What, then, will be the requisite standard of fault in this case?
- Will Simmons be able to prove the requisite standard fault?
- Are there other defenses the news site might consider?

(This assignment is entirely fictitious; the names, places and events were invented to create the above hypothetical.)

Online Resources

ADLAW

http://www.adlawbyrequest.com/
A good source of legal information for advertising and marketing researchers.

AEJMC Law Paper Abstracts

http://www.aejmc.org/_events/convention/abstracts/index.php
From the Association for Educators in Journalism & Mass Communication, this page lists accepted paper abstracts for AEJMC's law division, papers that were presented at the association's annual conventions.

Art of Public Records Searches

http://www.virtualchase.com/articles/public_records_research.html
How-to site with help in finding and searching public records repositories.

Citizen Media Law Project

http://www.citmedialaw.org
Legal resources for citizen media from the Berkman Center for Internet & Society.

Computers Freedom & Privacy Conference

http://www.cfp.org/
The Conference attempts to encourage public debate on the future of privacy and freedom in the online world.

Cyberlaw

http://www.cyberlaw.com/
Site contains the CyberLex and CyberLaw newsletters, sources for information and pointers to materials on law and computers.

Electronic Frontier Foundation (EFF)

http://www.eff.org/
EFF is a donor-supported membership organization that works to protect citizens' rights regardless of technology and to educate the press, policymakers and the general public about civil liberties issues related to technology.

"EFF Legal Guide for Bloggers"
http://www.eff.org/bloggers/lg/
A guide developed especially to inform bloggers of their legal rights in publishing online.

Electronic Privacy Information Center (EPIC)
http://www.epic.org
Established in 1994, EPIC is a public interest research center in Washington, DC, that tries to focus public attention on emerging civil liberties issues and to protect privacy, the First Amendment and constitutional values.

Federal Communications Commission
http://www.fcc.gov
FCC is charged with regulating interstate and international communications by radio, television, wire, satellite and cable. This site offers links to regulations, news, complaint forms, bureaus within the FCC and licensing information.

Federal Communications Law Journal
http://www.law.indiana.edu/fclj/index.shtml
Published by the Indiana University Maurer School of Law.

Federal Trade Commission's Privacy Page
http://www.ftc.gov/privacy/index.html
Protecting consumers' personal privacy is a duty of the FTC. This page outlines how the agency attempts to do this.

First Amendment Center
http://www.firstamendmentcenter.org/
A non-partisan foundation dedicated to free press, free speech and free spirit for all people founded by the Freedom Forum.

Freedom of Information Act
http://www.state.gov/m/a/ips/
Site explaining FOIA and how to use it, at the U.S. Department of State.

Free Expression Policy Project (FEPP)
http://www.fepproject.org/
Founded in 2000, FEPP provides research and advocacy on free speech, copyright, and media democracy issues.

How to File a FOIA Request
http://www.firstamendmentcenter.org/press/information/topic.aspx?
topic=how_to_FOIA
From the First Amendment Center, step-by-step instructions on how to use FOIA.

IPTAblog

http://www.iptablog.org/

Blogger Andrew Raff's thoughts about the relationships between law, communication, technology and the creative arts.

JDSupra

http://www.jdsupra.com/

Source for all sorts of legal documentation, cases, briefs and the like, a sort of WebMD of the legal profession.

Jim Romenesko's Media News

http://www.poynter.org/medianews/

This Poynter Institute site is updated daily with news from around the country about the media, often with news involving media law.

Journal of Information, Law & Technology

http://www2.warwick.ac.uk/fac/soc/law/elj/jilt/

Electronic law journal covering a range of topics relating to IT law and applications.

Jurist Legal News & Research

http://jurist.law.pitt.edu/

Published by the University of Pittsburgh School of Law.

Landmark Supreme Court Cases

http://www.landmarkcases.org/

Site developed to provide teachers with resources and activities to support the teaching of landmark Supreme Court cases.

Law.com

http://www.law.com

A daily news Web site for practicing lawyers, with search.

Media Law Resource Center

http://www.medialaw.org/

A non-profit information clearinghouse originally organized by a number of media organizations to monitor developments and promote First Amendment rights in the libel, privacy and related legal fields. The "Hot Topics" section is especially useful.

***New York Times'* Privacy in a Digital Age Page**

http://www.nytimes.com/library/tech/reference/index-privacy.html

Check out this section of the *Times* for a sense of the state of privacy law just before 9/11. For historical and anthropological reasons, this is an interesting collection of articles.

Politech

http://www.politechbot.com/

A blog by Declan McCullagh, an investigative journalist with *Wired* magazine. Topics include privacy, free speech, the role of government and corporations, antitrust, and more.

The Privacy Foundation

http://www.privacyfoundation.org/
This organization attempts to educate the public by conducting research into communications technologies and services that may pose a threat to personal privacy.

Privacy.org

http://www.privacy.org/
A site for news and policy developments in the area of privacy. The page is a joint project of the Electronic Privacy Information Center and Privacy International.

The Privacy Place

http://theprivacyplace.org/
Site for news on privacy-related policy developments.

Privacy Times

http://www.privacytimes.com
A subscription-only newsletter covering privacy and freedom of information law and policy; it is primarily for attorneys and professionals.

Reporters Committee for Freedom of the Press

http://www.rcfp.org/
A nonprofit organization dedicated to providing free legal assistance to journalists since 1970. Excellent source of news on free speech issues.

University of Iowa Library's Communication & Media Law Resources

http://bailiwick.lib.uiowa.edu/journalism/mediaLaw/index.html
The content here is precisely what the name suggests. Excellent search functionality by topic.

U.S. Copyright Office

http://www.copyright.gov
Copyright Office advises Congress on anticipated changes in U.S. copyright law; analyzes and assists in the drafting of copyright legislation and legislative reports and provides and undertakes studies for Congress; offers advice to Congress on compliance with international agreements and is where claims to copyright are registered. This site has links to copyright law, international copyright treaties, general information and copyright studies.

U.S. Supreme Court Blog

http://www.scotusblog.com/wp/
A surprisingly lively, very current blog and Web site, richly sourced with links to primary source documents such as briefs and precedent cases.

You Are Being Watched
http://www.youarebeingwatched.us/
This site dramatizes the high costs of camera surveillance systems, in terms of both money and civil liberties, and along the way is a good source for news on camera surveillance.

Sources

Andre Bacard, *The Computer Privacy Handbook* (Berkeley, CA: Peachpit Press, 1995).

David Banisar and Simon Davies, *Privacy and Human Rights 2000: An International Survey of Privacy Laws & Developments* (Washington, DC: EPIC, 1999).

Michael Barbaro, "Target Tells a Blogger to Go Away," *New York Times*, January 28, 2008, available: http://www.nytimes.com/2008/01/28/business/media/28target.html.

Committee of Concerned Journalists, "Reporting Tips from Pulitzer Winners," *Project for Excellence in Journalism*, July 29, 2006, available: http://www.concerned journalists.org/reporting-tips-pulitzer-winners.

Samuel Dash, *Unreasonable Searches and Seizures from King John to John Ashcroft* (Piscataway, NJ: Rutgers University Press, 2004).

Paul Farhi, "In the Tank," *American Journalism Review* (May/June 2008), available: http://www.ajr.org/Article.asp?id=4516.

Samuel Friedman, *Guarding Life's Dark Secrets: Legal and Social Controls Over Reputation, Propriety, and Privacy* (Palo Alto, CA: Stanford University Press, 2007).

Simson Garfinkel, *Database Nation: The Death of Privacy in the 21st Century* (Boston: O'Reilly & Associates, 2000).

Charles Jennings, Lori Fena, and Esther Dyson, *The Hundredth Window: Protecting Your Privacy and Security in the Age of the Internet* (New York: Free Press, 2000).

Lawrence Lessig, *Code and Other Laws of Cyberspace* (New York: Basic Books, 1999).

Kembrew McLeod, *Freedom of Expression®, Overzealous Bozos and Other Enemies of Creativity* (New York: Doubleday, 2005).

Steven Nock, *The Costs of Privacy* (Hawthorne, NY: Aldine de Gruyter, 1993).

Jeffrey Rosen, *The Naked Crowd: Reclaiming Security and Freedom in an Anxious Age* (New York: Random House, 2004).

Daniel J. Solove, *The Digital Person: Technology and Privacy in the Information Age* (New York: New York University Press, 2004).

Ben Worthen, "Best of the Business Tech Blog," *Wall Street Journal*, June 3, 2008: B6.

AFTERWORD
Core Values of Online Journalism

Free press can, of course, be good or bad, but, most certainly without freedom, the press will never be anything but bad.

Albert Camus, French novelist, essayist and dramatist

Were it left to me to decide whether we should have a government without newspapers, or newspapers without a government, I should not hesitate a moment to prefer the latter.

Thomas Jefferson

Below are definitions and descriptions of the core values of journalism, which hold true regardless of medium. These values include **accuracy, reasonableness, transparency, fairness** and **independence**.

Journalism Value 1: Accuracy

Without accuracy, what would be the point of journalism? The Society of Professional Journalists' Code of Ethics instructs journalists to maximize truth and minimize harm, making accuracy the starting point for good journalism. We get the facts, check and double-check them, then report with enough contextualization that the collection of facts can tell a truth, if not *the* truth. The accuracy tip sheet below was abstracted from the Knight Citizen News Network, an initiative of J-Lab: The Institute for Interactive Journalism.

Before Writing

1 Routinize your work. The best way to maintain accuracy is to develop a system and stick to it.
2 Take time to read back to an interviewee the spelling of his or her name. If you need an age, ask for a birth date and year.
3 Avoid using secondary sources to verify facts.
4 If you have to use secondary sources, find at least two and make sure they agree independently; don't simply ask one to confirm what the other said.
5 Verify phone/fax numbers, Web and email addresses. Plug the URL (Web address) into a browser to make sure it works. Call the phone number.

While Writing

1 Identify sources. Readers need to know where the information came from so they can judge for themselves its credibility. Online has put an even higher premium on this kind of transparency.

2 Do not confuse opinions with facts. Opinions make personal journalism lively, but make them clear to readers. It is easy to jump to conclusions when you are predisposed to believe something.

After Writing

1 Leave fact-checking and editing for last. For a thorough copyedit, print out the content. Spell-check your work. Read it backwards. Read the copy out loud. Try to see both the forest and the trees, so always read (at least) once for content and effect. Read (at least) once for mechanical errors, including those of grammar, punctuation and keystroke errors. And remember, errors often come with friends. Find one? Keep looking. There may be others.

2 Proofread corrections for readability, because error can be introduced even when correcting copy.

3 Assemble all source materials—notebooks, interview transcripts, tapes, books, studies, photos, everything used to report and write the story. Go over the story and compare it to the original sources. On projects and even on daily stories, some reporters make one printout for names and titles, another for quotes, a third for other details.

4 Fact-check. Many magazines use professional fact-checkers, and they still manage to make mistakes.

5 Call sources back and double-check key facts. When describing a financial transaction, a medical procedure or how a sewer bond works, there's nothing wrong with calling the source and asking him or her to listen to what you've written. Editors at *The Oregonian* in Portland concluded that the three most frequent sources of error are working from memory, making assumptions and dealing with second-hand sources. Avoid these whenever possible.

We should not rely on another person's figures. **Do the math.** If challenged by the complexity of the math or statistics or, say, how a survey was conducted (confidence level, margin of error, sample size, etc.), get some help. Do not pass along information you do not understand yourself, words of advice valid for much more than simply math.

Word processing has created great efficiencies. It has also made it a lot easier to leave off identifying information on first reference. Moving paragraphs around often results in a second or third reference becoming the first, so make sure you have full name and title on that first reference.

Check maps when providing geographic information, including routes and locations. Be careful with city and county names. The city of New York is in the county of New York, which is in turn in the state of New York.

Check for balance. Are the major perspectives or voices or points of view represented in the story? This is the Rule of Fair Comment, and it is aimed at avoiding one-sided or one-source stories, which are incomplete and therefore inaccurate. Talk to as many people as possible, even circling back and speaking again with previous sources after learning more from subsequent ones. Try not to allow the first source you speak with to frame the entire story.

Do your research. Read archived material on the topic. This important background material can provide corroboration for names and titles, and it can help you avoid misassumptions. It can also help spot inconsistencies and contradictions. With LexisNexis Academic and other online databases, checking the archives has never been easier.

Journalism Value 2: Reasonableness

Web content that exhibits reasonableness will be even-handed and will incorporate as many perspectives as is possible. In other words, the information will have no obvious conflicts of interest, or it will clearly acknowledge where potential conflicts might exist. The information will be consistent in presenting the facts and will clearly identify opinion when and where it is such. Here are a few questions to check a story's reasonableness: Is the article offering a balanced, reasoned presentation that incorporates the many sides of an issue or question or topic rather than one that is selective or slanted? Is the tone calm and reasonable? "Everyone in City Hall is a thief," for example, clearly lacks reasonableness, as well as plausibility. Check also for severe language ("Anyone who believes otherwise has no basic human decency") and sweeping generalizations ("This is the most important idea ever conceived!").

Journalism Value 3: Transparency

As described in Chapter 2, disclosure and transparency are crucial online to establishing and maintaining credibility. Blog readers, especially, want to know our motives, our experience and expertise, our background and, especially, any financial interest we have in the publication or dissemination of the story or article. So reporters and writers should be up front with this information. In addition, linking to source materials, providing brief biographical information somewhere on the page or site, and triangulating facts, figures and data can communicate thoroughness and transparency. Make it easy to be contacted, document your source material, and include however parenthetically any tie to or interest in these sources you might have. Readers will wonder:

- Where did the information come from?
- What sources did the creator use?

- How well is the information supported? Even if it is opinion, a sound argument will probably have other people who agree with it.

Corroboration uses information to test information. It is most important in cases where information is surprising or counterintuitive.

Transparency is needed in disclosing motives and potential conflicts of interest, and biases and subjective approaches should likewise be acknowledged. Transparency of process also contributes to credibility, which has to do with linking to documents, sources and supporting evidence. This transparency of process also serves to place the individual post or article in the collective, connective tissue of the online information space.

Transparency should also be the goal when things go wrong. When mistakes are made, publish an apology, take responsibility and correct the mistake. In addition to correcting the record, this kind of transparency shows that we all are human and that we are interdependent. We demand transparency in the institutions and organizations we cover; it only makes sense to offer that same transparency of process and of product to readers.

For more, see Cyberjournalist.net's blog on transparency in media (http://www.cyberjournalist.net/media_transparency/).

Journalism Value 4: Fairness

How many sides to an issue are there? Two? Think again. There are likely hundreds. Are your accounts providing as many of these perspectives as possible? What does balance look like in your story? Have you slanted the facts, or selectively, disingenuously included only certain ones to make a point? If you are attacking someone or a perspective, are you including different viewpoints? Are you giving the subject an opportunity to respond?

Balance and fairness are not about giving "equal weight to two sides." They have more to do with incorporating several different perspectives and giving relative weight to those different perspectives. An exposé on the toxic-waste dumping practices of an industrial manufacturer should not strive to give the company's public relations officers equal time or space to tout the wonderful things the company is doing in the community, for example. Balance and fairness are a bit more complicated than that. While giving the polluter an opportunity to respond, the story should maximize truth and minimize harm.

"Take readers to the margins and extremes, but do not dwell there at the exclusion of the 'middle'—report on ambiguity, consensus and ambivalence," the American Society of Newspaper Editors (ASNE) states on its Web site (asne.org). Understand that communities have many different layers and dimensions, and that we need to move between and within them to capture the mosaic of voices, viewpoints, events, problems and solutions that exist.

Balance and fairness also strive to reflect a community's diversity and wholeness, which will include, according to ASNE, "the good, the bad and the profoundly ordinary." The ASNE also recommends that writers and reporters:

- look beyond conflicts to explore underlying issues and perspectives— this will help engage people and create a greater sense of possibility;
- avoid falsely creating or overpresenting "sides" or points of view where they don't exist;
- step back and reflect on the patterns within news coverage and communities—provide balance over time, not just on a day-to-day basis.

Journalism Value 5: Independence

Ideally, we have no conflicts of interest when reporting, writing and publishing, because the "watchdog" responsibility of journalists requires independence. To hold the powerful accountable and cast the first stone requires an independence and purity of motive that only independence can produce. Independence is at the heart of journalism's essential role in a self-governing democracy, and it sets a standard for professionalism and ethical behavior. This value calls for us to guard and defend the role of a free press and to give a voice to as many perspectives as possible without favor and without being unduly influenced by anyone. Independence means avoiding membership in and associations with any group or individual who could compromise our integrity or credibility before our readers.

The SPJ built upon this language when it revised its code of ethics in the mid-1990s. SPJ's "Act Independently" principle includes the following: "Journalists should be free of obligation to any interest other than the public's right to know." The code also states that journalists should:

- avoid conflicts of interest, real or perceived;
- remain free of associations and activities that may compromise integrity or damage credibility;
- refuse gifts, favors, fees, free travel and special treatment, and shun secondary employment, political involvement, public office, and service in community organizations if they compromise journalistic integrity;
- disclose unavoidable conflicts;
- be vigilant and courageous about holding those with power accountable;
- deny favored treatment to advertisers and special interests and resist their pressure to influence news coverage;
- be wary of sources offering information for favors or money; avoid bidding for news.

These are guidelines, not absolute rules. They do not preclude tough calls, particularly when one or more of these imperatives are in tension with each other. In those situations, it helps to have a collaborative decision-making environment and a process of ethical decision-making already in place.

Online News Association

These core journalism values are reflected in the mission and vision statement of the Online News Association, which is composed largely of professional online journalists. The Association has more than 1,200 professional members whose principal livelihood involves gathering or producing news for digital presentation. Here is the Association's vision statement, reprinted with permission:

> ONA is a leader in the rapidly changing world of journalism; a catalyst for innovation in story-telling across all platforms; a resource for journalists seeking guidance and growth, and a champion of best practices through training, awards and community outreach.
>
> OUR VALUES:
> We believe that the Internet is the most powerful communications medium to arise since the dawn of television. As digital delivery systems become the primary source of news for a growing segment of the world's population, it presents complex challenges and opportunities for journalists as well as the news audience.
>
> Editorial Integrity: The unique permeability of digital publications allows for the linking and joining of information resources of all kinds as intimately as if they were published by a single organization. Responsible journalism through this medium means that the distinction between news and other information must always be clear, so that individuals can readily distinguish independent editorial information from paid promotional information and other non-news.
>
> Editorial Independence: Online journalists should maintain the highest principles of fairness, accuracy, objectivity and responsible independent reporting.
>
> Journalistic Excellence: Online journalists should uphold traditional high principles in reporting original news for the Internet and in reviewing and corroborating information from other sources.
>
> Freedom of Expression: The ubiquity and global reach of information published on the Internet offers new information and educational resources to a worldwide audience, access to which must be unrestricted.
>
> Freedom of Access: News organizations reporting on the Internet must be afforded access to information and events equal to that enjoyed by other news organizations in order to further freedom of information.

Sources

Bonnie Bressers, "Getting a Fix on Online Corrections" (ASNE, 2001), available: http://www.asne.org/kiosk/editor/01.march/bressers1.htm.

Mark Briggs, *Journalism 2.0* (Knight Citizen Journalism Network, 2007), available: http://www.kcnn.org/resources/journalism_20/.

Brian Carroll, "Culture Clash: Journalism and the Communal Ethos of the Blogosphere," *Into the Blogosphere* (University of Minnesota, 2003), available: http://blog.lib.umn.edu/blogosphere/culture_clash_journalism_and_the_communal_ethos_of_the_blogosphere.html.

Fred Fedler, *Reporting for the Media* (Oxford: Oxford University Press, 2001).

Bob Haiman, "Best Practices for Newspaper Journalists" (Freedom Forum, 2000), available: http://www.freedomforum.org/publications/diversity/bestpractices/best practices.pdf.

Knight Citizen News Network, J-Lab, University of Maryland (http://www.kcnn.org/principles/).

Bill Kovach and Tom Rosenstiel, *The Elements of Journalism: What Newspeople Should Know and the Public Should Expect* (New York: Three Rivers Press, 2007).

C. Max Magee, "The Roles of Journalists in Online Newsrooms" (Medill School of Journalism, 2006), available: http://www.editteach.org/downloads?download_id=167&filename=Roles%20of%20Journalists%20in%20Online%20Newsrooms.pdf.

The New York Times Ethical Journalism Handbook (September 2004), available: http://www.nytco.com/pdf/NYT_Ethical_Journalism_0904.pdf.

Poynter Guide to Accuracy, available: http://www.poynter.org/content/content_view.asp?id=36518.

INDEX